Susanne Jung
Bouncing Back: Queer Resilience in Twentieth
and Twenty-First Century English Literature and Culture

Susanne Jung, born in 1975, received her doctorate in English literature from the University of Tübingen. She studied English literature, musicology and pharmacy at universities in Tübingen, Norwich, and San Francisco.

SUSANNE JUNG

Bouncing Back: Queer Resilience in Twentieth and Twenty-First Century English Literature and Culture

[transcript]

Bibliographic information published by the Deutsche Nationalbibliothek
The Deutsche Nationalbibliothek lists this publication in the Deutsche Nationalbibliografie; detailed bibliographic data are available in the Internet at http://dnb.d-nb.de

© 2020 transcript Verlag, Bielefeld

Cover layout: Maria Arndt, Bielefeld

Print-ISBN 978-3-8376-5027-3
PDF-ISBN 978-3-8394-5027-7
https://doi.org/10.14361/9783839450277

Contents

Acknowledgments

My heartfelt thanks go to the following people who supported me throughout the writing of this book: My PhD supervisors Ingrid Hotz-Davies and Eveline Kilian, who both believed in this book project from the beginning. Christoph Reinfandt, Kaye Mitchell, Isabel Karremann and Jack Halberstam for critical and helpful input at various stages of the writing of this book. Ann-Katrin Zimmermann for never-wavering encouragement, immensely helpful comments and emotional support, always. This book would not have been possible without you. Kathrin Tordasi, Gero Bauer and especially Rebecca Hahn for helpful comments and support. Everyone who commented on my work at various colloquia in Tübingen and Berlin: Thank you. And finally, Gisela Jung and Friedrich Jung, Ulrike Rieber and Markus Rieber, Finn, Hannah and Samuel, Till Jung and Eberhard Jung for their continuing love and support.

Introduction
Towards a Theory of Queer Resilience

Consider the following: a world-renowned actor describing, in 2002, in an interview how he was able to cry – that is produce actual tears – on stage only after, in his late forties, he had come out to his parents as a gay man (McKellen, *Inside the Actor's Studio*). Something had obviously unlocked in him by his act of revealing his queer sexuality, which opened him up to a deeper level of connecting with his own emotions on stage. Consider also the matter-of-fact statement, two years later, of German football club FC St. Pauli's former president Corny Littman that, in his estimation, the ramifications of coming out currently as an active European top league gay male football player were bound to take too much of a toll on these young players' psychological health: "Ich würde keinem Profi raten, sich zu outen. Der soziale Druck wäre nicht auszuhalten [I would not recommend any professional player to come out. The social pressure would be unbearable, S.J.]" (qtd. in Walther-Ahrens 7). As of the writing of this book, two male football players have come out after retiring from European Premier Leagues, Robbie Rogers in 2013 and Thomas Hitzlsperger in 2014. Still, as of the last fifteen years, no active player in any of the major European leagues has dared to prove Littman's estimation wrong.[1] The question of whether LGBTQ individuals, even at the beginning of the twenty-first century, deem it safe to come out of the closet seems to depend,

---

1 Robbie Rogers has since come out of retirement and continued to play in a U.S. league as an active out-gay football player. Whether this proves that closeted players' fears around coming out in one of the top European leagues are unreasonable will have to remain to be seen (cf. Rogers). For some of the fears and presumed ramifications regarding a potential coming out in the *Bundesliga*, see Adrian Bechtold's 2012 interview with a closeted German gay male football player who wished to remain anonymous (cf. Bechtold). Thomas Hitzlsperger addressed his gay sexuality for the first time, after retiring, in an interview in German newspaper *Die Zeit* (cf. Hitzlsperger, "Homosexualität wird im Fussball ignoriert" and "I finally figured out that I preferred living with a man"). Openly gay ex-NBA basketball player John Amaechi blames the dirth of out-gay top league football players on the 'toxic' climate he makes out in the leadership and management of European Premier league football clubs (cf. Amaechi). No doubt, the 1998 suicide of Justin Fashanu, the first and to date only active openly-gay football player in the English Premier league, who came out in 1990, also still haunts some of these interviews. The situation seems to be slightly better in women's professional team sports.

still, on a number of factors, among them the environment they find themselves in, age and vulnerability of the individual in question, support systems available to them, and cultural and sociopolitical contexts, to name just a few. The two previous examples represent the two ends of a scale of what contemporary Western queer affective experience can look like as of the writing of this book and has, I argue, looked like for the better part of the last one hundred years. It is between these poles of queer affective experience and queer subjectivities and lives that this book wishes to situate itself.

I take as a starting point for my enquiry Eve Kosofsky Sedgwick's claim from her book *Epistemology of the Closet* that "many of the major nodes of thought and knowledge in twentieth-century Western culture as a whole are structured – indeed, fractured – by a chronic, now endemic crisis of homo/heterosexual definition, indicatively male, dating from the end of the nineteenth century" (1). In her work Sedgwick builds, among other theorists, on the ideas of Michel Foucault in *The History of Sexuality Vol. 1*. Foucault convincingly argued that our current system of categorizations of sexual identities dates from the nineteenth century. Earlier centuries, Foucault claimed, had not understood sexual deviancy in terms of identities, in terms of something that was believed to be innate to an individual, but as a set of deviant sexual acts that might potentially be undertaken by anyone. Says Foucault, "[t]he nineteenth-century homosexual became a personage, a past, a case history, and a childhood, in addition to being a type of life, a life form, and a morphology" (*History of Sexuality* 43). Recent historical research by David M. Halperin and others has corroborated the larger historical developments posited by Foucault, but historians have also found that the ontological shift from sexual acts to sexual identities already occurred over the course of the 'long' eighteenth century and was indeed mostly completed by the middle of the nineteenth century (cf. Halperin); it can furthermore be understood to have occurred within the context of the development of larger regimes of normalization and systematization that were taking place in European society and thought of the eighteenth and nineteenth centuries. Foucault developed his idea of the subject as being constituted by historically specific discourses as a direct countermodel to psychoanalytic understandings of the subject as ruled by instincts and drives, with non-heteronormative sexualities thought of as a developmentally early stage that needed to be overcome for the subject to reach full adulthood. Writing after Foucault the question remains, for queer theory but also presumably for other areas of poststructuralist thought: Can the subject and subjective experience as as a field of affective experience be redeemed – without necessarily recurring to the discourse of psychoanalysis? And in what language, with what kind of terminology, what kind of discourse can it be grasped, talked about, described, understood?

I take as premises for the present study two assumptions: One, that heteronormativity poses an affective challenge to queer peoples' lives. And two, the notion that queer people are not without means to deal with this challenge. My thesis is the following: Queer subjects have strategies of resilience at their disposal to help them cope with the challenge heteronormativity – as a power structure – poses to their affective lives.

Following Eve Kosofsky Sedgwick, I take queer, for the context of this study, to mean "a continuing moment, movement, motive – recurrent, eddying, *troublant*. The word 'queer' itself means *across* – it comes from the Indo-European root *–twerkw*, which also yields the German *quer* (traverse), Latin *torquere* (to twist), English *athwart*. [...] The immemorial current that *queer* represents is as antiseparatist as it is antiassimilationist. Keenly it is relational, and strange" (*Tendencies* xii). As Sedgwick has it, "one of the things that 'queer' can refer to" is "the open mesh of possibilities, gaps, overlaps, dissonances and resonances, lapses and excesses of meaning when the constituent elements of anyone's gender, of anyone's sexuality aren't made (or *can't be* made) to signify monolithically" (*Tendencies* 8). I also, more generally speaking, employ the term queer as an umbrella term for talking about LGBTQ subjectivities and lives.[2]

Previous theorists of queer affect, such as Ann Cvetcovich and others,[3] have for the past two decades been focussing mainly on the traumatic effects of hegemonic power structures on a given subject's internal experience when investigating the interior lives of queer subjects. However, there has been a slight change of focus in both neuroscientific and psychological research in recent years, moving away from the concept of trauma and focusing instead on a given subject's strategies of resilience when dealing with challenging life experiences.

The concept of resilience, as shall be explained in greater depth below, describes a subject's ability to withstand, deal and cope with a challenging life experience by drawing on a range of internal and external resources available to the individual at a given point in time. Some individuals, researchers claim, may be more resilient than others, at certain times, in certain contexts, but resiliency is also something which can be trained and learned. An individual may develop a range of strategies of resilience when dealing with stressful lifetime events.

This book aims at making the concept of resilience available to queer literary and cultural studies, looking at strategies of resilience in twentieth and twenty-first century cultural and literary texts. If the modern system of heteronormative power structures can be said to have been largely in place towards the middle

---

2 The capital letters stand for, variously, lesbian, gay, bisexual, transgender or transsexual and queer or questioning. As this by no means covers the whole range of human sexualities and genders beyond heteronormativity, an asterisk is sometimes added, indicating that the list could be expanded to include further terms of self-identification and self-description. The common usage of 'queer' as an umbrella term of the above list strikes me as eminently feasible.

3 Cf. e.g. Ann Cvetcovich, *An Archive of Feelings*; and Heather Love, *Feeling Backward*.

of the nineteenth century, as Foucault and others have argued, one should also be able to assume that queer subjects have always had or have concurrently been developing strategies of resilience in order to deal with this challenge to their affective lives. Looking at cultural texts from the nineteenth – and possibly even earlier – centuries lies, however, outside the scope of the present study. I take, for the purpose of this book, the Oscar Wilde trial and Wilde's conviction in 1895 on acts of 'gross indecency' as a turning point in history that catapulted (homo) sexuality to the forefront of people's consciousness. After the Wilde trial, I argue, normative and deviant sexualities took on a new form of visibility in the English speaking world.[4] If during the second half of the nineteenth century, one could, in the English speaking world, still evade having one's same-sex desires marked out (even to oneself), prosecuted and labelled as deviant, this proved to be much harder after the turn of the century. A case in point would be for instance Katherine Mansfield musing in Wellington, New Zealand, in her journal in 1907 on her newly developed feelings for her friend, the painter Edith Kathleen Bendal, with whom she had spent some time at her family's seaside bungalow. Katherine Mansfield explicitly links here her own feelings to the figure of Oscar Wilde and Wildean sexual deviancy. Claire Tomalin quotes Mansfield's journal at length in her biography *Katherine Mansfield: A Secret Life*.

> "Here by a thousand delicate suggestions I can absorb her – for the time. What an experience! And when we returned to town, small wonder that I could not sleep, but tossed to and fro, and yearned, and realized a thousand things which had been obscure ... O Oscar! Am I peculiarly susceptible to sexual impulse? I must be, I suppose – but I rejoice. Now, each time I see her to put her arms round me and hold me against her [sic]. I think she wanted to, too; but she is afraid and custom hedges her in, I feel. We shall go away again." (Mansfield qtd. in Tomalin 36)

I thus take the first decade of the twentieth century as the historical starting point for my enquiry into strategies of queer resilience, and Mansfield's short story "Leves Amores", written later in 1907, is the earliest literary text analysed in the present study.[5]

---

4 On the reception of the Wilde trial and the increased visibility of the discourse on same-sex desire after the turn of the century, cf. Joseph Bristow, "Introduction" and Gregory Woods, *Homintern* 31-41.

5 For a further discussion of Katherine Mansfield's treatment of same-sex desire in her life and her work as well as an analysis of "Leves Amores" see the chapter on spatial strategies.

The Turn to Resilience

Theorists of queer affect, such as for instance Ann Cvetcovich in *An Archive of Feelings: Trauma, Sexuality, and Lesbian Public Cultures* and Heather Love in *Feeling Backward: Loss and the Politics of Queer History*, have been focussing mainly on the negative effects of hegemonic power structures on a given subject's internal experience. Hegemonic power structures, such as heteronormativity, can undoubtedly have a traumatizing (in the sense of wounding; trauma in its original sense translated from the Ancient Greek means wound) effect on an individual's interior experience, and these negative feelings have indeed been explored in queer studies over the last fifteen years. Cvetkovich's book is more closely concerned with an archive of feelings that is produced inside one individual, whereas Love's project is more focussed towards larger historical structures of backward feelings and our present engagement with the legacy of bad feelings of queer subjects of the past. In their thinking, Cvetcovich and Love stand in a tradition with other queer critics' theorizations on negative affect, such as for example Eve Kosofsky Sedgwick's work on shame (cf. Sedgwick, *Touching Feeling*), Sara Ahmed's work on queer feelings of discomfort and grief in *The Cultural Politics of Emotion* and Judith Halberstam's work on failure (cf. *The Queer Art of Failure*).

Projects like Cvetkovich's and Love's books on trauma and backward feelings make important points: past and present experiences of social exclusion that many queers still face can indeed produce bad feelings. However, I do share critic Elizabeth Freeman's uneasiness with these traditions of thinking the negative in queer studies. In her essay "Time Binds, or Erotohistoriography", Freeman suggests that the turn in queer studies toward loss, failure, shame and negativity may be premature, asking where there might be a place for a politics of pleasure in all of this.[6] Her own countermodel of erotohistoriography suggests that "we might imagine ourselves haunted by ecstasy, not just by loss"; indeed, "residues", says Freeman, of "positive affect [...] might be available for queer counter- (or para-) historiographies" (66). Similarly, for José Esteban Muñoz in *Cruising Utopia: The Then and There of Queer Futurity*, "queerness exists [...] as an ideality that can be distilled from the past and used to imagine a future" (1). He contends that "[w]e must strive, in the face of the here and now's totalizing rendering of reality, to think and feel a *then and there*. [...] Queerness is a longing that propels us onward, beyond romances of the negative and toiling in the present" (1). Queerness is for Muñoz "an insistence on potentiality or concrete possibility for another world" (1). I wish to make a similar reparative argument to the one both Freeman and Muñoz make on the level of the collective or social, on the level of the individual by proposing a slight change of focus.

6 Cf. Freeman 58-59.

I am borrowing from a turn that has been happening in the neurosciences and in psychology over the course of the last fifteen years, where there has been a slight change of focus by scientists studying experiences of the negative, moving away from the concept of trauma and focussing instead on a given subject's strategies of resilience when dealing with challenging life experiences. I would like to offer the concept of resilience as a framework to theorize queer affect *alongside* the concept of trauma and feeling backward that has been predominantly used in conceptualizing queer affect so far.[7] The concept of resilience, in these disciplines of thinking, describes a subject's ability to withstand, deal and cope with a challenging life experience by drawing on a range of internal and external resources available to the individual at a given point in time. Some individuals may be more resilient than others, at certain times, in certain contexts, but resiliency is also something which can be trained and learned. An individual may develop a range of strategies of resilience when dealing with stressful lifetime events.[8]

Resilience, in its original sense derived from its Latin root (resilire), means bouncing back, to rebound, to spring back, so resilience might be termed the ability to bounce back, or spring back. The *Oxford English Dictionary* defines resilience as "elasticity; the power of resuming an original shape or position after compression, bending, etc.", as well as the "quality or fact of being able to recover quickly or easily from, or resist being affected by, a misfortune, shock, illness, etc.; robustness; adaptability".[9] As has become apparent in resilience research over the last three decades, human resilience can more aptly be grasped by figurative notions

---

7 In this book, I do not make a conceptual difference between 'affective experience' and 'emotional experience'. Both describe an individual's experiencing what is commonly referred to as 'feelings'. These 'feelings' also always co-occur in the human body/mind with what somatic researchers describe as 'bodily feelings' or 'sensations' (cf. Levine). I look at 'sensations' extensively in the chapter on bodily strategies. I am following Cvetkovich and others in not differentiating between 'affect' and 'emotion' (cf. Cvetkovich in Ahmed 205-206). I am aware that a different usage of these terms can be found in the work of some cultural theorists. A critical discussion, with which I would concur, of the so-called affective turn and of a conceptual differentiation between 'affect' and 'emotion' can be found in the second edition of Sara Ahmed's *The Cultural Politics of Emotion* (cf. 205-211). In the discipline of psychology, Silvan Tomkins differentiates between these terms, employing the term affects only to a limited number of emotions which are similar to the emotions described already by Charles Darwin as primary emotions and studied extensively by Paul Ekman and others. Emotions in this stricter definition of the term would then apply to an unlimited number of emotional states that one can make out to describe various shades of emotional experience (cf. Tomkins; Levine).

8 Cf. Fröhlich-Gildhoff and Rönnau-Böse, *Resilienz*; Masten and Wright, "Resilience over the Lifespan". For an easy-to-read yet still thorough introduction to the topic, I can also recommend Berndt, *Resilienz*.

9 Resiliency is similarly defined by the *Oxford English Dictionary* as "elasticity" as well as the "capacity to recover from misfortune, shock, illness, etc".

of elasticity and flexibility than by notions of hardness and hardiness. Resilience, in current research, is no longer regarded as an individual trait but is understood to be the result of a process involving an individual's capabilities, their interaction with their social environment as well as their being embedded in larger systems of relations, communities and cultures. Developmental psychologists Ann S. Masten and Margaret O'Dougherty Wright summarize current conceptualizations around human resilience as follows:

> "Resilience should not be conceptualized as a static trait or characteristic of an individual. Resilience arises from many processes and interactions that extend beyond the boundaries of the individual organism, including close relationships and social support. Moreover, an individual person may be resilient with respect to some kinds of stressors and not others, or be resilient with respect to some adaptive outcomes but not others [...]. Resilience itself also is dynamic: the same individual may show maladaptive function at one time and resilience later in development, or vice versa." ("Resilience over the Lifespan" 215)

Here are a few further definitions offered by a number of researchers studying human resilience in a number of academic disciplines, among them (developmental) psychology, pedagogy, social work and neurobiology: According to James Garbarino in the preface to the *Handbook for Working With Children and Youth: Pathways to Resilience Across Cultures and Contexts*, "resilience generally refers to an individual's ability to bounce back from adverse experiences, to avoid long-term negative effects, or otherwise to overcome developmental threats" (xi). Michael Ungar, in his introduction to the same volume, writes that in the context of a Western scientific community, "resilience has come to mean the individual capacities, behaviors, and protective processes associated with health outcomes despite exposure to a significant number of risks" (xvi). In their introduction to *The Resilience Handbook: Approaches to Stress and Trauma*, editors Martha Kent, Mary C. Davis and John W. Reich regard "resilience as a process rather than as a set of traits, outcomes, and risk, or protective factors", and see it as "composed of three elements: resilience as a sustained adaptive effort that prevails despite challenge, as a bouncing back and recovery from a challenge, and as a process of learning and growth that expands understanding, new knowledge, and new skills" (xii). Alex J. Zautra, in his essay "Resilience is Social, After All", points to the important role of the *"perceived* availability of social support" for human resilience which can foster feelings of connectedness and belonging, maintaining that "[s]ocial connections play a critical role in mitigating the effects of life's most stressful experiences" (185-186). In their introductory chapter to the *Handbook of Adult Resilience*, titled "Resilience: A New Definition of Health for People and Communities", Zautra together with John Stuart Hall and Kate E. Murray extend the framework of conceptualizing resilience by arguing that human resilience is not only about overcoming obstacles but also crucially about thriving. They offer "resilience as an integrative construct that provides an approach to understanding how people and their communities achieve and sustain health and well-being in the face of adversity" (4), adding that "*individual resilience* may be defined by the amount of stress that a person can endure without a fundamental change in capacity to pursue aims that give life meaning. The greater a person's capacity to stay on a satisfying life course, the greater his or her resilience. Whereas resilient *recovery* focuses on aspects of healing of wounds, *sustainability* calls attention to outcomes relevant to preserving valuable engagements in life's tasks at work, in play, and in social relations" (6). They conclude that the "capacity to mount effective responses to stress and to resist illness is a fundamental imperative. But survival is not enough for resilience. A fulfilling life is also fundamental to well-being, so changes that affect our plans and goals for ourselves, our families, and our communities need attention as well" (7). Margaret O'Dougherty Wright, Ann S. Masten and Angela J. Narayan make out four waves of research in resilience studies: The first wave regarded resilience as primarily residing in an individual, whereas the second wave understood resilience as a process and looked more closely into the interactions between an individual and their social environment; the third wave of research focused on implementing and evaluating programmes to help foster resilience in various settings, and the fourth wave now under way is trying to better understand the neurobiological underpinnings of individual resilience, investigating also the changes that occur in an individual (as regards e.g. biomarkers and gene expression) as a consequence of their interaction with their social environment (cf. "Resilience Processes in Development").

Several longitudinal studies are generally taken as the starting point for the current focus on and increasing scientific interest in the research on human resilience. The most famous and most often cited study was conducted by Emmy E. Werner and Ruth S. Smith on the island of Kauai. Werner and Smith conducted a study on child development, following the lives of 698 children from their birth till the age of forty, analysing the challenges they faced and looking at strategies they developed in order to deal with negative experiences. The model they developed showed that there were protective factors that could balance out risk factors in resilient children. Some of these lay within the children themselves, others were provided by the social environment of extended family, school or community (cf. Werner 36-38). Different children showed different levels of vulnerability, so there also proved to be a range of individual reaction to certain challenges. Some children might be more vulnerable than others, and would thus have a harder time dealing with a challenge than others. Werner and Smith, as well as other scientists who undertook similar kinds of research, isolated a number of resources individuals might have at hand that would help them cope with challenging situations or experiences; these resources might be available to them at the personal level, but also at a collective level.[10]

Resilience scholars differentiate between inner, or personal resources, and outer, or social resources. On the level of personal resources, Werner and Smith and others were able to make out certain resilience factors that would help determine an individual's resilience, such as e.g. self-efficacy, emotional and social competencies and problem solving skills.[11] In the wake of the publication of their and other scientists' studies, researchers have started employing the combined findings for the development of prevention programmes that aim at fostering children's and adolescents' resilience and help them learn and train basic skills as well as develop strategies for dealing with challenging situations. The most effective of these programmes intervene not only at the level of the individual children but also include parents and caregivers in their training and also try to positively influence school or preschool settings.[12]

Two caveats apply as concerns protective and risk factors, as more recent discussions in resilience research point out: things may be not as clear cut as researchers first believed, and what may function for one individual as a protective factor in one context may function for the same or another individual as a risk factor in another context (cf. Wright, Masten and Narayan 23-24). Furthermore, as Michael Ungar points out, definitions and conceptualizations of resilience may not work the same way cross-culturally. Ungar thus cautions against applying or mapping coordinates of resilience developed in one cultural context too easily onto another cultural context. His advice to fellow researchers is thus to keep an open mind about what resilience may mean in the context of the people and communities

10   For an excellent overview and extended discussion of protective factors and risk factors see Fröhlich-Gildhoff and Rönnau-Böse 20-57. Wright, Masten and Narayan provide a short list of promotive and protective factors (21), as do Lösel and Farrington (18). On a collective level, culturally based protective factors can include cultural traditions, ceremonies and rituals (Wright, Masten and Narayan 26-27).

11   Cf. Fröhlich-Gildhoff and Rönnau-Böse 43; Werner 35.

12   Cf. Fröhlich-Gildhoff and Rönnau-Böse 64-85; Werner 43-45; Wright, Masten and Narayan 27-30. In her essay "Risiko und Resilienz im Leben von Kindern aus multethnischen Familien", Emmy Werner remains cautiously optimistic as to the efficacy of social intervention programmes: "Es ist nicht anzunehmen, dass wir eine Patentlösung finden werden, ein einzelnes Interventionsprogramm, das *in jedem Falle jedem Jugendlichen* helfen kann, der unter schädigenden Bedingungen aufwächst. [...] Wir können aber Resilienz in einzelnen Kindern fördern. Dazu bedarf es keiner großen Summen, sondern einfach nur Zeit und Fürsorge. Wenn Kinder Personen begegnen, die ihnen eine gesicherte Vertrauensgrundlage bieten, sie zur eigenen Initiative ermutigen und ihnen zu Kompetenz verhelfen, dann können sie erfolgreich sein. Dieser Erfolg gibt ihnen Hoffnung, *realistische Hoffnung*. Dies ist ein Geschenk, das jeder von uns zuhause, im Klassenzimmer, auf dem Spielplatz und in der Nachbarschaft machen kann" (45).

they are studying and also about the factors they may find that help foster or promote resilience in this specific cultural context (cf. "Cultural Dimensions").[13]

Intervention programmes that aim at fostering individual resilience are not
only geared towards children and adolescents. There are also a number of psychologists working with adults who have taken up the concept of resilience.[14] Some
of them, like the German psychoanalyst Luise Reddemann, had previously been
working in the field of trauma therapy before recalibrating their focus towards
the concept of resilience.[15] The resilience approach offers these therapists a way to
focus not primarily on a patient's deficit or lack but on a patient's agency and ability
to help themselves. Apart from simply helping the patient mine the resources that
they already have, and train others that can be taught, Reddemann points to the
body of work of medical sociologist Aaron Antonovsky and his concept of a 'sense
of coherence' to help understand why some people in some situations seem to be
more resilient than others: Resilient individuals are able to attribute meaning to
whatever challenge they face (what Antonovsky calls a 'sense of meaningfulness').
They understand why whatever is happening to them is happening to them (what
Antonovsky calls a 'sense of comprehensibility'), and they are able to find ways of

---

13 To this end, Ungar provides an interview guide with questions that may help researchers inter-
viewing subjects and facilitates their arriving at a thick description of what resilience may mean
and how it can be achieved in a specific culture and context (cf. "Cultural Dimensions").

14 Martha Kent and Mary C. Davis provide an overview of current programmes and interventions
geared towards promoting or restoring adult resiliency (cf. "The Emergence of Capacity-Building
Programs and Models of Resilience"). Different scholars put different emphases when discussing the principles that should be developed in order to overall foster resilience. John W. Reich
argues for strengthening sense of control, coherence and connectedness in interventions following catastrophic events (Zautra, Hall and Murray, "Resilience" 20). Other researchers stress
first and foremost the restoration of a sense of agency. As Kent and Davis conclude, "resilience
is a response to challenge, just like stress and trauma are responses to challenge. Both occur in
similar contexts that are characterized by noncontingency, or contexts in which individuals have
little effect on that context or environment. Faced with an arbitrary, life-threatening event, the
resilient response is characterized by (1) an efficient stress response, (2) an approach/engage-
ment orientation, and (3) social relatedness" (442). Programmes geared towards fostering resilience will try to provide individuals with a skill set addressing all three aspects. Masten and
Wright, more generally, see "several strategies for intervention: reducing risk (e.g. [...] removing
landmines to prevent injuries to a population), increasing assets or resources (e.g. provision of
food programs, employment counselors), and mobilizing powerful protective systems (e.g. [...]
nurturing mentor relationships, empowering the leaderships of young people in rebuilding a
community after disaster or war)" (230). Angie Hart, Derek Blincow and Helen Thomas have
developed a form of resilient therapy geared specifically towards helping children in crisis (cf.
"Resilient Therapy"). For an overview of what is at stake in promoting resilience across the lifespan see also Rönnau-Böse and Fröhlich-Gildhoff, *Resilienz und Resilienzförderung über die Lebensspanne*.

15 Cf. Reddemann, *Überlebenskunst* and *Eine Reise von 1000 Meilen beginnt mit dem ersten Schritt*.

dealing with a challenging situation ('a sense of manageability'). The therapist can help the patient regain these senses when they have been lost.[16] Taken together, these three senses yield what Antonovsky calls a 'sense of coherence', a feeling which he describes as "a global orientation that expresses the extent to which one has a pervasive, enduring though dynamic feeling of confidence that (1) the stimuli deriving from one's internal and external environments in the course of living are structured, predictable and explicable; (2) the resources are available to one to meet the demands posed by these stimuli; and (3) these demands are challenges, worthy of investment and engagement" (*Unraveling the Mystery of Health* 19). Antonovsky employs the metaphor of life as a river that may run smoothly but that may also feature strong currents and swirls; in his work, he is first and foremost concerned with the question of how one may become a good swimmer – or help others become good swimmers – able to brace the currents regardless of conditions and circumstances (cf. Antonovsky).

Antonovsky is not the first to stress the importance of a restoration of a sense of meaningfulness to human health and well-being; this was already famously put forth several decades earlier by psychologist Viktor E. Frankl, who built his therapeutic intervention of logotherapy, which he developed in the interwar years, around the concepts of meaning and purpose. For Frankl, the "striving to find a meaning in one's life is the primary motivational force" in human beings, not the fulfilment of instinctual drives as Freud had argued and not a will to power as Adler had argued (*Man's Search for Meaning* 99). Frankl proposes that "the meaning of life always changes, but [...] it never ceases to be" (113). Meaning has to be discovered and can appear in several different guises. It can take the form of creating something or doing a deed; it can take the form of the experience of something or someone, which for Frankl boils down essentially to the experiencing of a value; and, if it is utterly unavoidable, even suffering can be rendered meaningful, as human beings are still always free to choose the stance they take towards the meaning of this suffering. Thus, Frankl says, one can find meaning even in suffering. Life, Frankl proposes, continues to throw questions at us, and we are called to continue to find answers to these questions.[17]

I suggest that in queer literary and cultural studies, the concept of resilience might prove to be a useful framework for the study of queer affect, not necessarily as a direct countermodel to the trauma approach, but as a model of framing human subjectivity and affect that could be in useful dialogue with it. Thus, I agree with the proponents of the trauma approach in queer studies that political activism working towards social change is still needed to lessen vulnerability fac-

---

16 Arguably, this is what the therapeutic intervention Reddemann has developed does when successfully employed (cf. *Imagination als heilsame Kraft*).

17 Cf. *Man's Search for Meaning* and *The Unheard Cry for Meaning*.

tors. Queer trauma studies does have its usefulness in pointing out how larger social and power structures can have a negative impact on queer individuals' actual (in the form of discrimination) and affective lives, and consequently a claim for social action can, and must, be made. However, I would also like to pose the question whether, as theorists of queer affect, we could imagine ourselves accepting and acknowledging the wound that queer stigma produces, and not cover it up with pride, and not remain in the victimized position either – and there is for me a danger with the trauma approach that it keeps us locked in a position of victimhood – but focus on agency on an individual and a collective level. Herein lies for me the usefulness of the concept of resiliency, which comes from a line of focussing not on being damaged but on salutogenesis, that is the study of the origin of being whole. Two points, I suggest, are useful for queer cultural studies: one, as resilience scholars stress, resiliency is something that can be trained and learned; and two: one might also look at queer historiography in that vein; to learn from past queer subjects; to find out what kinds of strategies they employed when faced with experiences of homophobic violence and/or social exclusion.

One might thus try to make out strategies of resilience in the works of the 'founding mothers and fathers' of queer theory – Michel Foucault, Judith Butler and Eve Kosofsky Sedgwick. Working with Antonovsky's concept of a 'sense of coherence', I would firstly like to suggest that the earlier works of Foucault, Butler and Sedgwick may have afforded their authors with just exactly the 'senses' Antonovsky describes as making up his 'sense of coherence': Michel Foucault's discourse analysis of how current regimes of sexuality came into being historically in *The History of Sexuality Vol. 1* affords him a 'sense of comprehensibility' of heteronormative power structures as he encounters them in 1970s and 1980s France. Similarly, Judith Butler's earlier works of *Gender Trouble* and *Bodies That Matter*, and Eve Kosofsky Sedgwick's *Epistemology of the Closet* might have helped their authors attain a 'sense of comprehensibility', and maybe to a lesser extent also 'manageability', through deconstructivist enquiry into the mechanisms of power, how our current sex/gender system came into being or by which means it is kept in place.

Secondly and maybe more interestingly, one can make out quite a number of what I would like to call resilience strategies in all of these writers' later work. One might thus read Michel Foucault's notion of 'heterotopia' in his essay "Different Spaces" and his concept of potential forms of queer community in "Friendship as a Way of Life" as possible outer, social resources for queer subjects.[18] As for inner, or personal resources, I suggest that one might productively read the later Foucault's work on technologies of the self in terms of internal strategies of queer resilience.[19]

---

18 I take up Foucault's notion of 'heterotopia' in the chapter on spatial strategies.

19 I expand on this in the chapter on emptiness.

In the case of Eve Kosofsky Sedgwick, her privileging the haptic sense in her introduction to *Touching Feeling* might be read as a somatic or bodily resilience strategy, and one could include her notion of the usefulness of periperfomative utterances as a form of performative or communicative resilience strategy for queer subjects.[20] Her discussions of gay shame, which include the idea (which she derives from Silvan Tomkins' work) that different subjects possess different shame theories, i.e. that there are people who have a high shame theory, whereas other people have a low shame theory, furthermore corresponds directly with resilience scholars' ideas about people possessing different levels of vulnerability as well as susceptibility: some people are more vulnerable than others, and different people are differentially susceptible or sensitive to contextual influences, beneficial or adversary (cf. Masten and Wright 216).[21] Finally, Judith Butler's notion in *Undoing Gender* of a subject beside itself, which is also a subject open to transformation, a subject in open-ended process, corresponds to resilience scholars' notion of the self as processual rather than static: the resilient self is a self in progress, and risk factors interact with protective factors, determining an individual's resilience in a given situation at a given point in time.[22]

Work on queer resilience so far has been undertaken mainly in the disciplines of sociology and psychology as well as social work. Kimberly F. Balsam in her introduction to the anthology *Trauma, Stress, and Resilience Among Sexual Minority Women* lists social support, the identification of sources of oppression, the confrontation of oppressive situations as well as reframing one's sexual identity as unique or a gift as strategies of resilience employed by the individuals studied in this collection of essays (cf. Balsam 6-7).[23] Marion Brown and Marc Colbourne have investigated queer youth resilience in a youth project in Nova Scotia, look-

---

20 I further elaborate on the sense of touch in the chapter on bodily strategies, and I draw – among other theories – on Sedgwick's discussion of the periperformative in the chapter on performative strategies.

21 Cf. Sedgwick, *Touching Feeling*.

22 Cf. also Aranda et al. for a discussion of Butlerian concepts of performativity and recognition and how they can be linked to ongoing theorizations around resilience ("The resilient subject").

23 For a description of resilience strategies that take into account not only instances of heterosexism but also of racism see the essay by Bowleg et al. in the same volume (cf. "Triple Jeopardy and Beyond: Multiple Minority Stress and Resilience Among Black Lesbians"). For an in-depth discussion on gender and resilience see Judith V. Jordan's essay "Relational Resilience in Girls" in the *Handbook of Resilience in Children*. Jordan argues convincingly that "resilience resides not in the individual but in the capacity for connection. [...] Mutual empathy, empowerment, and the development of courage are the building blocks of this resilience" (73). While she focuses on the importance of relational resilience in girls, she also posits that "growth-fostering connections are the source of resilience for both boys and girls" (73). For an in-depth discussion on the situation of transgender youth see Zeeman et al., "Promoting resilience and emotional well-being of transgender young people"; Singh, "Transgender Youth of Color and Resilience: Negotiating

ing at protective mechanisms at the level of the individual, family environment and gay and ally communities (cf. "Bent But Not Broken"). Their findings included that on the level of the individual youth, a belief in their right to "express truth in their being" (272) and a sense of personal agency contributed to youth resilience, as well as a "familiarity with being on one's own in some area of one's life" as this could help temporarily weather feelings of isolation; also helpful was a "personal orientation toward rejecting the negativity and myths promoted by heterosexism and homophobia" (273). Brown and Colbourne note that families of origin that welcomed and affirmed LGB youth contributed to their resilience, but more often family members that were supportive were likely to show only conditional support. Brown and Colbourne made out a precarious "marginal freedom" in families where same-sex sexuality remained invisible and unaddressed (274). They emphatically stress the importance of gay and ally communities for queer youth: "Locating and securing the means to break social isolation, accessing the gay and ally community, and sharing identity are cornerstones in naming protective features that contribute to resilience" (274). Gay and ally communities provide a peer group that validates a queer youth's identity as well as a safe space for self-expression and a place to "explore one's identity and its meanings" (274). There, information about LGB issues can be accessed and role models can be found. These "iterative and interactive relationships between self, family, and the gay and ally community" all contribute to queer youth resilience (274).

A study conducted by Michael Sadowski and Lisa Machoian with LGBTQ adolescents in a large northeastern U.S. city and later also in a rural area of the U.S. came to similar conclusions. As Michael Sadowski writes, "[f]inding spaces such as school- or community-based LGBTQ youth groups *that felt genuinely safe* and relationships in which they could *communicate openly, be themselves, and have their identities affirmed* was associated for many with the cessation of risk behaviours and a greater sense of self-acceptance" (*In a Queer Voice* 10). For the participants of Sadowski's study, gay-straight alliances at school and/or community-based LGBTQ youth groups provided a space to feel safe, supported and where they belonged as well as sites of personal empowerment, besides giving them access to "that rare, safe adult to whom [...] an LGBTQ student could talk confidentially 'about anything'" in the form of an adult GSA advisor or youth project facilitator (157). This was especially important as for numerous participants of Sadowski's study, school did not prove to be a space free of discrimination or harassment (cf. 155-156). Furthermore, in situations "in which youth felt the most isolated", such as e.g. living in a rural area, "the Internet provided a virtual lifeline. Most important [...] it served as a springboard to other forms of communication" (163-164). Again

---

Oppression and Finding Support"; and Singh, Meng and Hansen, "'I Am My Own Gender': Resilience Strategies of Trans Youth".

echoing Brown and Colbourne's findings, Sadowski reports that family support, when it was available, was rarely unconditional. His findings "suggest that (1) when LGBTQ youth report that their parents are supportive, terms such as *support* and *supportive* can have vastly different meanings based on their expectations, and (2) open communication about being lesbian, gay, bisexual, transgender, or queer is frequently absent even from otherwise supportive relationships between LGBTQ youth and their parents" (164). Sadowski consequently points towards a need for parents and families to develop a new language for talking about gender and sexuality: "Being able to be in true dialogue with the people to whom they feel closest – and having their real voices resonate in these relationships – requires that the traditional silences about sexuality and gender that pervade our society be broken" (165). Analysing interviews with the participants of his study who had been found via (and had therefore found their way already to) LGBTQ youth groups, Sadowski comes to the conclusion that even those youths "who endured severe harassment and isolation found ways to survive, and there is strong evidence to suggest that key relationships have made an important difference in this regard" (151). Some of the participants had "supportive parental relationships that incorporated open acceptance of their LGBTQ identities", others had "supportive relationships at school with their peers" or with adults or with both (151-152). Every youth seemed to have found "that 'one good relationship' – or set of relationships – that can help make a young person resilient in the face of risk and to progress on a positive developmental pathway. Ideally, of course, young people benefit from a multiplicity of relationships that interconnect across the ecology of their lives"; still, Sadowski's research highlights "the compensatory power that one adult or peer can play within a social environment that a young person otherwise experiences as unwelcoming" (152).[24]

The first German nation-wide study on the situation of LGBTQ youth, which was initiated by the federal government and saw the participation of 5000 adolescents and young adults, was carried out in 2014. In the final report on the findings, Claudia Krell and Kerstin Oldemeier diagnose a heightened vulnerability for LGBTQ youth and young adults. They present an extensive analysis of the study, which comprised an online survey and forty personal interviews with study participants aged fourteen to twenty-seven, and provide a very good overview of the current situation of LGBTQ adolescents and young adults in Germany (Krell and

---

24 Sadowski provides in-depth follow-up case studies of six of the participants in his study. Their detailed accounts demonstrate the myriad forms of context-specific resilience strategies queer youth and young adults have come up with – singular strategies that worked in the specific situations they found themselves in – to survive in a hostile environment and thrive later on in their lives (cf. 17-130). For information on how to make school environments more LGBTQ friendly, see Sadowski, *Safe Is Not Enough* and van Dijk and van Driel, *Sexuelle Vielfalt lernen*.

Oldemeier, *Coming-out – und dann...?!*). The study focused on finding out how participants had experienced their coming out processes, as well as learning about discriminatory experiences in families, schools, at work, with friends and in participants' every-day lives. The report reveals that roughly fifty percent of study participants reported having experienced discrimination at school, at work and with their immediate family (cf. 103-115; this number was higher for trans youth in some contexts, cf. 163-177). Study participants reported that having emotional support available as well as being in contact with other LGBTQs and being able to have access to information on LGBTQ issues helped them successfully navigate their coming out journeys (cf. 92). In the coming out process, which roughly seventy-five percent of all youth and young adults experienced as stressful, friends and family were described as being an asset when they were supportive of the youths' emerging LGBTQ identities (75; 126-127). Krell and Oldemeier provide an overview of conditions that either supported adolescents and young adults in their coming out journeys or made their lives more difficult, while also noting a number of strategies study participants used to better cope with their situation, to minimize stress and to take control of their lives, by e.g. actively choosing the point in time to come out to friends or family, by moving to a different environment, by hiding their queer sexuality in circumstances deemed unsafe, and by reframing discriminatory experiences to experience them as less stressful (cf. 124-134; 183-192). In a final extensive chapter, the authors call on policy makers and schools as well as youth project service providers to take measures to reduce vulnerability for LGBTQ youth and young adults (cf. 213-220).[25]

This book is the first extensive study approaching queer resilience from a literary and cultural studies perspective. By incorporating literary and cultural texts from the last 110 years, I open up a historical dimension to the available data on queer resilience. What is more, the human need to make art and to experience art, all art, goes back roughly 35,000 years, and can thus be regarded as one of the fundamental needs of human beings.[26] The experiential dimension of art is an aspect of human existence that is not extensively covered in considerations

---

25 For recent reports on the situation of LGBTQ youth and (young) adults in, variously, the U.S. and the U.K. see also the Human Rights Campaign's youth survey report *Growing Up LGBT in America*, which delineates the experiences of 10,000 thirteen to seventeen year-olds, and Nodin et al., *The RARE Research Report LGB&T Mental Health – Risk and Resilience Explored*, which analyses context specific risk and resilience factors among 2000 U.K. study participants with attention to three specific health issues: suicide attempts and self-harm among LGBT youth under twenty-six, alcohol misuse among lesbian and bisexual women, and body image issues including eating concerns among gay and bisexual men. Both studies used state-of-the-art mixed-methods approaches, that is they combine surveys of a large number of study participants with personal interviews of a smaller number of study participants.

26 Cf. Conard; Conard, Malina and Münzel; Sinclair.

of queer resilience in psychological and sociological research. This study seeks to also address this void, primarily as regards the art of literature.

In this study, I analyse literary texts as cultural artefacts, that is to say I work with the assumption that literary texts can be regarded as much as a mirror of and a valid source material for inquiring into what is at stake in a society at a given point in time as texts of the historical archive or sociological data or an ethnographer's thick description of a culture.[27] Still, literary texts possess aesthetic qualities that historical texts may lack. These will also be analysed as part of the close reading of specific literary works in the following chapters. However, literary texts and acts of writing and reading can also be employed more generally to further one's resilience, as a number of writers and readers have explored.

A short sketch of answers to the question what writing can do, what reading can do, that is to say how both can be used to promote resilience on a more general level, might read as follows: As philosopher Martha C. Nussbaum has argued, reading novels can teach empathy and help develop the moral imagination of the reader, both prerequisites for a just society; it can make many different, possibly conflicting points of view accessible to the reader in the same textual universe (cf. Nussbaum). Poet Billy Collins maintains that reading poetry can provide comfort in times of crisis, arguing that "the formalized language of poetry can ritualize experience and provide emotional focus. Poetry is thus seen as a kind of floatation device for those who find themselves at sea on troubled waters"; what is more, poetry "can assure us that we are not alone; others, some of them long dead, have felt what we are feeling. They have heard the same sea, watched the same sky; looked up to see the same moon" (Collins xvi). In a similar vein, bibliotherapists Ella Berthoud and Susan Elderkin, in their introduction to *The Novel Cure*, reason that a treatment consisting of reading one or more novels may be able to help you, whatever difficult situation you may find yourself in or whatever you may be suffering from. "Some treatments will lead to a complete cure. Others will simply offer solace, showing you that you are not alone. All will offer the temporary relief of your symptoms due to the power of literature to distract and transport"; indeed, sometimes "it's the story that charms; sometimes it's the rhythm of the prose that works on the psyche, stilling or stimulating. Sometimes it's an idea or an attitude suggested by a character in a similar quandary or jam" (2). Reading may thus become a resource to someone in distress or in a situation of heightened vulnerability. It is not just the content but also the aesthetics of the work that contribute to this experience. The reader who resonates with a work of art activates not only the prefrontal cortex but also the limbic system and evolutionarily older regions of the brain. The reception of a work of art is a whole brain activity that

---

27 I follow the premises of both new historicism and cultural materialism in this regard (cf. Brannigan).

draws on rhythm, image, metaphor and symbol as well as content for the individual to arrive at last at a deriving of meaning and insight, epiphanic or mundane (cf. Paul). This is regardless of whether the intent of reading is therapeutic or not. As novelist Ursula K. Le Guin notes in *The Wave in the Mind*, reading is "an active transaction between the text and the reader", and thus both an active experience and a creative act; to "read a story is to participate actively in the story. To read is to tell the story, tell it to yourself, reliving it, rewriting it with the author, word by word, sentence by sentence, chapter by chapter" (269). For Le Guin, the reader is active, agent, the co-creator of the book.

> "Story is a collaborative art. The writer's imagination works in league with the reader's imagination, calls on the reader to collaborate, to fill in, to flesh out, to bring their own experience to the work. Fiction is not a camera, and not a mirror. It's much more like a Chinese painting – a few lines, a few blobs, a whole lot of blank space. From which *we* make the travellers, in the mist, climbing the mountain towards the inn under the pines." (Le Guin 276)

For Jeanette Winterson in *Art Objects*, an encounter with a work of art can provide a range of experiences: insight, rapture, transformation, joy, as well as shock, for "the calling of the artist, in any medium, is to make it new" (12). Winterson may be a late modernist in this regard, but one of her points is that the artist is actually in this way connected to the past and makes him- or herself a connection to the future (12). The reader, or the recipient of any work of art, is then called upon to bring attention and patience to the table as well as curiosity and openness. They will partake of this connection, but this may entail a "series of jolts, or perhaps I mean volts, for art is an extraordinarily faithful transmitter. Our job [as recipients, S.J.] is to keep our receiving equipment in good working order" (13). The interactive process that occurs between a work of art and a recipient, say, a reader is finally never over. "There is a constant exchange of emotion between us, between the three of us", Winterson writes: between the artist, the work of art and the one beholding the work of art; she is here echoing Le Guin's notion of the process of engaging with a work of art as being a collaborative one; for Winterson, the "totality" of the work of art – in her case a picture, but it can be assumed this applies to all art – "comments on the totality of what I am. The greater the picture the more complete this process is" (19). The result of art as not only object but also as process is then manifold: an illuminating, potentially transformative encounter for the reader with open ended result; an experience of present aliveness, the "energy in being" (19); and a connection to 'truths' past and present (if one is inclined to follow Winterson who defines 'truth' in her epigraph as "that which lasts"), since art, "all art, is the communication cord that cannot be snapped by indifference or disaster. Against the daily death it does not die" (20). The encounter with art, which may

work as a training ground for curiosity and attention and invites active participation, can then act as a transformational experience, a catalyst for the resilient
self in process.

And what can acts of writing do for the one undertaking them? How can writing help promote resilience? As art therapists point out, artistic practices such as
writing can help externalize inner, psychic landscapes; these can be worked on
and transformed and then again internalized in a changed form, thus giving the
one who writes agency over his or her internal experience as well as helping them
make sense of and transform difficult feelings and experiences (cf. Susanne Lücke
in Reddemann, *Imagination als heilsame Kraft* 152-153; DeSalvo 29-46). Why do
writers write in general? To solve a problem, to conduct a thought experiment, to
think about an issue more deeply – these are some of the reasons Le Guin provides
for her own artistic practice (cf. Le Guin 279). Margaret Atwood, in *Negotiating
with the Dead*, has compiled a whole two-page list of reasons she has found writers provide for why they engage in the act of writing (cf. Atwood xx-xxii). Clearly,
motives writers find for writing are near endless. But what exactly happens in the
act of writing? For Le Guin, writing fiction results from "imagination working on
experience" (265). For her as a writer of stories and novels, "fictional 'ideas' arise
from a combination of experience and imagination that is indissoluble and unpre-
dictable and doesn't follow orders" (276). And by the experiential she means personal experience, personal observation as well as reading about others' personal
experiences (cf. 276-278). This applies even to the realm of the magical and the
fantastic.

> "Experience is where the ideas come from. But a story isn't a mirror of what hap-
> pened. Fiction is experience translated by, transformed by, transfigured by the
> imagination. [...] In a novel [...] the raw materials are not only selected and shaped
> but fused, composted, recombined, reworked, reconfigured, reborn, and at the
> same time allowed to find their own forms and shapes, which may be only indi-
> rectly related to rational thinking. The whole thing may end up looking like pure
> invention. [...] But there's no such thing as pure invention. It all starts with expe-
> rience. Invention is recombination. We can work only with what we have. There
> are monsters and leviathans and chimeras in the human mind; they are psychic
> facts. Dragons are one of the truths about us. We have no other way of expressing
> that particular truth about us. People who deny the existence of dragons are often
> eaten by dragons. From within." (268-269)

The starting point from which a story or a novel unfolds may be different for
every writer. Still Le Guin, following Virginia Woolf, proposes that one element
comes first in the act of writing for a lot of writers: a deep attention to a sense of
rhythm. "Beneath memory and experience, beneath imagination and invention

[...] there are rhythms to which memory and imagination and words all move; and the writer's job is to go down deep enough to begin to feel that rhythm, to find it, move to it, be moved by it, and let it move memory and imagination to find words" (281). Aesthetic qualities of a work of fiction, such as rhythm, are then inevitably bound up with content, may indeed precede or precipitate content for at least Ursula Le Guin and Virginia Woolf, and Woolf employs the metaphor of a wave to describe this sense of underlying rhythm that one is trying to capture in writing.[28] The attention to rhythm from which art originates, Le Guin proposes, can create a resonance that takes on an almost somatic quality, an experience of felt sense connecting writers and readers through the medium of the art object.

> "None of us is Virginia Woolf, but I hope every writer has had at least a moment when they rode the wave, and all the words were right.
>   As readers, we have all ridden that wave, and known that joy.
>   Prose and poetry – all art, music, dance – rise from and move with the profound rhythms of our body, our being, and the body and being of the world. Physicists read the universe as a great range of vibrations, of rhythms. Art follows and expresses those rhythms. Once we get the beat, the right beat, our ideas and our words dance to it, the round dance that everybody can join. And then I am thou, and the barriers are down. For a little while." (282)

Louise DeSalvo has written extensively on what life writing can do for the one undertaking it. For her, too, aesthetic qualities of the written narrative provide one pillar of the sustaining power she attributes to life writing. DeSalvo emphasises the usefulness of employing metaphor when describing experiences that are seemingly beyond words. "Because metaphors say one thing while meaning another, they are important vehicles for conveying information that seems beyond the limits of language", she maintains, claiming that metaphor not only "compacts meaning, but it also evokes emotion, so it enables us to express nonliteral experiences in a highly individualized way. Its use presents one solution to the challenge of how to render extreme situations" (166). It renders sayable what has remained unsayable and it also helps link events to feelings, thus promoting an integration of a traumatic event into one's life narrative. In *Writing as a Way of Healing*, DeSalvo advocates employing life writing to help deal with challenges

---

28 This is Virginia Woolf in a letter to Vita Sackville-West from 16 March 1926: "As for the *mot juste*, you are quite wrong. Style is a very simple matter: it is all *rhythm*. Once you get that, you can't use the wrong words. [...] Now this is very profound, what rhythm is, and goes far deeper than words. A sight, an emotion, creates this wave in the mind, long before it makes words to fit it; and in writing (such is my present belief) one has to recapture this, and set this working (which has nothing apparently to do with words) and then, as it breaks and tumbles in the mind, it makes words to fit it" (qtd. in Le Guin 280).

present and past. She is drawing and expanding on the work of James W. Pennebaker, who conducted a number of writing experiments with college students, finding that students who had taken part in a study consisting of writing about a previous challenging event in their lives for fifteen minutes a day during four consecutive days, with a focus on describing what had happened to them, the impact this event had had on their lives as well as what their feelings regarding this event were then and now, improved their health in the long term (cf. DeSalvo 17-28; Pennebaker). DeSalvo advises on how to approach longer life writing projects but also posits the benefits of engaging in the act of writing itself on a regular basis:

> "What [...] if writing weren't [...] a luxury? What if writing were a simple, significant, yet necessary way to achieve spiritual, emotional, and psychic wholeness? To synthesize thought and feeling, to understand how feeling relates to events in our lives and vice versa? What if writing were as important and as basic a human function and as significant to maintaining and promoting our psychic and physical wellness as, say, exercise, healthful food, pure water, clean air, rest and repose, and some soul-satisfying practice?" (6)

Benefits of a regular writing practice, according to DeSalvo, may include: becoming a witness, an observer of one's own life; writing as a centering ritual when one sets up a regular schedule of writing in a relaxed way; learning to let the process be the guide by keeping a process journal; in time, DeSalvo says, writing will yield surprising benefits; it can be engaged in as a form of self-care and act as an agent of transformation (cf. 69-107). Approached in this way, writing can become an engagement in an "act of creation that energizes and enlarges us"; it is then a "gift that comes to us. A gift we give ourselves. A gift we give to others" (92). DeSalvo is one of a growing number of writers and therapists positing that engaging in life writing can promote resilience. What is at stake is not only a working through of experience but also, critically, the expression of a self in language. As DeSalvo and also trauma therapist Bessel van der Kolk have argued, engaging in any artistic practice, whether writing or doing theatre, can open up pathways to navigating difficult experiences and their aftermath by providing avenues for expressing oneself, for finding a voice, giving testimony and giving a voice to experience.[29] What acts of writing and reading can do specifically for queer subjects, then, will be discussed extensively in the following chapter.

---

29 Cf. van der Kolk, *The Body Keeps the Score* 230-247; 330-346.

The Art of Bouncing Back

The current study presents and analyses an archive of literary and cultural texts from the twentieth and early twenty-first centuries, among them short stories, novels, poems, plays and films as well as published interviews with queer artists and, sometimes, activists. These texts, I argue, showcase a whole range of strategies of queer resilience that queer artists and cultural workers have been able to come up with, in their life and in their art, for the past 110 years to help them deal with the challenge heteronormativity, as a power structure, poses to their affective lives. In this book I analyse these strategies in terms of how they relate to cultural concepts around narration, performance, space and bodies; I furthermore present a strategy of dealing with modern subjectivities in a way that is conducive to queer resilience that I term the art of emptiness.

In the first chapter, I discuss what I term narrative strategies of queer resilience. This chapter shows how queer subjects employ identificatory, disidentificatory and deconstructive narrative practices in order to establish themselves, that is their narrative identities, as queer subjects. The narrator of Jeanette Winterson's *Oranges Are Not the Only Fruit* serves as a literary example for this mode of queer becoming and being. I furthermore show how novelists, such as Michael Cunningham in *The Hours*, as well as queer historiographers employ intertextual narrative strategies to work towards extending existing queer textual archives. Another narrative resilience strategy can be found in queer reception processes of narrative media. Readers and spectators can read a narrative against the grain, and can even derive new narratives from this act of reception. Meaning thus turns out to be a field co-created by both producers and consumers of cultural texts, potentially opening up any (heteronormative) cultural text to the insertion of queer subjectivities and contents.

The second chapter presents 'other' ways of 'doing' queer subjectivities. Following Louis Althusser's notion that an individual becomes a subject by being hailed into an ideological subject position, thus becoming recognized as a subject, I pose the question whether queer artists and theorists might not have discovered ways by which one might disregard ideology's interpellating call. I present two forms of 'doing' subjectivity in another way while still being recognizable to oneself as a subject: the art of emptiness and the art of self-care. What I term the art of emptiness is basically a way of letting go of the need to be recognized as a subject. This is a stance towards human subjectivity that is best known from Buddhist epistemologies, but I suggest that the same gesture can be found in the queer subjectivities of some of the poetic personas of contemporary poet Mary Oliver and in the queer subjectivities of a number of characters in novels by Sylvia Townsend Warner from the 1920s and 1930s, especially *Lolly Willowes* and *Summer Will Show*. In a postscript, I present Michel Foucault's model of practices of self-care as a viable alternative to knowledge practices of the self. Foucault finds notions of doing subjectivity in another way in the writings of Greek and Roman philosophers of late antiquity. These technologies of the self, as he calls them, and particularly the stance of privileging the care of the self over the knowing of the self, serve for Foucault as models of potentially doing subjectivity in another way.

In the third chapter I discuss performative strategies of queer resilience. I take a look at how queer subjects make use of both performance and performativity as strategies of queer resilience. I show how a number of contemporary queer cultural icons consciously publicly perform their queer sexuality, by (i) using patterns of disclosure and non-disclosure of their queer sexuality, by (ii) employing the performance and publication of a song as an act of creative sexual citizenship, or by (iii) drawing on the periperformative in comedic stand-up performances. For this I draw on published interviews of the actors Ian McKellen and Zachary Quinto as well as on art by musician Melissa Etheridge and writer and performance artist Lynnee Breedlove. I furthermore trace patterns of the strategic disclosure and non-disclosure of his queer sexuality in the life of George, the protagonist of Christopher Isherwood's early 1960s novel *A Single Man*. Lastly, I present a close reading of actor and playwright DeObia Oparei's play *Crazyblackmuthafuckin'self*, tracing how its protagonist Femi employs camp performance, performativity and ritual as strategies of queer resilience.

The fourth chapter deals with spatial strategies of queer resilience. In this chapter I look at how fictional characters and actual cultural workers and authors make use of the spaces they travel to, create or inhabit, spaces both metaphoric and real. I apply Foucault's notion of heterotopic space as a space of utopian possibility that already exists within the real to earlier texts of the twentieth century, namely two short stories by Katherine Mansfield and Elizabeth Bowen, which use the trope of the garden as a heterotopic queer space, and a poem by Robert Duncan in which an interior heterotopic space emerges as a safe space. Queer space, I contend, can be understood to be one form of heterotopic space. I furthermore trace the emergence of actual queer spaces in the city of San Francisco from the beginning of the twentieth century to the late 1970s. This decade saw the development of whole residential neighbourhoods with openly LGBTQ residents, fostering a sense of connection among an emerging LGBTQ community and providing a space for many to feel safe and belong and from which a political movement could eventually emerge.

In the final chapter I outline what I term bodily strategies of queer resilience. In this chapter I take a look at what I call the art of postpornography, that is queer works of art that purposefully disregard the interpellating call of the pornographic vs. the non-pornographic binary. These works of art depict sexual bodily acts and subjects of a variety of sexual identities, demonstrating the ideological investment underlying the art/porn binary, which turns out to be invested with heteronormative interests. I trace this in a close reading of *Shortbus*, a narrative feature film, and in a poem by Mark Wunderlich. I also trace an epistemology privileging bodily sensations and feelings and the sense of touch in poems by May Swenson, Thom Gunn, Pat Parker and Carol Ann Duffy, which I link to current neuroscientific research regarding the body and to somatic therapies that can be employed to promote resilience. Bodily experiences emerge in this chapter in a number of ways as potential resources for queer subjects.

Hegemonic power structures, such as heteronormativity, may thus have a challenging and sometimes also traumatizing (in the sense of wounding) effect to an individual's interior experience, but the individual subject, as I argue, is not without both internal and external resources. Strategies of queer resilience similar to the ones that I am going to discuss in the following can hopefully be learned and employed by any given subject. In this book I am presenting writers and artists, and characters developed by writers and artists, that have become good swimmers, to use Antonovsky's metaphor; queer subjects that have come up with a myriad of strategies to answer the question that life, that is living in a heteronormative society, posed – and continues to pose – to them, as Viktor Frankl might have phrased it. May their creativity inspire yours.

Narrative Strategies

How do we come to tell ourselves the story of who we are? What is, more generally, the role of narrative and narration in (queer) people's lives? And how can acts of reading and writing help to further the resiliency of queer subjects? These are some of the questions the following chapter traces. "Most fundamentally, to *narrate* is to tell a story", says literary theorist Julian Wolfreys ("Narrative" 162). The human being is a meaning making animal, and narrative is, according to Wolfreys, "that which produces a particular identity or meaning through the singular arrangement of a temporal and spatial series of incidents, figures, motifs and characters" (163). Wolfreys characterizes narrative as being "fundamental to most, if not all societies and cultures throughout history, whether the act of narration is carried out orally, through pictures or pictograms, through staging or ritual, in film, or in writing. Narration offers patterns and images which acts of reading seek to comprehend in ways that see in narrative a mediation of individual or social beliefs, habits, or ideologies" (163). Anthropologists, such as Nigel Rapport and Joanna Overing, come to similar conclusions (cf. "Narrative").

Sexual identity then, like any other facet of one's personal identity, requires a narration which the subject provides for itself to comprehend itself as a subject. Identity, whether individual or collective, is always mediated through narration. Paul Ricoeur has coined the term 'narrative identity' to in some form capture this basic feature of human experience. For Ricoeur, "[t]he constitution of narrative identity, whether it be that of an individual person or of a historical community", is the site of a "fusion between narrative and fiction" ("Narrative Identity" 188). Taking autobiography as an example, Ricoeur argues that "self-knowledge is an interpretation; self interpretation, in its turn, finds in narrative, among other signs and symbols, a privileged mediation; this mediation draws on history as much as it does on fiction, turning the story of a life into a fictional story or a historical fiction" ("Narrative Identity" 188). In "Life in Quest of a Narrative", he argues that "[i]t is [...] by means of the imaginative variations of our own ego that we attempt to obtain a narrative understanding of ourselves, the only kind that escapes the apparent choice between sheer change and absolute identity. Between the two lies narrative identity" (33). According to Ricoeur, subjects accomplish this feature by the narrative act of emplotment, a concept Ricoeur borrows from Aristotle, that is, they become the creators of their own, "well constructed" stories by a process that is "an operation, an integrating process" ("Life in Quest of Narrative" 21). This process of both narration and meaning making is an ongoing process; narrative identities are thus always provisional and constantly open to rewritings, in flux, renegotiable; a doing, not a being. One constantly rewrites the story of one's life, and even the signifying systems themselves may change over time. It is also by means of narrative that human beings arrive at what Aaron Antonovsky calls a 'sense of meaningfulness' and a 'sense of coherence', both important preconditions for resiliency in Antonovsky's conception of salutogenesis (cf. *Unraveling the Mystery of Health*). Viktor Frankl's logotherapy, with its emphasis on discovering meaning in life, equally makes use of narrative (cf. *Man's Search for Meaning* and *The Unheard Cry for Meaning*).[1]

Subjects thus narrate themselves to themselves, creating their own (ever evolving) personal narrative identities or stories of self. At the same time, they are tied to larger structures of social and cultural collectives also by the medium of narrative. Mythology, literature, as well as historiography can perform this function for the subject. Indeed, as Laurence Coupe points out in *Myth*, "'mythology', the body of inherited myths in any culture, is an important element of literature, [...] and literature is a means of extending mythology. That is, literary works may be regarded as 'mythopoeic', tending to create or recreate certain narratives which human beings take to be crucial to their understanding of their world" (4).[2]

Queer subjects in a heteronormative cultural context may, however, run into trouble when trying to create their own narrative identities, or when trying to integrate their personal identities into larger relational narratives of the cultural and the social. As minoritarian subjects, queer subjects may on occasion find it difficult to locate cultural subject positions that are readily available to them via simple processes of identification. Still, identification – that is establishing a similarity between oneself and someone else that one knows (of) – is probably the easiest way of locating oneself culturally, and queer artists and other well-known queer people often cite this as one of their reasons for coming out publicly: they want to offer themselves as role models or as sites of identification for LGBTQ youth (see e.g. the example of Zachary Quinto in the chapter on performative strategies).

However, often more complex processes of partial identifications have to be employed by queer subjects in order to make sense of their own lives, and also

---

1   See the introduction for a further elaboration of Antonovsky's and Frankl's ideas and how they pertain to the concept of resilience.

2   For examples of the function and role of myth in various cultures see also Rapport and Overing, "Myth". Willie Erskine and Rodney Frey provide interesting takes on the role of myth and storytelling from a modern-day indigenous point of view.

of their lives in terms of a larger social and cultural context. Various critics have attempted to describe these processes of partial identifications.[3] José Esteban Muñoz' concept of 'disidentification' – which he developed in the context of queer of colour criticism, where simple processes of identification are even harder to come by – is the model that maybe best describes the complex processes involved in narrating a self that lies outside the bounds of hegemonic discourse. For Muñoz, disidentification is at the same time "a hermeneutic, a process of production, and a mode of performance" (*Disidentifiactions* 25). Muñoz writes, "[t]he fiction of identity is one that is accessed with relative ease by most majoritarian subjects. Minoritarian subjects need to interface with different subcultural fields to activate their own senses of self" (5). To disidentify "is to read oneself and one's own life narrative in a moment, object, or subject that is not culturally coded to 'connect' with the disidentifying subject" (12). It is also, "[l]ike melancholia, [...] an ambivalent structure of feeling that works to retain the problematic object and tap into the energies that are produced by contradictions and ambivalences" (71). Muñoz provides an example for this when he relates his own memory of seeing Truman Capote on a TV show, who left a lasting impression on his "pre-out consciousness" (4); yet, struggling to locate and verify Capote's comment years later, he discovered that "my memory and subjectivity reformatted that memory, letting it work within my own internal narratives of subject formation" (4). Disidentification can be regarded as both a narrative and a performative affective strategy for minoritarian subjects. I am most concerned with narratives of the self, here, but for Muñoz, disidentification is also a modality of performance and performance art, one that he ascribes a worldmaking power to.[4]

A further alternative narrative strategy to queer subjects' exclusion from larger heteronormative cultural narratives may be the deconstruction of hegemonic narratives by e.g. the use of parody by queer subjects or authors.[5] Outlining the cultural work parody can do for feminist enquiry, Linda Hutcheon has described this narrative practice in her book *The Politics of Postmodernism*.

> "As a form of ironic representation, parody is doubly coded in political terms: it both legitimizes and subverts that which it parodies. This kind of authorized trans-

---

3 Cf. Muñoz, *Disidentifications* 13-15.

4 In this sense, disidentification is for Muñoz "a performative mode of tactical recognition that various minoritarian subjects employ in an effort to resist the oppressive and normalizing discourse of dominant ideology. [It] resists the interpellating call of ideology that fixes a subject within the state power apparatus. It is a reformatting of self within the social. It is a third term that resists the binary of identification and counteridentification" (*Disidentifications* 97).

5 I agree with Nicholas Royle, who characterizes deconstruction as being "concerned with the ludic, patient attempt to trace what has not been read, what remains unread or unreadable within the elaboration of concepts and workings of institutions" (160).

gression is what makes it a ready vehicle for the political contradictions of post-modernism at large. Parody can be used as a self-reflexive technique that points to art as art, but also to art as inescapably bound to its aesthetic and even social past. Its ironic reprise also offers an internalized sign of a certain self-consciousness about our culture's means of ideological legitimation. How do some representations get legitimized and authorized? And at the expense of which others? Parody can offer a way of investigating the history of that process. In her feminist pacifist work *Cassandra* [...] Christa Wolf parodically rewrites Homer's tale of men and war. [...] Because we only know Cassandra through male representations of her, Wolf adds her own feminist representation, one that is equally the 'creation' of a writer, of course.

In feminist art, written or visual, the politics of representation are inevitably the politics of gender. [...] Postmodern parodic strategies are often used by feminist artists to point to the history and historical power of those cultural representations, while ironically recontextualizing both in such a way as to deconstruct them." (97-98)

The use of parody as outlined by Hutcheon is equally useful for queer cultural enquiries, I propose, and indeed Hutcheon makes much the same argument in an epilogue to the second edition of her book (cf. 178-179).

The following chapter aims at looking at narrative resilience strategies employed by queer subjects. These include, I propose, the following: narrations of self that employ strategies of identification and disidentification when narrating the self; strategies of deconstructing hegemonic narratives by making use of, for instance, pastiche and parody; the act of writing and rewriting one's story; furthermore, intertextual strategies that utilize or work towards extending queer textual archives; and finally, reception processes that generate new narratives which include queer subjectivities or viewpoints which the original narrative lacked or obscured. In the following, I will present readings of Jeanette Winterson's *Oranges Are Not The Only Fruit*, Michael Cunningham's *The Hours* as well as the works of queer historiographers such as Valerie Traub and Carolyn Dinshaw, Amy Fox' *Heights* and, finally, queer fan fiction in light of these narrative queer resilience strategies.

Narrating the Self in Jeanette Winterson's *Oranges Are Not The Only Fruit*

Jeanette Winterson's novel *Oranges Are Not The Only Fruit* presents the fictional autobiography of the narrator 'Jeanette', an account of her life from birth to adulthood. It is both a coming-out and a coming-of-age novel of a lesbian teenager raised in a strictly religious community of Evangelical Christians.[6] By Winterson's own admission, the novel "offers a complicated narrative structure disguised as a simple one [...]. This means that you can read it in spirals. As a shape, the spiral is fluid and allows infinite movement. But is it movement backwards or forwards? Is it height or depth? Draw several, each drifting into each and all this will be clear" (*Oranges* xiii). By presenting the reader with layers of narratives, both Winterson and her narrator Jeanette can be found to be employing all three of the above-mentioned strategies for narrating the self: identification, disidentification, and deconstruction. The act of writing itself appears, finally, as another quite powerful resilience strategy for the author Jeanette Winterson.

As a mythopoeic text, the Bible serves as the narrative foundation for both practices of identification and disidentification for the character of Jeanette in *Oranges Are Not The Only Fruit*. The structuring of the novel into chapters, named after the first eight books of the Old Testament, yields us the narrative of Jeanette from birth in the novel's first chapter, accordingly called "Genesis", to her achieving a state of fully-formed adult narrative identity of lesbian sexual subjectivity in the novel's final chapter "Ruth". On the structural level of the division of chapters, both Winterson and Jeanette here identify with the Bible as a mythopoeic text. "Genesis" presents us with an account of Jeanette's first seven years of her life, describing her origins, the family environment she grows up in (she is an adopted child) and the community of Evangelical Christians who make up her – and her mother's – entire world. In "Exodus", she has to leave the familiar environment of being home-schooled by her mother behind to join a regular school, "the Breeding Ground" (17), as her mother calls it, a place where Jeanette finds herself mystified and bullied and essentially lost in the wilderness – much like the Israelite tribes in the desert in the second book of the Pentateuch. "When the children of Israel left Egypt, they were guided by the pillar of cloud by day, and the pillar of fire by night. For them, this did not seem to be a problem," the narrator relates. "For me, it was an enormous problem. [...] The daily world was a world of Strange Notions, without form, and therefore void" (*Oranges* 47).[7] "Leviticus", which in the Bible outlines laws such as purity laws and the nature of various sins, depicts the notion of sin as Jeanette's mother and various local religious authorities understand it – from sex and the "Heathen [...] Next Door" (51) to the Society of the Lost's sermon on

---

6 Sonya Andermahr places the novel in the generic and historical context of "a specifically lesbian reworking of the Bildungsroman genre or novel of development" (50), while Lyn Pykett reads *Oranges* as "Winterson's *A Portrait of the Artist as a Young Man*, rewritten as a portrait of the artist as a young working class lesbian who flees the nets of religion and community and refuses to subdue her own inner light and sexuality [...] to serve the craven world of heterosexual respectability" (58).

7 This is also a reference to Genesis 1. The narrator employs biblical language and metaphor to render her experience.

being flawed as the opposite of perfection; perfection, in the words of the local pastor, is "a thing to aspire to. It was the condition of the Godhead, it was the condition of man before the Fall" (58). Here, however, Jeanette finds herself developing her "first theological disagreement" (58), not doubting the merit of perfection as a thing to aspire to itself, but questioning her congregation's definition of perfection as flawlessness. Perfection, the narrator maintains (via the means of a fairy tale inserted into the main narrative), is not flawlessness but rather a balance of qualities and strengths (cf. 62). "Numbers", which in the Bible contains the genealogy of the tribes of Israel, outlining generations of fathers and sons, has Jeanette pondering the merits of heterosexual marriage – neither the marriages of various neighbours nor the marriages in her immediate family environment inspire much confidence in the hailed union of man and woman, from which such offspring might follow. It is not until Jeanette finds herself developing feelings for Melanie, a girl she meets at the local market, that she understands what such a union, what love might be. She brings Melanie with her to church, and spends the night with her. "And it was evening and it was morning; another day", the narrator announces this transformative experience (86), again making use of biblical symbolism: falling in love with and having sex with another woman is presented as another genesis, a story of creation, a rebirth for Jeanette into an other subjectivity. "Deuteronomy", which in the Bible contains three sermons by Moses – a summary of the history of the people of Israel so far as well as the presentation of divine rules to live by such as the Ten Commandments and delivered shortly before the people of Israel are to enter Canaan, the Promised Land – contains a metanarrative by an unidentified narrative voice, a meditation thematically linked to both Jeanette's story and the book of the Old Testament: a meditation on time, making sense of one's past, the truth values of history writing and storytelling, the order and balance to be found in stories.

In "Joshua", the first of the Bible's history books named after the religious leader Joshua, the successor of Moses, Jeanette aptly becomes a religious leader in her own right, serving as a preacher in her congregation and as a tent missionary in Blackpool. However, the walls (of Jericho) fall, and her mother discovers Jeanette's affair with Melanie, prompting an exorcism to be performed on her in order to get rid of the demon that, this is the doctrine of her church, has befallen her and led her astray. In another inset story, an Eden-like secret garden appears "on the banks of the Euphrates", containing an orange tree. To eat the fruit of this tree of (sexual) knowledge "means to leave the garden because the fruit speaks of other things, other longings. So at dusk you say goodbye to the place you love, not knowing if you can ever return, knowing you can never return by the same way as this" (120). The story of sexual awakening of same-sex love is again couched by the narrator in biblical imagery and language. For Lauren Rusk, this passage equally "speaks of deepest longings, danger, and banishment; it invokes the central religious ideas of Eden and the Eucharist; and it centers around the oranges of the title which often appear at emotionally laden moments in Jeanette's life" (119). In the Bible's second history book, Judges, a number of powerful religious leaders (such as Deborah, Gideon, Samson) emerge while the tribes of Israel fight against enemies, are unfaithful and therefore punished. The themes of power struggles and powerful religious leaders, of sharp dividing lines between friends and perceived enemies dominate this chapter in the novel as well. Jeanette, a successful preacher in her own right by now, finds herself cast out of her congregation – and home – once more after her next relationship with Katy, another female member of her church, comes to light. Out of his depth this time around, the pastor appeals to the church council for further advice. The council decrees that the "real problem, it seemed, was going against the teachings of St Paul, and allowing women power in the church" (*Oranges* 131). Taking a man's place in the pulpit, the pastor and Jeanette's mother agree, has led Jeanette to "flout God's law and [try] to do it sexually" as well (131). This time Jeanette refuses to repent and is thrown out by her mother. "'You'll have to leave,' she said. 'I'm not havin' demons here'" (134). Jeanette leaves, taking with her "my books and my instruments in a tea chest, with my Bible on top" (134). The Evangelical congregation is left behind but not the faith, nor its foundational book of stories. "At that time I could not imagine what would become of me", the narrator concludes, "and I didn't care. It was not judgement day, but another morning" (134).

In the Old Testament, the Book of Ruth finally contains the story of Ruth and Naomi, arguably the Bible's most well-known proto-lesbian couple, and a story of loyalty among women and of choices made in the name of love. It is Ruth who is unwilling to let go her mother-in-law Naomi after her husband's death, promising to leave her own native Moab and accompany Naomi to her native Judaea: "Intreat me not to leave thee, or to return from following after thee: for whither thou goest, I will go; and where thou lodgest, I will lodge: thy people shall be my people, and thy God my God. Where thou diest, will I die, and there will I be buried: the Lord do so to me, and more also, if ought but death part thee and me" (*King James Bible*, Ruth 1.16-17). In Winterson's chapter "Ruth", Jeanette finishes school while working various jobs and living with a teacher. She eventually moves to the city, where she tries to leave her past behind, coming to realize however, that instead of trying to run from her past or disavow it, she had much better confront it and integrate it into her current life and the person she has become, a self-identified lesbian and a writer. She ponders her choices, again making use of biblical metaphors.

"'What would have happened if you had stayed?'
I could have been a priest instead of a prophet. The priest has a book with the words set out. Old words, known words, words of power. Words that are always

on the surface. Words for every occasion. The words work. They do what they're
supposed to do; comfort and discipline. The prophet has no book. The prophet is a
voice that cries in the wilderness, full of sounds that do not always set into meaning. The prophets cry out because they are troubled by demons. [...] I came to this
city to escape.
If the demons lie within they travel with you." (156-157)

The writer-prophet is the one without a known script. The writer-prophet is the
one who turns weaknesses into strengths, exploring the abject, disavowed parts of
him- or herself, her "demons", to emerge with the story (stories) of her self or selves
in an autoethnographic fiction aiming at finding the narrative truth(s) of her narrative identity to find an answer to the question, Who am I? And how did I come to
be the person that I am? At the end of the novel, Jeanette returns home one Christ-
mas to find her mother unchanged (except for the fact that she has gone electric
and has become an amateur radio missionary now), and Melanie playing down
her past feelings for her. Both occasions are experienced as emotional betrayals
by Jeanette, which she connects with her past life within the Evangelical Christian
community both her mother and Melanie belong to. "By betrayal, I mean promising to be on your side, then being on somebody else's" (166). It is in the world of
the city that she hopes to find both the kind of same-sex loyalty and love among
women embodied in the story of Ruth and Naomi and a more successful same-sex
relationship than the ones she previously had.

> "I miss God. I miss the company of someone utterly loyal. I still don't think of God
> as my betrayer. The servants of God, yes, but servants by their very nature betray.
> I miss God who was my friend. [...] I want someone who will be on my side for
> ever and ever. I want someone who will destroy and be destroyed by me. There
> are many forms of love and affection, some people can spend their whole lives
> together without knowing each other's names. Naming is a difficult and time-con-
> suming process; it concerns essences, and it means power. But on the wild nights
> who can call you home? Only the one who knows your name. Romantic love has
> been diluted into paperback form and has sold thousands and millions of copies.
> Somewhere it is still in the original, written on tablets of stone. I would cross seas
> and suffer sunstroke and give away all I have, but not for a man, because they want
> to be the destroyer and never be destroyed. That is why they are unfit for romantic
> love. There are exceptions and I hope they are happy." (164-165)

By the novel's close she is still searching for love and recognition, by a beloved
other, by a divine Other, and through the telling of her story, a recognition by herself of her own self. For this is what the activity of narrating the self provides: a
recognition of oneself, the knowing and the naming of oneself, provisionary as it

may be, that is necessary for the subject to experience him- or herself as a coherent subject.[8] Queer theorists such as Judith Butler and Donald E. Hall make much the same point: "The Hegelian tradition links desire with recognition", says for instance Judith Butler in *Undoing Gender*, "claiming that desire is always a desire for recognition and that it is only through the experience of recognition that any of us become constituted as socially viable beings" (2). And Donald Hall in his book *Reading Sexualities* maintains that "[s]exual identity is a narrative we tell ourselves and we tell about ourselves" (1).[9] Complex and open to change as it may be, it is still a story that has to be narrated and read by us in order for us to understand and make sense of our selves and our world.

If at the level of discourse, biblical language and imagery is invoked again and again in an identificatory manner in Winterson's novel, at the story level, Jeanette of course encounters severe problems when her teenage relationship with Melanie, another girl of the same congregation, comes to light. The pastor singles both of them out for a public revelation and confrontation with their purported sins. Jeanette here successfully employs the narrative strategy of disidentification. That is, she identifies only with some aspects of, in this case, the biblical text and her congregation's reading of it, while actively and consciously discarding other aspects that may be harmful to her emerging queer subjectivity.

> "'These children of God,' began the pastor, 'have fallen under Satan's spell.'
> His hand was hot and heavy on my neck. Everyone in the congregation looked like a waxwork.
> 'These children of God have fallen foul of their lusts.'
> 'Just a minute ...,' I began, but he took no notice.
> 'These children are full of demons.'
> A cry of horror ran through the church.
> 'I'm not,' I shouted, 'and neither is she.'
> 'Listen to Satan's voice,' said the pastor to the church, pointing at me. 'How are the best become the worst.'
> 'What are you talking about?' I asked, desperate.
> 'Do you deny you love this woman with a love reserved for man and wife?'
> 'No, yes, I mean of course I love her.'

---

8 Naming is also an act of creation and an expression of power and agency. In Genesis 1 it is God who bestows names unto entities and creatures. In Genesis 2, Adam gets to name all creatures. The act of naming creates and establishes a bond. It is an expression of power but also entails responsibility towards those one has named.

9 Hall, however, is more interested in acts of reading than acts of writing, and in treating "our sexual narratives as occasions for reading and, more to the point, readerly response" (2).

> 'I will read you the words of St Paul', announced the pastor, and he did, and many
> more words besides about unnatural passions and the mark of the demon.
> 'To the pure all things are pure,' I yelled at him. 'It's you not us.'" (102-103)

Jeanette identifies only with those parts of the Bible and the Christian faith that
leave her subjectivity intact. Her love for Melanie is love, the same kind of love
which is described in the biblical quotations she is familiar with, even if those
provide only examples of heterosexual love. She rejects all notions of abjection,
maintaining that to the "pure all things are pure", a direct quote from the New
Testament (Titus 1.15; *English Standard Version*).[10] The biblical passages quoted to
her by the pastor, the notions of 'good' sexual subjectivity transported by the biblical passages written by St Paul the pastor refers to (presumably Romans 1.26),[11]
are not part of her mythology. Laura Doan sees this as one of the strengths of
Winterson's novel. "Jeanette's strength and the strength of this coming-of-age/
coming-out novel, emerges from a profound and unshakeable conviction that her
lesbianism is right and that any attempt to condemn or despise her – a celebrant
of the most natural of passions – constitutes perversion" (137).

Already before their public outing, another instance of disidentification
occurs when Jeanette, together with Melanie, ponders their emerging attraction
to each other.

> "'Do you think this is Unnatural Passion?' I asked her once.
> 'Doesn't feel like it. According to Pastor Finch, that's awful.' She must be right, I
> thought." (86)

At this point, both girls trust their feelings more than the pastor's and Jeannette's
mother's interpretation of the Bible. Jeanette considers Melanie "a gift from the
Lord, and it would be ungrateful not to appreciate her" (*Oranges* 102). She stresses
that she loves both Melanie and the Lord even when the pastor tells her that she
cannot do so (cf. 103). Jeanette's disidentificatory act is even articulated metaphorically in the novel through an inset fairytale describing a feast by the elect
("Father Son and Holy Ghost") set in a Winter Palace about to be stormed by rebels
(cf. 86-87). Disidentification becomes an act of rebellion here. During the exorcism that follows their public outing, Jeanette experiences a vision of her "demon",
who tells her that "everyone has a demon [...] but not everyone knows this, and not
everyone knows how to make use of it" (106). Demons are not evil, her – orange –

---

10 Another translation renders Paul's Epistle to Titus thus: "Everything is pure to those whose
    hearts are pure" (*New Living Translation*).

11 There are no direct quotes from the Bible in the pastor's speech. He merely employs the diction
    of biblical verse while drawing on some ideas outlined in Romans 1.

demon maintains. "We're here to keep you in one piece, if you ignore us, you're quite likely to end up in two pieces, or lots of pieces, it's all part of the paradox" (106). In other words, knowing about and integrating one's disavowed aspects is better than fighting them in oneself (and others). "But in the Bible you keep getting driven out", Jeanette says (106). "Don't believe all you read", her demon tells her, thus supporting the disidentificatory strategy Jeanette is already employing. In a similar vein, Sonya Andermahr reads Jeanette's demon "as a 'daemon', an aspect of herself which, in an internal dialogue, allows her both to express qualms about her lesbianism and to receive reassurance of its positive value" (55). Jeanette's dis-identification becomes finally fully articulated in "Judges": "While some of our church forgave me on the admittedly dubious grounds that I couldn't help it [...], my mother saw it as a wilful act on my part to sell my soul"; falling in love with a girl had for her, first "been an accident. That accident had forced me to think more carefully about my own instincts and others' attitudes. After the exorcism I had tried to replace my world with another just like it, but I couldn't. I loved God and I loved the church, but I began to see that as more and more complicated" (*Oranges* 126).

As a postmodern text, Winterson's novel makes use of the Bible at the same time as an intertext and a foil. The deconstructionist, parodic aspects of the novel are already conveyed in "Genesis", with a seven-year-old Jeanette rewriting the story of Daniel in the Lion's Den using Fuzzy Felt figures – in her version, Daniel is swallowed by the lions (cf. *Oranges* 12). Likewise, in "Exodus" she drowns one of the animals (a detachable chimpanzee) of a collage of Noah's Ark (cf. 24); and at a hyacinth growing competition in primary school, she names her ensemble of pink hyacinths "The Annunciation" because "the blooms were huddled up close, and reminded me of Mary and Elizabeth soon after the visit by the angel" (45). When contrary to her expectations, the ensemble does not win a prize, she feeds "The Annunciation" to her rabbit, even though "I was a bit uneasy afterwards in case it was heresy, and the rabbit fell sick" (45). Biblical stories, foundational texts of the Old and New Testament are deconstructed and work no longer as authoritative texts for either the seven-year old Jeanette or the adult narrator.[12] With its inter-

---

12　I regard disidentification and deconstruction as two separate strategies, as I see in the act of disidentifying still a holding onto and affirming a part of something (while discarding other parts), i.e. a partial identification; whereas deconstruction renders visible the cracks in the logic, dismantling that something, not holding onto any part of it. I furthermore see the kind of parody that Hutcheon outlines in *The Politics of Postmodernism* and that Winterson employs in *Oranges* as making use of primarily modes of deconstruction and not modes of disidentification, as the position employed is one of ironically subverting a source text, here the Bible. The affirmative gesture, the love, the emotional investment that I connect with modes of disidentification is markedly absent.

woven narrative layers of fairytales and strangely rewritten Arthurian myths, as well as deconstructed Bible scenes, the novel serves as both a mythopoeic text and at the same time deconstructs, through the use of parody, mythology as a basis for any cultural authority – and hegemonic notions of identity.[13]

The following rewriting of Sir Thomas Malory's *Le Morte D'Arthur* and Sir Perceval's quest for the Holy Grail may serve as a second example of Winterson's use of parody in her novel, by which she casts doubt on the project of going on heroic quests – in search of ultimate truths meant to bring ultimate peace to the seeker.

> "On his last night at Camelot, he found Arthur walking in the garden, and Arthur had cried like a child, and said there was nothing. […] On the first day and the second day and the third day, Perceval could have turned back, he was still within the sphere of Merlin. On the fourth day, the woods were wild and forlorn, and he did not know where he was, or even what had driven him there. Now Sir Perceval lay on the bed and fell asleep.

---

13   Other critics have found a diverse range of functions the story inserts can be argued to perform in relation to the main narrative. For Susana Onega, the "interpolation of the Perceval story adds a mythical and archetypal dimension to Jeanette's autobiographical life story, providing the unitary quest pattern into which the other subsidiary texts can be integrated" (26), while Andermahr sees *Oranges* arguing "for the validity of different, competing definitions of the real, endorsing discredited cosmologies and mythologies, and imbuing them with fresh explanatory power: folk tales, Greek myth, Grail legend, old wives tales are all seen as repositories for a human wisdom and way of knowing the world which is as truthful as orthodox, rational versions of reality" (56). Rusk and Paulina Palmer, on the other hand, link the fantasy episodes to psychological realism. For Palmer, they "are an integral part of the novel […]. The interplay of narratives which they create highlights the part which fantasy plays in the construction of the adolescent psyche and gives a more complex and multifaceted representation of subjectivity than is usually found in the Coming Out novel" (101). And Rusk sees these "allegorical sections correspond to adjacent events in the narrative, figuratively expanding on the psychological implications of those happenings. The early chapters each include one fairy tale, but after Jeanette is outed, the fantasies increase, which suggests that she must use all her imaginative resources to interpret and cope with the social repercussions of her private life" (107). Isabel Gamallo, finally, merges the two strands of criticism to some extent, claiming that by "her interweaving of fabulous narratives, Winterson manages to build up a parallel and alternative plot that replicates and complements, while simultaneously problematizing, the realistic coming-of-age story. These fantastic tales comment on, explain, displace, condense, and/or allegorise some of the crucial elements displayed in the linear progression of realistic events, subverting the possibility of a single, authoritative reading of her fiction" (126); with her inclusion of mythical tales, thus "discarding a single, autonomous, unitarian model of subjectivity, Winterson also conveys a clear awareness that experience – even autobiographical experience – cannot be explained or legitimised by a single overarching narrative and that there is no one single established and accepted path through experience. […] Since the act of storytelling itself is the most basic of all techniques for establishing an identity, the self becomes a constantly shifting entity, a product of language and narratives, and ultimately, a narrative in itself" (127).

He dreamed of that supper time, when there was a great cracking and crying of thunder and in the midst of the blast entered a sunbeam seven times brighter than the day. Each of them saw the other as they had never seen before, and every man was struck dumb. Then into the hall came the Holy Grail covered with white samite. They had vowed there and then to seek it, and not to rest until they had obtained a full view of it, and Arthur had sat silent looking out of the window.

When Perceval awoke, the sun was sinking. He must wash and greet his host. He would speak of the Grail, but not of his reason for seeking it. He had seen the vision of perfect heroism and, for a fleeting moment, the vision of perfect peace. He sought it again, to balance him. He was a warrior who longed to grow herbs." (161)

Winterson's Perceval is a "warrior who longed to grow herbs". He will later wonder about the purpose of his journey: "His journey seemed fruitless, and himself misguided" (168). Winterson's rewriting seems to suggest that maybe the quest for the Holy Grail – of narrative identity, of narrative queer identity or any other kind of narrative sexual identity – is not all that important. That a Perceval who abandons his quest might be the happier Perceval. Or a Perceval who never set out on his quest to begin with, who has stayed with King Arthur, who seems to be, in this reimagining, the only character who might prize the company of his knights higher than their leaving him for their individual quests, possibly never to return. Hence the king's expression of sadness. Happiness for Winterson's knights seems to lie in the present moment, of a dinner between knightly companions, of retired knights growing herbs in a garden, not in the setting out for quests and heroic adventures.

Winterson does not intend to provide the reader with a readymade solution to the problems around the role of narrative in humans' lives, to questions of authority and truth and definitive narrative identities. "[W]hen someone tells me what they heard or saw, I believe them", the narrator maintains in "Deuteronomy", "and I believe their friend who also saw but not in the same way, and I can put these accounts together and I will not have a seamless wonder but a sandwich laced with mustard of my own" (*Oranges* 93). What might even work as some sort of philosophical conclusion is, however, immediately ironically subverted. "Here is some advice. If you want to keep your own teeth, make your own sandwiches ..." (93).

This does not make the task easier for literary critics of Winterson's work. For Paulina Palmer, "*Oranges Are Not the Only Fruit*, while rejecting a unitary model of subjectivity in favour of a delineating of fantasy identities and multiple selves, also [...] envisages and depicts subjectivity itself in terms of narrativity. Jeanette, instead of uncovering a single, static identity, constructs for herself a series of shifting, fluid selves by means of the acts of storytelling and fabulation in which she engages" (101), while for Laurel Bollinger, "[i]n blending Biblical references with Jeanette's story, Winterson deliberately challenges the distinction between fact and fiction as well as between the novel she is writing and the Biblical texts she uses for her parody. These Biblical texts are already problematic; not quite history and not quite story-telling, their position on any kind of fact-fiction continuum changes with the point of view of the observer" (365). I see Winterson, with her making use of deconstruction as a textual strategy which she employs most prominently in the metatextual chapter "Deutoronomy", as partaking in the project of postmodernism, which declared the merits of grand narratives of any kind to be questionable (cf. Malpas). However, I do agree with Lyn Pykett who proposes that "Winterson's postmodernism is post-Modernist not in the sense of constituting a break with Modernism or superseding it, but rather as a collaborative dialogue with Modernism" (53); for, "despite the fact that it disrupts all sorts of foundationalist assumptions Winterson's early fiction is nevertheless very affirmative, especially of such universals as art, the imagination, and romantic love" (56).[14] Similarly, Andermahr sees Winterson writing "about desire *per se*", claiming that "this depiction is frequently grounded in lesbian experience, using that experience as a take-off point, continually reaching beyond particular bodies, selves and actions for the universal" (23); still, Winterson "represents 'reality' and 'identity' as radically unstable concepts, whereby the 'self' and the world it inhabits are continually in flux" (25). As my analysis has shown, the narrator in *Oranges Are Not the Only Fruit* tries out and successfully employs various modes of engaging with authoritative cultural texts in her quest for a viable narrative sexual identity, among them modes of identification, disidentification and deconstruction. Winterson's novel is therefore both: a lesbian novel, delineating with the character of its narrator Jeanette narrative strategies of queer resilience. At the same time it is a postmodern (post-Modern) text, tentatively questioning the usefulness of rigidly set constructions of narrative identity for any kind of subject.

It is, finally, the act of writing itself which may serve as a resilience strategy for queer subjects, here for the author Jeanette Winterson. "Is Oranges an autobiographical novel? No not at all and yes of course", she maintains in the novel's introduction (*Oranges* xiv). She elaborates on this in an interview with literary critic Margaret Reynolds: "In *Oranges* the narrator has my name, because I wanted to invent myself as a fictional character. [...] [A]ll writing is partly autobiography in that you draw on your own experience, not in a slavish documentary style, but in a way that transforms that experience into something else. I saw myself as a

---

14 Onega also regards Winterson as an heir to high modernist writers such as Virginia Woolf, Ezra Pound and T. S. Eliot, but sees her writing as also influenced by Gabriel García Márquez, Italo Calvino and Isabel Allende, as well as British writers Angela Carter, Sara Maitland and Marina Warner.

shape-shifting person with many lives, who didn't need to be tied to one life" (qtd. in Reynolds and Noakes 16-17). In the same interview Winterson also reveals that the act of writing serves another purpose for her. She uses writing as an epistemological tool; her intention is to understand – herself and the world she lives in. "I also write so that I can explain the world to myself, because writing becomes a third person – it becomes something which is separate from yourself. It's no longer you, although it's generated by you, and when it returns to you it explains things. It explains you to yourself and it explains the world" (11-12). Applied to *Oranges Are Not the Only Fruit*, Winterson says, this means:

> "I was trying to explain [to myself] where I'd come from. I was trying to make sense of a bizarre childhood and an unusual personal history. And I was trying to forgive. I don't think it's possible to forgive unless you can understand, and one of the things that writing can do – that literature can do, that all art can do – is to help you understand. It can put you in a position which is both inside and outside of yourself, so that what you get is a depth of knowledge, otherwise not possible, about your own situation, and a context in which to put that situation, so you're no longer alone with feelings that you can't manage. People's powerlessness comes from feelings that they can't manage, and especially those that they can't articulate. Being able to write a story around the chaos of your own narrative allows you to see yourself as a fiction, which is rather comforting, because, of course, fictions can change. It's only the facts that trap us. I've always thought that if people could read themselves as fictions they would be much happier." (qtd. in Reynolds and Noakes 12)

Writing, the creation of narrative, for Winterson promotes self-understanding as it makes conscious what had before remained unconscious, enabling one to find shape and meaning in what emerges on the page. "I'm always trying to understand life as a story"; this is how she characterizes one of her key themes in her work (qtd. in Reynolds and Noakes 25). In her case, as in *Oranges* for example, there is often not only one story but there are several. What kinds of truths can then narrative, even multiple and sometimes conflicting narratives offer the reader? "The writer will say, 'Here's a possibility, here's a set of clues, here's a pattern which may or may not be useful to you.' And in those hesitations and gestures, I think, we come closer to a truth than in any possible kind of documentary objectivity. [...] [Writers] do not claim to have that certainty and that knowledge, but they do claim to have a map, passed down from hand to hand, redrawn, uncertain, but the buried treasure is really there" (21). The reader's job, then, or the writer's job when reading their own narrative, is to collect the clues, recognize the pattern, and see if it provides meaning, if it promotes their understanding – of the work, of themselves and of the world.

It is not just writing, but also *rewriting* one's own story, that can serve as a narrative resilience strategy: recreating what should have been and thereby healing the past, that is, acknowledging neglected needs of a past self and imaginatively providing for them. Winterson makes use of this in *Oranges* as well when she introduces the character of Elsie, an elderly member of the congregation who steps in when her mother fails Jeanette and who, over time, becomes Jeanette's only champion and friend. When Jeanette, aged seven, loses her hearing and has to undergo an operation to have her adenoids removed, it is Elsie who regularly visits her in hospital, reading her the Bible, Swinburne, Rossetti's *Goblin Market*, telling stories and providing nuggets of wisdom. "She said stories helped you to understand the world", the narrator says (*Oranges* 29). "What looks like one thing", says Elsie, "may well be another" (30). Another time, she tells Jeanette: "'There's this world,' she banged the wall graphically, 'and there's this world,' she thumped her chest. 'If you want to make sense of either, you have to take notice of both'" (32). When Jeanette's needlework project does not win a prize in school (in fact, it is derided by the teacher), Elsie offers a different framework to think about Jeanette's creative project to the one provided by the teacher. "Once a thing was created it was valid for all time. Its value went not up nor down. Perception, she said was a fraud; had not St Paul said we see in a glass darkly, had not Wordsworth said we see by glimpses? [...] I knew what she meant. It meant that to create was a fundament, to appreciate, a supplement. Once created, the creature was separate from the creator, and needed no seconding to fully exist" (45). Later, Jeanette spends time with Melanie at Elsie's. Elsie knows of and approves of the relationship, and does what she can to protect Jeanette. She is unable to prevent either the exorcism after Jeanette and Melanie are discovered or the religious quarantine Jeanette is put under after her relationship with Katy comes to light. Nevertheless she remains a calming presence for Jeanette amid the chaos wreaked by her mother and the pastor. "We didn't talk about *it*", the narrator relates, "not the rights or wrongs or anything; she looked after me by giving me what I most needed, an ordinary time with a friend" (130).

In her memoir *Why Be Happy When You Could Be Normal?*, published twenty-five years later and another story written in order to understand some of the same territory as the one covered in *Oranges*, Winterson reveals that Elsie, in the semi-autobiography that is *Oranges*, is a fiction:

> "I am often asked, in a tick-box kind of way, what is 'true' and what is not 'true' in *Oranges*. Did I work in a funeral parlour? Did I drive an ice-cream van? Did we have a Gospel Tent? [...]
>
> I can't answer these questions. I can say that there is a character in *Oranges* called Testifying Elsie who looks after the little Jeanette and acts as a soft wall against the hurt(ling) force of Mother.

I wrote her in because I couldn't bear to leave her out. I wrote her in because I really wished it had been that way. [...]
There was no Elsie. There was no one like Elsie. Things were much lonelier than that." (6-7)

Winterson says of her own story, of adoption, of her unknown origin, of being raised by Mrs Winterson: "There are markings here, raised like welts. Read them. Read the hurt. Rewrite them. Rewrite the hurt" (*Why Be Happy* 5). That is what she is doing in *Oranges*: rewriting her past as it could have – should have been. And that is also what she is doing with the invention of a character like Elsie. "To avoid the narrow mesh of Mrs Winterson's story I had to be able to tell my own. Part fact part fiction is what life is. And it is always a cover story. I wrote my way out" (*Why Be Happy* 5-6).

Acknowledging neglected needs of a past self and imaginatively providing for them: the principle Winterson uses is also one that is employed by therapists such as Luise Reddemann and others, who encourage clients to use their imagination in healing past trauma by, for instance, providing imaginatively in the form of a loving adult self for a younger self that has been overwhelmed by a past event, thus creating the trace of trauma. If this imaginative scenario is engaged in repeatedly, the traumatic memory will over time lose its emotional charge, that is, the network of neural pathways that make up the traumatic memory in the brain will reorganize itself.[15] Using the present to heal the past works because one can be in both at the same time. Winterson acknowledges this contemporaneity of the past and the present for the act of writing. It presumably also extends to the psychic space of therapy. When writing, Winterson says in her interview with Reynolds, "[y]ou really are in the place, at the moment, but that moment itself is fully expanded because you are travelling in time and in imagination to all sorts of other moments. In itself, the act of writing is proof that time is neither constant nor straited ... that it is this vast moving thing, entity, energy, that none of us can fully realise and that our only chance is to inhabit it as best we can" (qtd. in Reynolds and Noakes 24).

Narrating the Past: Michael Cunningham's *The Hours* and Queer History Writing

Queer presents and queer pasts meet up quite spectacularly in another late twentieth-century novel, Michael Cunningham's *The Hours* from 1999, which imaginatively engages on several levels with Virginia Woolf's 1925 novel *Mrs Dalloway*,

---

15 Cf. Reddemann, *Imagination als heilsame Kraft* and *Psychodynamisch Imaginative Traumatherapie*.

and which – via intertextual narrative strategies – works towards producing and extending existing queer textual and cultural archives. Always under threat of either neglect or even complete erasure from mainstream cultural archives, the recuperation of queer texts of the past and the production of and continuing engagement with queer textual and cultural archives has been of utmost importance to queer cultural workers for the past several decades. For, as Judith Halberstam notes in her book *In a Queer Time and Place*, the queer archive "is not simply a repository; it is also a theory of cultural relevance, a construction of collective memory" (169-170).[16] In what follows, I want to propose both queer intertextual novel writing and queer history writing as possible forms of narrative resilience strategies for queer subjects.

Woolf's novel tells the story of a day in the life of two characters walking the streets of London on a day in June in 1923: Clarissa Dalloway, fifty-two-year-old wife of Richard, a moderately successful MP, who is about to give a party on the same night; and Septimus Warren Smith, a shell-shocked war veteran and failed poet, on the brink of suicide and searching for a doctor who can cure him. Both ponder their past and present (usually, a sensual perception of the present prompts a sense memory of the past and the narration of the past event takes off from there), meet old acquaintances and reflect on life, love and the decisions they have made. Both are made transparent to the reader with the help of evocative, poetic language and innovative modernist storytelling techniques such as stream-of-consciousness narration and rapidly changing points of view. Throughout the day, Clarissa's mind takes her back to another day at her childhood home Bourton, when she was eighteen and being courted by both Richard and Peter Walsh (another character who is to reappear in the novel's present). But it is her friend Sally Seaton who really captured the eighteen-year-old Clarissa's heart. "[H]er relation in the old days with Sally Seaton. Had not that, after all, been love?" the middle-aged Clarissa ponders (*Mrs Dalloway* 35). Sally's "charm was overpowering, to her at least, so that she could remember standing in her bedroom at the top of the house holding the hot-water can in her hands and saying aloud, 'She is beneath this roof ... She is beneath this roof!'" (37); Sally makes her feel "as she crossed the hall 'if it were now to die 'twere now to be most happy'. That was her feeling – Othello's feeling" (37-38). And on a stroll along the terrace at Bourton comes "the most exquisite moment of her whole life passing a stone urn with flowers in it. Sally stopped; picked a flower; kissed her on the lips. The whole world might have turned upside down! The others disappeared; there she was alone with

---

16 Ann Cvetkovich importantly also points to queer archives as archives of feelings that can also be "archives of emotion and trauma"; for "that gay and lesbian history even exists has been a contested fact, and the struggle to record and preserve it is exacerbated by the invisibility that often surrounds intimate life, especially sexuality" (242).

Sally" (38). Clarissa's (queer) moment of happiness will, of course, not last. She will eventually marry Richard Dalloway, thus becoming Mrs Dalloway, the novel's titular heroine.

Regarding Woolf's treatment of lesbian and gay subject matter in both her life and her fiction, literary critics have over the last two decades done away with stereotypes of a repressed lesbian sexual subjectivity and have instead come to the conclusion that, as Patricia Cramer puts it, "[e]xternal censorship – not personal inhibition – is the primary cause for Woolf's circumspect treatment of lesbian themes in her writing" (120); indeed, not in the least "the 1928 trial and banning of Radclyffe Hall's lesbian novel, *The Well of Loneliness*, made clear to Woolf and other women writers of her generation that any public defense of lesbianism could result in legal retaliation" (Cramer 119). Woolf therefore had to resort to the use of allusions, or to employ lesbian metaphors and codes in much of her writing intended for publication during her lifetime, while her letters and diaries afforded her a greater amount of freedom to discuss lesbian themes (cf. Cramer 121-124). Eileen Barrett convincingly traces several discourses around female same-sex desire prevalent in the 1920s which make their appearance in *Mrs Dalloway*: the discourse of romantic friendship in Clarissa's relationship with Sally Seaton, and the discourse of sexual inversion which can be found in Clarissa's reactions to the figures of Miss Kilman and Lady Bruton, both minor characters in *Mrs Dalloway*; Barrett also points to the homoerotic desire between Septimus Smith and his deceased friend Evans – Septimus remains, throughout the novel, "haunted by his love for his comrade Evans" (Barrett 152).[17] Kate Haffey also analyses the relationship between Clarissa and Sally Seaton, focussing on the effect the memory of the kiss between the adolescent Sally and Clarissa continues to have on the adult Clarissa Dalloway: "In the process of recollecting this memory of Sally, Clarissa is able to actually experience again the feelings that she had when she was eighteen years old. The feeling attached to this memory seems to rupture the divisions between Clarissa's past and her present" (141). Haffey argues that moments such as these "seem to do a few things in *Mrs. Dalloway*. Rather than merely recalling the past, they make visible the very presence of that past. Moments also function to dissolve the difference between Clarissa's childhood, adolescence, and adulthood" (145). The discourse of romantic female friendship in *Mrs Dalloway* can therefore not be reduced to the description of one moment, one kiss between two women thirty-four years prior; it continues to figure prominently in the novel's present and for the fifty-two year old Clarissa Dalloway.

---

17 For an overview of lesbian readings of *Mrs Dalloway*, see Eileen Barrett, "Unmasking Lesbian Passion: The Inverted World of *Mrs. Dalloway*" and Patricia Cramer's introduction to *Virginia Woolf: Lesbian Readings*. For a very early lesbian reading of the novel see Shalom Rachman, "Clarissa's Attic: Virginia Woolf's *Mrs. Dalloway* Reconsidered".

Cunningham's *The Hours* engages with Virginia Woolf and her novel *Mrs Dalloway* in three interlinked stories, all of which take place during a single day: in 1990s New York City, Clarissa Vaughan, a modern-day Clarissa Dalloway, prepares to throw a party for her dying friend Richard, a writer who suffers from AIDS; in Los Angeles shortly after the end of the second World War, housewife and mother Laura Brown bakes a cake for her husband's birthday while intermittently reading Woolf's novel *Mrs Dalloway* throughout the day;[18] and in Richmond in 1923, Virginia Woolf starts working on a new novel about a character called Mrs Dalloway. In his novel, Cunningham emulates Virginia Woolf's aesthetics (her focus on perception and stream of consciousness narration), and takes up some of Woolf's themes (love, life, death, writing, living moment by moment, making and maintaining connections). He rewrites Woolf's triangular relationship between Clarissa, Richard and Sally in his 1990s storyline – where Clarissa is married to Sally and still a close friend of Richard, her onetime lover – and foregrounds queer desires and kinship structures that had partly already been present in Woolf's novel even if their potential remained underdeveloped, such as Clarissa's infatuation with Sally Seaton, and expands on them. Furthermore, Cunningham's reader in the 1940s storyline, Laura Brown, and Cunningham's writer in the 1920s storyline, Virginia Woolf, are also haunted by queer desires which is expressed in the recurring motif of the (same-sex) kiss. Here is Cunningham reimagining Virginia Woolf, towards the end of the day at Hogarth House, musing about the heroine of her new book:

> "Clarissa Dalloway will have loved a woman, yes; another woman, when she was young. She and the woman will have had a kiss, one kiss, like the singular enchanted kisses in fairy tales, and Clarissa will carry the memory of that kiss, the soaring hope of it, all her life. She will never find a love like that which the lone kiss seemed to offer." (*The Hours* 210)

What prompts this creative decision in Cunningham's revisioning is the character Virginia Woolf's memory of a kiss between herself and her sister Vanessa of the same day – Cunningham here follows Woolf biographer Hermione Lee's assessment that her sister Vanessa was the 'great love' of Virginia Woolf's life.[19] "The kiss was innocent – innocent enough", Cunningham's Virginia thinks; "but it was also full of something not unlike what Virginia wants from London, from life; it was full of a love complex and ravenous, ancient, neither this nor that. It will

---

18 Laura Brown's surname can be read as a nod to an essay by Woolf, "Mr Bennett and Mrs Brown", which outlines some of her thoughts on how modern novelists should best approach characterization.

19 Cf. Castle, *Literature of Lesbianism* 776.

serve as this afternoon's manifestation of the central mystery itself" (*The Hours* 209-210). Earlier, in the kitchen, in the presence of Nelly, the cook, "[s]he, Virginia, has kissed her sister, not quite innocently, behind Nelly's broad, moody back" (210). In 1990s New York City, Cunningham's Clarissa also kisses her partner Sally after returning home from her outing to buy flowers for the party. "They kiss quickly, on the lips. They are always generous with kisses" (89). But Clarissa's thoughts return throughout the day to another kiss she shared with Richard at age eighteen, beside a pond in Wellfleet, when Richard had loved both her and Louis – "Louis the farm-boy fantasy, the living embodiment of lazy-eyed carnality" (11).[20] The relationship did not last, neither Clarissa's with Richard nor Richard's with Louis. But what "lives undimmed in Clarissa's mind more than three decades later is a kiss at dusk on a patch of dead grass, and a walk around a pond as mosquitoes droned in the darkening air. [...] That was the moment, right then. There has been no other" (98). Woolf's central image around desire of the (same-sex) kiss in *Mrs Dalloway* is fur-thermore taken up in the 1940s storyline, where Laura Brown kisses her neighbour Kitty, former member of the in-crowd at their local high school where "Kitty and her friends [...] were the queens of the various festivals, the cheerleaders, the stars of the plays" (102). Kitty pays Laura an unexpected visit, disclosing to Laura that she has to undergo an operation and is suffering from a quite possibly terminal ill-ness. During the intimate embrace that follows, "Kitty lifts her face, and their lips touch. They both know what they are doing. They rest their mouths, each on the other. They touch their lips together, but do not quite kiss" (110). Laura's thoughts will return to the incident later in the day, when she is all by herself:

"She touches her lips, where Kitty's kiss briefly resided. She doesn't mind so much about the kiss, what it does and does not imply, except that it gives Kitty an edge. Love is deep, a mystery – who wants to understand its every particular? Laura desires Kitty. She desires her force, her brisk and cheerful disappointment, the shifting pink-gold lights of her secret self and the crisp, shampooed depths of her hair. [...] She can kiss Kitty in the kitchen and love her husband, too." (143)

The various kisses stand in emblematically for queer desires and form one of the elements linking the three stories. The original image from *Mrs Dalloway* is taken

20 "It was 1965; love spent might simply engender more of the same. It seemed possible, at least. Why not have sex with everybody, as long as you wanted them and they wanted you? So Richard continued with Louis and started up with her as well, and it felt right; simply right. Not that sex and love were uncomplicated" (96).

up by Cunningham and reworked, expanded, brought into play again and again over the course of the three stories, symbolically linking them.[21]

On the level of story, too, Woolf's *Mrs Dalloway* is repeatedly evoked. Laura Brown, when reading Woolf's novel as a means of escaping for a moment a stifling existence in post-war Los Angeles, is drawn in by Clarissa Dalloway's love of life. Woolf's novel is quoted at length in Cunningham's story, and the reader reads Woolf alongside Laura Brown: "*In people's eyes, in the swing, tramp, and trudge; in the bellow and the uproar, the carriages, motor cars, omnibuses, vans, sandwich men shuffling and swinging, brass bands; barrel organs; in the triumph and the jingle and the strange high singing of some aeroplane overhead was what she loved; life; London; this moment of June*" (*The Hours* 41; Cunningham's italics indicate that this is a direct quote from *Mrs Dalloway*). Both the image of the flying aeroplane and Woolf's phrase "*life; London; this moment of June*" (111), full of dactyls and alliterations, will come back to Laura over the course of her day, anchoring her like a talisman in a reality which to her does not quite feel real at all, "[t]he world, this world", which "feels suddenly stunned and stunted, far from everything" (111). In fact it is the reality of the book which feels more real to her at times; she yearns for a life beyond the one she is already living. Reading Woolf's novel both stabilizes and inspires Laura Brown, and she will, over the course of the novel, come to change her life.[22] In the New York City storyline, Cunningham's characters use Woolf's characters as icons. It is Richard, the writer, who comes up with the literary nickname for Clarissa Vaughan.

> "The name Mrs. Dalloway had been Richard's idea – a conceit tossed off one drunken dormitory night as he assured her that Vaughan was not the proper name for her. She should, he'd said, be named after a great figure in literature, and while she'd argued for Isabel Archer or Anna Karenina, Richard had insisted that Mrs. Dalloway was the singular and obvious choice. There was the matter of her existing first name, a sign too obvious to ignore, and, more important, the larger ques-

---

21 Haffey also analyses Cunningham's use of the image of the (same-sex) kiss in *The Hours*. However, her argument is largely concerned with notions of queer temporality. "Like Woolf, Cunningham uses the kiss as a vehicle that is able to cut across time and connect two disparate moments. The kiss between Clarissa and Sally thus becomes a model for a type of queer moment that Cunningham himself further develops" (150). Haffey argues that if "Laura's kiss takes her outside the script she feels she is following each day of her life, and if the memory of Clarissa's kiss returns her to a moment when 'anything could happen', then the kiss between Virginia and Vanessa combines and extends these aspects" (155).

22 As Maria Lindgren Leavenworth puts it, "[r]eading becomes a place in which [Laura] can find herself and escape the pressures from her life" (517). Leavenworth elucidates how the changes made in the film adaptation of *The Hours* help flesh out Laura Brown's storyline and further trace her decisions' complex ramifications for the life of her son.

tion of fate. She, Clarissa, was clearly not destined to make a disastrous marriage or fall under the wheels of a train. She was destined to charm, to prosper. So Mrs. Dalloway it was and would be." (10-11)

In the novel's present, Richard's intuition has proven correct: Clarissa Vaughan has prospered and continues to charm.[23] The nickname also has stuck; Richard continues to call her "Mrs Dalloway". Like her literary namesake, Clarissa Vaughan enjoys playing the role of hostess and throwing parties to foster connections among people.[24] She has deliberated at length who to invite and who not to invite for the party she is giving in honour of Richard's being awarded a prestigious poetry prize. "She will give Richard the best party she can manage. She will try to create something temporal, even trivial, but perfect in its way. She will see to it that he is surrounded by people who genuinely respect and admire him [...]; she will make sure he doesn't get overtired. It is her tribute, her gift" (123). In the same diligent manner she employs for organizing a social event, Clarissa devotedly looks after and cares for the dying Richard; queer kinship ties extend here beyond the immediate family circle formed by Clarissa, Sally and their daughter Julia. However, before the party is about to commence, Richard kills himself by jumping out of a window, thus mirroring the suicide of Septimus Warren Smith in Woolf's *Mrs Dalloway*.[25] The final tableau of the New York City storyline sees Clarissa, Sally and Julia welcoming Richard's mother into their home – and symbolically also into the web of extended queer kinship and family around Clarissa, Sally and the deceased Richard. Richard's mother turns out to be Laura Brown, the housewife and mother of the Los Angeles storyline, who the reader learns left both

---

23 Clarissa lives with Sally in an apartment, "[t]wo floors and a garden", in the West Village; "[t]hey are rich, of course; obscenely rich by the world's standards; but not *rich* rich, not New York City rich. They had a certain amount to spend and they lucked into these pine-planked floors, this bank of casement windows that open onto the bricked patio where emerald moss grows in shallow stone troughs and a small circular fountain, a platter of clear water, burbles at the touch of a switch" (91).

24 Mary Joe Hughes links the recurring imagery of water and waves, as well as the plunge, in both *Mrs Dalloway* and *The Hours* to the theme of connections and connectedness: Woolf "clearly intends the imagery of waves and water" in *Mrs Dalloway* "to suggest the vast concentric circles of interconnection that unite the disparate characters of the novel, as well as the unfathomable depths beneath the surface of their thoughts and actions" (351). Both Clarissa Dalloway and Clarissa Vaughan enjoy throwing parties and furthering connections among people, offering occasions where "one individual's being ripples out into others, drawing them from their isolation into something more general. [...] Clarissa's offering is to help further this 'radiancy' through her parties" (Hughes 353).

25 Richard's suicide can be read either as the deliberate choice of a terminally ill man or as the unfortunate result of his mixing a number of medications which are not meant to be taken simultaneously.

her husband and son (and a life which had become unbearable to her) to become a librarian in Toronto. Clarissa's final musings once again echo her famous literary namesake's affirmation of life in the face of death:[26]

> "Yes, Clarissa thinks, it's time for the day to be over. We throw our parties; we aban-
> don our families to live alone in Canada; we struggle to write books that do not
> change the world [...]. We live our lives, do whatever we do, and then we sleep [...]. A
> few jump out of windows or drown themselves or take pills; more die by accident;
> and most of us, the vast majority, are slowly devoured by some disease or, if we're
> very fortunate, by time itself. There's just this for consolation: an hour here or there
> when our lives seem, against all odds and expectations, to burst open and give us
> everything we've ever imagined, though everyone but children (and perhaps even
> they) knows these hours will inevitably be followed by others, far darker and more
> difficult. [...]
> Heaven only knows why we love it so." (225-226)

Living life fully means, says Clarissa Vaughan (says Clarissa Dalloway, says Virginia Woolf, says Michael Cunningham), accepting that death is not on the outside but inevitably forms a part of it. The fullness of life can be grasped by truly being open to experiencing and cherishing it, moment by moment, both the challenging and the exhilarating times. One will inevitably follow the other but neither will last forever. And a full life will inevitably consist of both. Thus Cunningham's Clarissa Vaughan concludes:

> "Forgive us, Richard. It is, in fact, a party, after all. It is a party for the not-yet-dead;
> for the relatively undamaged; for those who for mysterious reasons have the for-
> tune to be alive.
> It is, in fact, great good fortune." (226)

Earlier in the day, Clarissa Vaughan had pondered which book to buy for an acquaintance. "You want to give him the book of his own life, the book that will locate him, parent him, arm him for the changes" (21-22). Presumably, such a book is Woolf's *Mrs Dalloway* for the writer Michael Cunningham.

But what drew Cunningham to Virginia Woolf, and to her novel *Mrs Dalloway* in particular? Why write about her of all writers? "Because she was a genius and a visionary, because she was a rock star, because she was the first writer to split the atom, because I'm in love with her, because she knew that everyone, every single person, is the hero of his or her own epic story", says Cunningham ("Michael Cunningham after Hours" 30). He discovered *Mrs Dalloway* while still in high

---

26 Cf. Woolf, *Mrs Dalloway* 202-203.

school, "and the book just nailed me; I've thought about it almost constantly ever since" ("Michael Cunningham: New Family Outings" 53).[27] For the writer Michael Cunningham, writing – and thus reimagining – Virginia Woolf writing *Mrs Dalloway* can therefore perform several functions. It can be a way of being, imaginatively, close to a writer he loves. It can be a way of imaginatively inhabiting the life of the author Virginia Woolf, a walking in someone else's shoes and seeing the world from someone else's (Virginia Woolf's) perspective. The novel creates and expresses a form of kinship between Woolf and Cunningham, who share aesthetics, thematic concerns, attitudes and beliefs. Cunningham's novel is an expression of a queer love affair over time, a declaration of kinship. It fosters an imagined community of queer writers past and present. Woolf's text provides Cunningham with a mirror of love in which he finds recognition and self-recognition as a (queer) writer: what he finds when reading Woolf, what he sends back when writing to (about) Woolf. *The Hours* is a love letter to Virginia Woolf. It is also a translation of Woolf's novel for modern-day readers. As a piece of intertextual writing it furthers the creation of (it constructs, it produces) a queer textual archive.[28]

What I have so far argued for queer intertextual novel writing can also be argued for queer history writing: both acts of narration can serve as narrative resilience strategies for queer subjects. If we consider, following Hayden White,[29] history writing as an act of narration, then several questions open up: Why are we interested in history? What use is there in knowing about our individual and collective past, where we come from and how the world that we live in came to be, to us today? History writing can provide meaning and orientation for us:[30] a place to belong along the arrow of time and a community to belong to over time. Historiography has the power to explain to us how the world and the culture we live in came to be the way it is, thus providing us with an understanding of our present and locating us as being part of a bigger whole. I am, then, part of a continuing line of ancestors, even if they are ancestors in spirit. It provides us with an internal map of our world and shows us our place in it. If Michael Cunningham's novel

---

27 Margret Fetzer reads such authorial statements on Cunningham's part as conveying that "instead of giving the known facts of [Woolf's] life, he wrote about the effect the known facts, as well as the reading of *Mrs Dalloway*, had upon him" (69). Accordingly, Fetzer reads Cunningham's novel as "an innovative contribution to theories of reading and writing. Reading and writing are important topics not only within the novel [...]: they are also strongly implicated in the making of the book itself [...]. On both these levels, reading and writing feature as creative and potentially procreative processes" (65).

28 For further examples of intertextual novels that engage with a queer past see Jodie Medd, "Encountering the past in recent lesbian and gay fiction".

29 Cf. White, *Metahistory*.

30 For history writing as providing orientation cf. Jörn Rüsen, *Historische Orientierung*.

forms part of and at the same time produces a queer textual archive and an imagined community of queer writers and readers past and present, it also forms part
of and produces a site of queer cultural and collective memory and carries this
memory forward in time.[31]

Likewise, queer historiography can do several things at the same time. It can
provide a corrective lens to a mainstream historiography which ignores the discourse and fact of same-sex desire and which, at its worst, projects current majoritarian (i.e. heteronormative) discourses onto the past and thus falsifies the discourse of desire and the history of sexuality itself.[32] Queer historiography can also
provide queer subjects with a narration of who they are culturally, individually,
collectively. Queer history writing can, most importantly for the purpose of this
study, provide a stabilizing mirror for queer individuals, providing (self-)recog-
nition of the transhistorical occurrence of same-sex desire – it can admittedly at
times also work at disorienting queer individuals who cling too narrowly to an
identity-based conception of sexual subjectivity, a model of sexual subjectivity
which cannot necessarily be shown to exist transhistorically as a majoritarian discourse.[33] Historians such as David M. Halperin, Valerie Traub and Carolyn Dinshaw have traced various discourses around same-sex desire as they pertain to
different historical time periods in Western culture.[34] How do they conceptualize
what their insights can do for contemporary queer subjects? This is, for instance,
Valerie Traub, in the introduction to her book *The Renaissance of Lesbianism in Early
Modern England*:

> "*The Renaissance of Lesbianism in Early Modern England* is simultaneously an act of his-
> torical recovery and a meditation on the difficulties inhering in such an act. My
> desire is to explore our historical differences from early modern women while

---

31 On the notion of cultural memory cf. Jan Assmann, *Das kulturelle Gedächtnis*; Aleida Assmann,
    Erinnerungsräume; and Astrid Erll, *Kollektives Gedächtnis und Erinnerungskulturen*. On the notion of
    imagined communities, cf. Benedict Anderson, *Imagined Communities*. I am here borrowing An-
    derson's concept, which was originally developed in the context of theorizing the nation-state.

32 For an example of what such a process of negotiation between mainstream and queer historiog-
    raphy can look like in a German context, see the curatorial statement of the joint 2015 exhibition
    of the *Deutsches Historisches Museum* and the *Schwules Museum** Berlin (cf. Birgit Bosold, Dorothée
    Brill and Detlef Weitz, "Wildes Wissen").

33 For an overview of the history of various discourses on male same-sex desire and their trans-
    historical continuities and discontinuities see David M. Halperin, "How to Do the History of Male
    Homosexuality" (Halperin 104-137). For a brief overview of the transhistorical continuities and
    discontinuities of discourses around female same-sex desire from the seventeenth century to
    the twentieth century see Valerie Traub's "Afterword" (Traub 355-361).

34 Cf. Halperin, *How to Do the History of Homosexuality*; Traub, *The Renaissance of Lesbianism in Early
    Modern England*; and Dinshaw, *Getting Medieval*.

showing how distant representations of female-female intimacy can be correlated, though not in a linear fashion, to modern systems of intelligibility. The methodological difficulty we face is not the absence of homoerotically desiring women, but tools adequate to crack the code organizing early modern conceptual categories. [...] One of the consolations my book offers to those looking for historical affirmations of gay identity is this: although we will not find contemporary *lesbians* in early modern England, neither will we find contemporary heterosexuals.

Even as I enact a critical method deliberately disengaged from questions of *lesbian* subjectivity, I recognize that the desire to discover *lesbians* in the past cannot be simply disavowed. [...] In certain contexts, both pedagogical and political, the illumination of homoeroticism as a salient force in history and culture may necessitate temporarily suspending alterity in the name of transmitting vital cultural information, personal affirmation, homo life support. The needs are real, and nothing I advocate in this book is intended to minimize them. But in the context of scholarship, I have found it more enabling to work with and through, rather than concede, the intractability of our desire for a useable past." (26-28)

Traub's research, then, tries to do both at the same time: be available as an affirming mirror for contemporary lesbian subjects while also providing an accurate account of the genealogy of female-female homoeroticism, that is tracing various discourses around female same-sex desire as they can be shown to exist in England for the early modern period.[35] As she argues, she has "tried to keep open the question of the relationship of present identities to past cultural formations – assuming neither that we will find in the past a mirror image of ourselves nor that the past is so utterly alien that we will find nothing usable in its fragmentary traces" (32). This becomes visible, not in the least, by her strategic use of the term *lesbian*, in italics, to describe female same-sex desire irrespective of the time period she is discussing. "[B]ecause the nouns 'lesbian' and 'lesbianism' clearly are relevant to the histories, figures, and investments addressed herein, linking disparate phenomena as well as the past to the present, my solution, from this point on, is to italicize these terms. My hope is that the persistent typographical strangeness of *lesbian* and *lesbianism* will remind readers of their epistemological inadequacy, psychological coarseness, and historical contingency" (16). For she is, with her research about the *lesbian* past, of course also trying to stage an intervention in the *lesbian* present:

"[M]y genealogy of the terms of *lesbian* representation is not pursued as a purely historicist aspiration, but as an intervention in contemporary understandings and

---

35 Traub lists the figure of the tribade and the figure of the friend as discursive sites at which early modern female same-sex desires can be shown to become visible and intelligible.

opportunities. Although history will not provide the redress to *lesbian* invisibility, I
do believe that its manifold complexities could render less dangerously presump-
tive the meaning of women's erotic desires and practices, both in the early modern period and our own time. Composed in the impassioned space of wanting, of
longing, of imagining that *lesbians* can have a history without submitting to the
deformations of identity or the double-binds of visibility, this book is offered in
the name of history as well as in the name of a different futurity – of what Jonathan
Goldberg has called 'the history that will be.'" (34-35)

While Valerie Traub analyses representations of female same-sex desire in seventeenth century England, Carolyn Dinshaw, in her book *Getting Medieval: Sexualities and Communities, Pre- and Postmodern*, goes even further back in time to
fourteenth and fifteenth century England. Dinshaw, too, follows what she calls
"a queer historical impulse, an impulse toward making connections across time
between, on the one hand, lives, texts, and other cultural phenomena left out of
sexual categories back then and, on the other, those left out of current sexual categories now. Such an impulse extends the resources for self- and community building into even the distant past" (1). Her project is about "making relations with the
past, relations that form parts of our subjectivities and communities; it is about
making affective connections, that is, across time" (11-12). For Dinshaw, "queer
histories are made of affective relations", and her aim is "to make such histories
manifest by juxtaposition, by making entities past and present touch" (12). Indeed,
it is by "using this concept of making relations with the past [that] we realize a
temporal dimension for the self and of community" (21). Dinshaw is much more
vocal than Traub on the usability of history to modern subjects:

"I want to state in no uncertain terms that this kind of queer history can be usable
history – usable to (among others, I hope) lesbians, gays, bisexuals, transgenders,
queers forming selves and communities; to medievalists seeking to broaden the
narratives of the field; to cultural theorists in search of new times. [...]
        I am concerned in this book to demonstrate ways in which a historical past
can and does provide material for queer subject and community formation now.
[...] My use of the term [community] draws on the concept of partial connection
that I developed in regard to historical relations – thus I regard partial connections
across time as constitutive of communities [...]." (22)

One of the examples Dinshaw provides for her notion of the usable past, for making entities past and present touch, is the archive of letters of the historian John
Boswell, author of the – not uncontroversial – book *Christianity, Social Tolerance,
and Homosexuality: Gay People in Western Europe from the Beginning of the Christian
Era to the Fourteenth Century*, published in 1980 and one of the first books con-

cerned with finding traces of homoeroticism in the distant past. Dinshaw looks at Boswell's archive of letters, written to him by readers of his book, "to see how people talked about making use of this history" (23). What she finds is quite a range of responses. The letters come from within and outside the U.S. For Dinshaw, "the letters witness an expanding gay public discourse and institutional presence in the United States" (24). They come from gay clergy, from lawyers, from Christian counsellors in the army. "The appeal of the book from this institutional point of view was not its argument that there was a distinct gay subculture in the high Middle Ages but that gayness was accepted in dominant ancient and medieval institutions that are still authoritative today" (Dinshaw 25). Some of the letter writers had not even read the book but only its *Newsweek* review.

> "For some the very existence of *Christianity, Social Tolerance, and Homosexuality*, a chunky university press history book – read or unread – whose author taught at Yale, was enough to strengthen gay claims to cultural legitimacy. [...] In the eyes of many letter-writers, the assertion of a history – *some* kind of history – seemed fundamental to the mainstream acceptance of gay people now in the United States." (25)

But most importantly as regards history writing as a narrative resilience strategy, as Dinshaw relates, the letters "also reveal the intense, personally enabling effects" of Boswell's book; "some of these letters, nominally concerning the book, provided the occasions of brief, private, supportive contact with another gay man, creating a tiny and temporary community of two" (27-28). As the letters demonstrate, Boswell's book also enabled the experience of queer communities across time:

> "In yet another deeply felt response based this time on a close engagement with the book's argument, a philosophy professor reflects on the book's effect on him of creating something like a gay community across time: 'Whereas I have often felt intellectual 'friendships' across the centuries – historical thinkers with whom I have felt such strong affinities that I feel I know them and that we speak for one another, I had never felt – until I read your book – that I had *gay* friends across the centuries.' For this reader, history becomes a source – directly, itself – of gay community, a community of affinities, of friends, even perhaps (given this letter's impassioned tone) of lovers." (28)

Boswell's book – and his approach towards doing the history of (male) homosexuality – have subsequently been discussed quite controversially among historians of sexuality. A valid point may be made that he errs too much on the side of stressing historical continuities of discourses around same-sex desire while disregarding the discontinuities and historical alterities of queer sexualities past and present.[36] Nonetheless, the book's legacy is remarkable, as Dinshaw relates: "The book still sells about two thousand copies a year in the United States and has proved not only enabling of individuals but has helped move oppressive institutions toward reform: [...] it infiltrated church, military, courts, and schools [...] on the ground level" (31-32). It even influenced, as Dinshaw convincingly shows, Michel Foucault, who took away from Boswell's work the notion that "[s]exual behavior is not, as is too often assumed, a superimposition of, on the one hand, desires which derive from natural instincts, and, on the other, of permissive or restrictive laws which tell us what we should or shouldn't do. Sexual behavior is more than that. It is also the consciousness one has of what one is doing, what one makes of the experience, and the value one attaches to it" (Foucault qtd. in Dinshaw 33-34). Reading the traces of Boswell in Foucault, says Dinshaw, will "extend and complicate the relations that we trace as we hand down a history of researchers on sex in the Middle Ages. In tracing those relations, queer medievalists are not only doing history – our own – but also [...] constructing a community across time" (34). As for her own work, on Margery Kempe, on the Pardoner in Chaucer's *Canterbury Tales*, on the heretical Lollards, on John/Eleanor Rykener, Dinshaw intends to show "with these new pieces of history [...] that queers can make new relations, new identifications, new communities with past figures who elude resemblance to us but with whom we can be connected partially by virtue of shared marginality, queer positionality" (39). And with a close reading of Roland Barthes writing about French historian Jules Michelet, Dinshaw even traces how "the historian manages thus, by writing, to 'touch' bodies across time" (47).[37]

As I have shown, queer intertextual novel writing and queer history writing both work towards creating and extending existing queer textual and cultural archives. Writers of both intertextual novels and histories thus create connections and communities, foster relationships and create kinship structures over time, and they also make these kinship structures accessible and available for readers of their work. Connections are a central concern for Virginia Woolf's Clarissa Dalloway; and the "queer, extended, post-nuclear family", as he himself puts it, is a recurring motif in Michael Cunningham's novels ("Michael Cunningham: New Family Outings" 53). Connection is also a protective factor in most models of resilience, where it occurs variously as the relational aspect of resilience, as the resilient aspect of community or of the unwavering support by an individual other.[38] What queer historian Carolyn Dinshaw describes with her notion of *getting*

---

36 See Halperin, *How to Do the History of Homosexuality* and Alan Bray, *The Friend* for more recent discussions of Boswell's work.

37 Cf. Dinshaw 40-53.

38 Cf. Michael Sadowski, *In a Queer Voice*, esp. chapter 7 and 8; and Alex J. Zautra, "Resilience Is Social, After All". The resilient aspect of connection has been shown to work on a physiological

medieval thus serves as another narrative strategy of resilience for queer subjects: "using ideas of the past, creating relations with the past, touching in this way the past in our efforts to build selves and communities now and into the future" (206).

Resilient Readings: Queer Visions of Sexuality and Kinship in Amy Fox' *Heights*

Several things may happen when a queer reader encounters a text. One possibility is that the (closeted) queer reader may discover in an overtly queer text visions of a world beyond his or her immediate surroundings, thus providing him or her with a sense of hope and possibility. Queer theorist Donald E. Hall provides an example for this in his book *Reading Sexualities* when he describes his "journey from depressed young queer" in rural Alabama "to fully self-assured proto-queer-rights activist" (18), which was deeply influenced by his happening upon and covertly reading "a copy of *The Happy Hooker* by Xaviera Hollander", a memoir of a New York author and call girl which provided him with a vision of a world where same-sex relationships as well as "pleasant, relatively uninhibited sexual encounters and a supportive community of like-minded friends and partners" did exist (20). The encounter with Hollander's text changed him in that "Hollander's autobiography demonstrated to me that what I saw before me did not have to *be*, that one day, if I persevered, I too might travel the world, meet other people with desires like mine, find a fulfilling niche for myself, and even perhaps cross paths with Xaviera [...]. *The Happy Hooker* allowed me to imagine a narrative for my own life that did not end in an Alabama beauty parlor and/or suicide" (19). The experience of encountering a text that opens up a whole new set of possible ways of being in the world is one that is probably shared by many LGBTQ people whose coming-out predates the advent of the internet, especially ones raised in rural communities. (I know that a seminal text for me proved to be Rita Mae Brown's *Rubyfruit Jungle*, as well as a biography of the bisexual singer Joan Baez). Hall goes on to employ Hans-Georg Gadamer's theory of hermeneutics for describing what happens when we read texts and find ourselves changed by them: "my processing of [Hollander's] narrative helped me change my perspective on my self and possible ways of being in a world beyond the boundaries of my rural locale. My horizon was shifted in new directions" (29). Hall goes on to describe what can happen in transformative encounters and conversations with others in terms of Gadamer's

level, too. If we experience connection and a safe social contact, the human body produces oxytocin, a neuropeptide which helps the body to regulate and modify physiological stress and fear responses (cf. Jessie L. Frijling et al., "Promoting Resilience After Trauma: Clinical Stimulation of the Oxytocin System").

hermeneutics as well. "Our life narratives, imperfectly expressed and never clear even to ourselves, are entangled with those of many others, all inviting our active interpretations, and leading, through their critical juxtaposition and interaction, to a process of endless alteration and reevalution" (29). The prerequisite for such transformational encounters and conversations is an attitude of openness and of being prepared to really listen to one another. Hall sees a chance in these processes for transformational change in society, even if the pace of that change may be much slower than the quick, radical shifts in attitudes hoped for by many queer activists.

But what can also happen when queer readers encounter texts is that the reader may in the act of reading do something with a text, circumnavigating dominant readings and reading the text against the grain, teasing out new meanings and thus opening up the text to new, queer perspectives. This is the mode of reading the present chapter will be concerned with. I argue that the performing of queer reception processes of narrative media, reception processes that may generate new narratives which include queer subjectivities or viewpoints the original narrative lacked or obscured, may serve as a strategy of resilience for queer subjects, helping LGBTQ readers to affirm their subject position by finding a point of entry into a text that, at first glance, seemed to exclude them. This mode of reading, then, constitutes what Eve Kosofsky Sedgwick refers to as "a reparative reading position" (*Touching Feeling* 150). As Sedgwick writes in an essay which had previously been published as an introduction to an anthology of queer readings: "What we can best learn from [reparative reading] practices are, perhaps, the many ways selves and communities succeed in extracting sustenance from the objects of a culture – even from a culture whose avowed desire has often been not to sustain them" (*Touching Feeling* 150-151).

Modern reader response theorists regard reception as a meaning making process that involves both reader and text. "What we call *reading* is an active participation with a piece of writing or an image for the purpose of producing meaning, or, more generally, to 'translate' the book or image […] from its condition as a perceived ensemble of potential signs to a text on which the process of interpretation is brought to bear", says for instance Julian Wolfreys ("Reader/Reading" 212-213).[39] And for Hélène Cixous, "[w]riting and reading are not separate, reading is a part of writing. A real reader is a writer. A real reader is already on the way to writing" (20). Maria Pramaggiore describes what can happen when queer reading practices, here even more specifically bisexual reading practices, are brought to bear on a – in her case filmic – text:

---

39   See also Roland Barthes, "The Death of the Author" and Wolfgang Iser, *The Act of Reading*.

"Bisexual reading practices are dynamic processes involving both textual address and a motivated readership. In theories of film spectatorship, this posited inter-action encompasses the narratives and images projected upon the screen (high-lighted in structural or apparatus approaches) and the audience's activities of and investment in interpreting those images (emphasized in cultural studies and ethnographic approaches). Apparatus models present cinema as a seamless ideo-logical machine, whereas reception studies emphasize readings and responses of historical spectators whose activity of watching is assumed to construct the text's meaning, often in opposition to culturally authorized interpretations. Studies of gay and lesbian film spectatorship, of particular relevance here, often rely implic-itly on the assumption that gay and lesbian audience members are uniquely will-ing and able to read against the grain of mainstream texts to rewrite heterosexual endings or to elucidate homoerotic or homosexual elements which the narrative elides or represses." ("Straddling the Screen" 279)

Queer spectators thus become co-creators in the meaning-making process. In the following two subchapters, I trace resilient and reparative reading practices. First I will provide an exemplary reading of a narrative film and the play it is based on, Amy Fox' *Heights*. I argue that the movie rereads the central conflict between the main characters put forth by the play in a manner conducive to a bisexual reading position. At first glance, *Heights* seems to offer a standard, if somewhat tortu-ous, coming-out narrative of Jonathan, its (presumably) gay male protagonist. I want to offer an alternative reading that understands Jonathan not as gay but as bisexual. The movie adaptation of the play, it seems to me, strengthens this read-ing position. In the subsequent subchapter I will present fan fiction as a genre of writing that actively engages with popular cultural narratives by not only reading texts, often against the grain, but by generating new texts in the act of reading which include LGBTQ subjectivities; this constitutes, as I argue, a resilient and reparative reading practice.[40]

In Amy Fox' one-act play *Heights*,[41] three twenty-something characters find them-selves trapped on a Manhattan rooftop in the middle of the night in contemporary New York City: Jonathan, a lawyer, his fiancée Isabel and his lover Alec. Over the

---

40 I understand resilient readings to constitute acts of reading that promote a reader's resilience, as well as texts derived from these acts of reading.

41 *Heights* premiered in January 2000 at the Ensemble Studio Theatre in New York City as part of an evening of short plays by Youngblood, the theatre's collective of emerging professional play-wrights under the age of thirty. Ismail Merchant, executive producer of Merchant Ivory, com-missioned Fox to turn her thirty-minute play into a ninety-minute feature film. Merchant Ivory is best known for elaborate costume dramas set in the Edwardian period, such as the screen adaptations of E. M. Forster's *A Room with a View*, *Maurice* and *Howard's End*, or Henry James' *The*

course of the night it emerges that all three characters currently find themselves stuck in various aspects of their lives. Isabel, who is troubled by frequent bouts of insomnia, cannot quite work out what is going wrong both in her own life and in her relationship with Jonathan. Alec desperately wants Jonathan to finally come clean with Isabel about their affair. And Jonathan is seemingly unwilling or unable to choose between his lover and his fiancée, his "two favorite people in the world" (*Heights* 20). What appears at first glance to be no more than a standard coming-out narrative is revealed to be much more multilayered if one follows each character's motivations and desires separately. Viewed through the eyes of Alec, an out-gay man, Jonathan appears to be a conservative closeted gay man who is on the point of choosing the hegemonic relationship model of monogamous heterosexual union – the kinship model that his chosen profession presumably advocates. However, a different picture emerges from Jonathan's own utterances, and especially from those moments in the play when his words fail him. In my reading I argue that Jonathan finds himself unable to voice and express his desires because he has hit a dead end in discourse. His 'stuckness', if you will, is an epistemological stuckness of the symbolic order through which Jonathan's subjectivity constitutes itself. There is no room in neither Alec's nor Isabel's – nor Jonathan's – imaginary which follows late twentieth-century binarisms of gay and straight sexual identities and a heteronormative understanding of kinship relations, for the conception of shifting, bisexual, or queer identities and subjectivities, or for a polyamorous or any other form of queer system of kinship ties.

The following is an example of a scene where Jonathan fails to find words to express what it is, exactly, that he wants from Alec and Isabel, and in his frustration turns to resorting to physical violence instead. – Alec and Jonathan are here fighting over the batteries to Alec's cell phone. Alec's phone is the only way they have of contacting someone to open the locked door to the rooftop for them. Until that happens, they are all trapped on the roof together, and Alec is trying to use this situation to his advantage to get some answers from Jonathan.

"Isabel: What are you doing?

Alec: Things happen for a reason. People get stuck for a reason.

Jonathan: We're not stuck.

Alec: Everyone's always running away. Until one day they get stuck. They have to face things.

Jonathan: We're not stuck. Just give us the batteries.

Alec: Of course. Just give us some answers.

Jonathan: Give me the fucking batteries.

Wings of the Dove. *Heights* constitutes a bit of a departure for Merchant Ivory in terms of their usual subject matter for filmmaking (cf. Fox, "*Heights*: A Merchant Ivory Film").

Alec:	No. *(Jonathan lunges for the batteries, the two men struggle violently, nearing the edge of the roof. Jonathan has lost control; Alec attempts to defend himself. Isabel watches, attempting to stop them.)*
Isabel:	Stop it – please – what are you doing? ... STOP IT! I said – JONATHAN! *(Isabel comes between them.)* Stop it. Both of you. We're twelve stories up.
Jonathan:	*(To Alec)* What is it you want? What do you fucking want?
Alec:	I want you to figure it out. You're in the same goddamn fog you were the night we met. [...]" (23-24)

Jonathan's frustration and speechlessness culminates here in a physical struggle between him and Alec. Due to the rooftop setting this part of the scene is very dramatic for the audience, as there is always the possibility that one character might throw the other character accidentally or not-so-accidentally over the railing in a physical fight. But try as he might, Alec does not get a simple answer from Jonathan over the course of the following exchange between the characters; all he gets are only more revelations about Jonathan's past which neither Alec nor Isabel had previously been aware of.

Yet the possibilities opening up beyond heterosexual hegemony are hinted at and glimpsed by Isabel towards the end of the play when, standing close to the edge of the rooftop – "too close to the edge" as per the stage directions – she apprehends the possibilities of being more than 'just' the wife of a New York lawyer.

"Jonathan:	Isabel, what are you doing?
Isabel:	Were you ever scared of heights? [...]
Jonathan:	Please come away from the edge.
Isabel:	Most people are terrified. They call it vertigo.
Jonathan:	Alec, the batteries. Now, before something happens.
Alec:	She'll be all right.
Jonathan:	How do you know?
Alec:	Because she's leaving you.
Isabel:	Vertigo. I'm looking. At all the windows. I just want ... I just want to look." (26)

Standing on the edge of the rooftop, Isabel does not proceed to commit suicide, as Jonathan fears, but chooses to take on the future whatever it may bring her. As for Jonathan, forced by Alec to choose between himself and Isabel,[42] Jonathan in the end chooses Alec, but it is left open whether Alec will actually take him back at the end of the play, as over the course of the play it has also emerged that Jonathan

---

42 Alec dares Jonathan to propose to Isabel, but Jonathan finds himself unable to do so (cf. *Heights* 26).

has not been entirely truthful with Alec about his previous sexual history. Alec is not, as Alec always assumed, Jonathan's first male lover, and thus – as it turns out – Jonathan has been stuck in his existential limbo for much longer than Alec assumed. As I read it, this is not just a momentary period of confusion the previously-straight Jonathan has to pass through to come out at the other end – with a little help from Alec – confident and proud as a gay man. Alec phrases it somewhat differently, but this is in effect how he has regarded Jonathan from the beginning of their affair five months earlier (cf. *Heights* 24). As regards the play, a point can probably be made to read Jonathan as either gay or bisexual; this will depend not in the least on the reading position of the viewer. The movie, however, provides further scenes which, as I argue below, can be read much more promisingly as elucidating a bisexual rather than a gay male subjectivity for Jonathan. "Welcome to the roof", says Isabel to Alec towards the end of the play. "It's a scary place" (26). In the end, nothing is as it seemed, and seeing the beloved other in the clear light of day – or night – stripped of all projections and preconceptions turns out to be a scary, but ultimately liberating, experience for all three characters. Jonathan's situation of stuckness and confusion is taken to new heights in the movie adaptation of the play. The way this final confrontation scene between Alec, Isabel and Jonathan is played out in the movie is as follows: Alec meets up with Jonathan on the rooftop and asks him to tell Isabel about their affair. Jonathan says, "I can't. What I have with her is good". Alec asks, "Is it real?" Jonathan says, "It's close enough", but then kisses Alec. Isabel enters the rooftop and sees this kiss, turns around and flees back down the stairs. Jonathan comes after her. Isabel confronts him in the staircase, demanding an explanation, and this is what Jonathan tells her: "I don't know what to say to you. I've been needing to figure things out, and I didn't tell you because I was ashamed. I'm so sorry. I want you to know that I want to be with *you*". This is when Isabel breaks up with him. The thirty minute rooftop scene in the play is condensed to a four minute scene in the movie, and in a way this confrontation scene between these three characters is what the whole movie leads up to (cf. *Heights*).

In the movie version of the play dating from the year 2005, for which Amy Fox and Chris Terrio wrote the screenplay and which was directed by Chris Terrio, several more characters are added to the main cast. Among them are Diana, Isabel's mother portrayed by Glenn Close, a successful actress who is in an – albeit troubled – open relationship with her husband which leaves her free to pursue younger men, among them Alec, now an aspiring actor; and Peter, a British journalist who has come to New York to interview various male models and ex-lovers of the openly gay, and wildly promiscuous star photographer Benjamin Stone. Peter himself is involved – in fact he is caught up in – an emotionally abusive relationship with Benjamin Stone; Jonathan, as it turns out, is one of Stone's ex-lovers, a secret aspect of his past which Jonathan throughout the course of the movie desperately tries to prevent from coming out.

In the movie, the main characters all cross paths several times over the course of a twenty-four hour period, sometimes because they already know each other, other times by chance. Alec, for example, runs into Diana, Isabel's mother, when he auditions for a part in a new play for an Off-Broadway production, his opportunity for a big break, for which Diana happens to be the director. In the audition, Alec has to portray a character who is "gay, but not-gay" in the words of the playwright. Alec himself describes the character to a fellow actor as "just confused". The way the scene is linked to the previous scene – Alec's monologue starts as a voiceover to the final outside shot of the previous scene of Jonathan working in his office at his law firm – is also clearly meant to draw a parallel between the character's situation in the play and Jonathan's own situation of 'stuckness' or confusion; Alec clearly bases his portrayal of this character on Jonathan, and goes for motivation presumably for the character being gay but still struggling to come out – even to himself – as a gay man, since that is clearly what he believes is Jonathan's problem. This is an adequate dramatic realization of the character in the audition monologue (cf. *Heights*). However – Alec's perception of Jonathan aside – Jonathan himself, it seems to me, is readable more promisingly in terms of a critical analysis, as a bisexual man, or even still, at this stage of Jonathan's character development, as a self-identified heterosexual man who occasionally has affairs with other men.

There have been a number of efforts over the course of the last sixty years by scholars from various disciplinary fields to map the field of contemporary Western bisexual identity, behaviour and desire. Biologists like Alfred Kinsey and psychiatrists like Fritz Klein have come up with various graphs for helping people pinpoint their exact location on the map of human sexuality (cf. Storr, *Bisexuality*). Social scientists and bisexual activists have variously pointed out that there is not, in fact, one kind of bisexual experience but there are many different ones: There is the question of whether one should focus on bisexual identity or on bisexual behaviour in conducting research on bisexuality – not everybody who has or has ever had same-sex experiences may choose to identify as bisexual (cf. Storr, "Introduction"). Furthermore, some bisexual people may choose to live in monogamous kinship arrangements, whereas others may favour polyamorous kinship arrangements. Also, one's desires may change over the course of one's lifetime, raising questions about the temporality and the mutability of desire. The gender of one's desired object may be deeply important to some bisexual people; it may be irrelevant to other bisexual people, or to quote Eve Kosofsky Sedgwick's famous commonsensical first axiom in *Epistemology of the Closet*, "People are different from each other" (22). Sedgwick provides a whole list of how people might experience their sexuality in quite different ways, ranging from, "even identical genital acts mean very different things to different people", to the aforementioned, "Some people, homo-, hetero-, and bisexual, experience their sexuality as deeply embedded in a matrix of gender meanings and gender differentials. Others of each sexuality do not" (25-26). Or one may come, as a bisexual subject, to reject the notion of a binary gender system altogether, and consequently also come to reject the term 'bi-sexual', preferring to identify as 'pansexual' instead, or remain forevermore fashionably 'questioning'. One can simply subsume one's bisexual identity under the broader notion of a 'queer' identity and refuse the interpellating call to further differentiate one's desire, or one may come to follow, as a bisexual subject, Sedgwick's call, also from *Epistemology of the Closet*, for nonce taxonomies and playfully describe one's currently favoured flavour of (bi)sexuality in ever changing ways.

A number of scholars have come up with various metaphors in order to describe contemporary bisexual experience and systems of bisexual knowledge formation. Clare Hemmings talks in her early work about the 'revolutionary double agent' who moves across boundaries and potentially transfers knowledge from one sexuality and community to another (cf. Hemmings, "Extract from *Locating Bisexual Identities*"). Maria Pramaggiore posits an 'epistemology of the fence' for the bisexual subject, theorizing the fence as "a place of in-betweeness and indecision" and claiming that "bisexual epistemologies have the capacity to reframe regimes and regions of desire by deframing and/or reframing in porous, nonexclusive ways" ("Extracts from *Epistemologies of the Fence*" 146). – This is of course formulated in analogy to Sedgwick's *Epistemology of the Closet*, which famously pointed to structures of knowing and not-knowing, visibility and invisibility that have pervaded Western culture as a whole at least since the second half of the nineteenth century, and that have at their centre a binary structure of human sexuality, the homo/hetero dyad (in which power is however unequally distributed) that, as Sedgwick claims, informs all aspects of twentieth-century Western knowledge formation.[43] One of the problems with the metaphors of the 'double agent' or the 'epistemology of the fence' is, of course, that the whole system of heteronormative and patriarchal power structures that Sedgwick so convincingly analysed, also shapes the culture the contemporary bisexual subject moves in and is, in turn, shaped by (cf. e.g. Hemmings, *Bisexual Spaces*). Bisexual people, too, will not be exempt from having to learn ways of knowing how to navigate closet structures, and can potentially become the victims of or fall prey to homophobic or (in the case of bisexual women) sexist acts of violence, discrimination or insult. Also, not all behaviourally bisexual subjects may favour such an epistemology of the fence. Merl Storr, for instance, points to a different epistemology which may for example underlie the

---

43 Cf. Sedgwick, *Epistemology of the Closet*. Epistemology is the study of knowledge formation. It
   generally uses a genealogical and historiographic approach, investigating how we come to
   know who we think we are.

ways of knowledge formation of men who have sex with men but prefer to identify as straight, an "epistemology of compartmentalization and splitting, of keeping discrete areas of life and thought separate from one another", where it may conceivably be exactly the "thrill of the illicit" that may be an important part of this (behaviourally bisexual) subject's erotic life ("Introduction" 9-10).

My aim in this reading is not to pinpoint as accurately as possible where exactly the character of Jonathan in *Heights* might be located in all of this. An argument could probably be made in his case for several of the abovementioned bisexual epistemologies. Rather, I want to open up possibilities of reading Jonathan as a bisexual subject as such, however epistemologically located and locatable, moving beyond the confines of reading him teleologically as a subject that is not yet fully gay but definitely getting there. However, as a subject who is shown, in his daily and in his professional life, to be moving overwhelmingly through either exclusively straight spaces (his office environment, his home life with Isabel, the religious community he belongs to) or, in his past and in his student life overseas for a limited period of time in exclusively gay spaces (the circle of admirers, students and models around the photographer Benjamin Stone), Jonathan definitely shares in what Hemmings describes as "the consistent partiality of bisexual experience" (*Bisexual Spaces* 42). Bisexual subjectivity, Hemmings points out in *Bisexual Spaces*, in contemporary Western cultures is formed almost exclusively in lesbian, gay or straight spaces: "Passing as lesbian, gay or straight (whether intentionally or not) is inevitably a formative part of what it means to become bisexual", says Hemmings, adding that, "epistemologically, the insistent partiality of bisexuality makes visible the process by which we all become sexual and gendered subjects" (43).

Jonathan himself experiences the situation of 'stuckness' and confusion he finds himself in, what one might call with Hemmings inevitably aspects of an always 'partial' and 'transitive' bisexual subjectivity, as frustrating and painful. Jonathan Dollimore, in *Sex, Literature and Censorship*, speaks to this potential suffering of the bisexual subject, outlining how desire always has a tendency to undermine identity, potentially producing destructive confusion and "wrecking the rational subject" (35). He argues that "[b]isexuality may on occasions (contingently, not necessarily) resonate even more acutely than homosexuality or heterosexuality with the difficult, fascinating complexities which ineradicably mark any human desire which is vulnerably alive" (33), adding that, "[t]o be alive is to desire; to desire is to be deeply and maybe destructively confused, sooner or later" (36). Dollimore asks what the potential psychic cost for such a partial bisexual subjectivity might be for the individual, wondering what exactly happens if, analysing bisexual subjectivity, one is in the end "left with a mass of tangled desires and identifications" (31). He goes on to inquire:

"Do we ever simply desire the person we love, or is our desire not also partly an identification with him or her? Simply put, the 'I want you' of desire is complicated by
the 'I want to be you' of identification. This seems especially plausible when we
realize that the process of identification we are talking of is not necessarily, nor
only, with the lover, but the 'other' which he or she stands for. Who might this other
be? Someone completely different from us, or someone obscurely familiar to us:
an actual parent or sibling perhaps, or maybe the parent or sibling we wanted but
didn't have? And if this sounds too incestuous for those of us with, say, gay identifications well outside of the conventional 'family romance', we might still wonder
whether (for example) the person desired might resemble the person we once
were; or the person we always wanted to be; or the person others wanted us to be,
or the person we would still like to be? It's sometimes assumed that identification
is especially strong in same-sex relationships; I suspect that it may be particularly
complex in some expressions of bisexuality, conscious or otherwise. But if Freud
is right in thinking not just that we are all inherently bisexual, but that *all sexual
acts* are so as well, then the potential for complex identification is there for all of
us." (27-28)[44]

In the following, I want to take a closer look at one such "mass of tangled desires
and identifications", a passionate encounter between Isabel and Jonathan taking
place in the hallway of their apartment which exemplifies a moment of triangulated desire since it is haunted by the specters of both Alec, Jonathan's lover, and
Mark, Isabel's ex-boyfriend.

The context of the scene is as follows: Alec has accidentally left his jacket when
he auditioned for Diana, and Diana has given the jacket to her daughter Isabel
since Isabel and Alec, though not acquainted with each other, turn out to be living
in the same building, and Isabel is about to return the jacket to Alec. Both Isabel
and Jonathan are in a bad mood and have been fighting previous to this scene
and have been taking their frustrations out on each other. – Jonathan has just
returned from meeting up with Peter, the British journalist who wants to interview him about his relationship with Benjamin Stone, and Isabel has just been
offered to work on a feature for the *New York Times* together with her ex-boyfriend,
which could have been her big break as a photographer, but she has chosen to turn
down the offer because it would have meant she would have to reschedule her

---

44 Dollimore quotes Sigmund Freud from a letter to Wilhelm Fliess: "But bisexuality! You are certainly right about it. I am accustoming myself to regarding every sexual act as a process in which
four individuals are involved. We have lots to discuss on this topic" (qtd. in Dollimore 174). Dollimore further contends: "Identity, we know, is formed socially, not just in the here and now but
also, and much more so, by the past. So too is desire. To a degree that we can never exactly know,
our conscious desires of the here and now are constituted by the history of what we have desired
and perhaps lost in the past" (34).

meticulously planned fairy-tale wedding with Jonathan. This is the scene in question: Jonathan, in this scene, sees Isabel with Alec's jacket and is momentarily confused, and Isabel, to tease him about his jealousy regarding her past relationships with other men, specifically here her ex-boyfriend Mark whom she has just met up with, puts on the jacket. Jonathan demands she take it off, and when she refuses to do so, starts to fight with her over Alec's jacket until he ends up throwing her against the wall. Suddenly, the frustration and their physical fight morphs into sexual tension between Isabel and Jonathan; they kiss and make out against the wall (with the jacket now mostly forgotten) until they are interrupted by a phone call from Diana that goes directly to voicemail but which still effectively breaks the mood and ruins the moment for both of them.

Several questions beg to be asked: For one, who exactly is the object of Jonathan's desire in this scene? The image and texture, the feel and maybe even smell of the jacket, which Jonathan holds onto, which Jonathan and Isabel wrestle about, is probably meant to evoke for Jonathan sense memories of Alec wearing that jacket, maybe even evoke memories for him of a larger, more masculine frame underneath his hands, if one takes note of the way he manhandles Isabel, throwing her against the wall. He is quite rough with her in this scene, which Isabel, however, does not particularly mind or object to. Is Jonathan then properly attracted to Alec here, or to a cross-dressing Isabel, or to a fantasy subject that is both Alec and Isabel at the same time? And how does Jonathan's jealousy of Isabel's previous boyfriend play into all this? Reading the scene with Sedgwick's theories about male homosocial desire from *Between Men* in mind, Isabel primarily serves here as a conduit for Jonathan's desire for other men. Jonathan is linked here to the chain of his fiancée's past lovers via his current relationship with Isabel in an economy of desire where women primarily serve as exchange value for affective bonds between men.[45]

---

45 Here is another question: Is the shame Jonathan will mention later to Isabel when she confronts him in the staircase, and that he cites as the reason for not telling her sooner about his affairs with Alec and Benjamin Stone, merely the shame that Jonathan experiences around his same-sex desires and the clandestine natures of his affairs with men, or is it also linked to the conflicting emotions he clearly experiences when finding himself, as here in the hallway, drawn to and desiring an Isabel who is wearing Alec's jacket? One could certainly argue that Jonathan may very well in this moment be haunted by what Dollimore calls 'daemonic desires' (cf. *Sex, Literature and Censorship*), i.e. desires that have been excluded from a stable identities favouring, unitary subject, experiencing a moment of negation, of being outside of, or beside himself, of finding himself to be an 'ec-static subject' (as Butler would say), beyond recognition to himself or to Isabel (cf. Butler, *Undoing Gender*). Butler is drawing on Hegel's theories on negation and recognition for her notion of the 'ec-static subject'. Her view on the possibility of mutual recognition between different subjects is much more pessimistic than Jessica Benjamin's, which I will discuss in the following section.

And who is conceivably the object of Isabel's desire in this scene? She is obviously getting off on, and playing into, Jonathan's jealousy over her ex-boyfriend and enjoys using him as bait here. Or is Isabel still attracted to Mark and would maybe not at all mind having sex with both of them? Does she simply like it rough? Do both characters simply like make-up sex?[46] Both characters certainly egg each other on with their triangulated desires and fantasies (and the ones they think the other person is indulging in), and one could argue that the fact that they quite successfully play into each other's fantasies constitutes a successful negotiation of the zone of intersubjectivity which, following Jessica Benjamin's theories on recognition, is always a field comprising *two* subjectivities, *two* centres of self where one self may at any moment be temporarily dislocated by the desire of the Other of the other. For Benjamin, human interactions are always simultaneously structured by both complementarity, i.e. subject-object interaction, or relation in the intrasubjective realm, and mutuality, i.e. subject-subject (or: self-other) interaction, or relation in the intersubjective realm. Benjamin suggests that a constant tension between the processes of recognition and destruction underlies any successful interaction between two subjects. Interestingly, aggression and destruction are intrinsic to Benjamin's model of intersubjectivity: the moment when the object, i.e. the subject's fantasies and projections of the other, is shattered by the encounter with the real external other (who, for instance, behaves differently than the subject assumed) becomes the moment of true recognition of the other as separate, external other. This negation is the prerequisite, for Benjamin, for the subject's relating to the other as a separate being and for recognizing difference, but also then for empathic identification *with* the external other, for understanding the other's point of view and interest (which will probably be different from the subject's own), what and how the other feels about the interactive situation, which then enables both subjects to truly interact successfully socially in the intersubjective zone and reach a moment of mutual recognition (cf. *Like Subjects, Love Objects* and *Shadow of the Other*). These momentary breakdowns, these moments of negation are, for Benjamin, par for the course for successful intersubjectivity, for successful communication between two subjects. Without being confronted with the other as external other (a process which necessarily destroys the subject's fantasized or projected other-as-internalized-object), mutual recognition would not be possible. It's what you do with these breakdowns, how you act after they have happened, that is important. Mutual recognition is possible, says Benjamin, but it's a process; there is an ongoing tension between the intersubjective realm (i.e. self-other relations) and the intrasubjective realm (i.e. subject-object relations) that has to be learned to be navigated and mastered by the subject if the subject

---

46 That is a question the film does not provide enough detail on to be finally answerable.

truly wants to successfully relate to an other subjectivity and reach a moment of mutual recognition.

In this scene, the characters – rightly or wrongly – read each other, and I would argue that the moment when the jacket is finally discarded by both Jonathan and Isabel constitutes such a moment where the characters have successfully navigated the process of intra- and intersubjectivity and reached a moment of mutual recognition in the sense that Benjamin suggests. However, the framing of the final shot of this scene certainly suggests also that the fantasies, even though they can be indulged in at this point on an individual basis and can also contribute to a successful interaction between the characters, still need to be finally disavowed: The camera is slightly removed from the characters, capturing their actions in the hallway from the living room through an open doorway, while in the background of the scene, another half-open doorway leads to Isabel's darkroom – Isabel happens to be a professional photographer in the movie – where her photography equipment is stored. Symbolically, the characters find themselves slightly removed here from both the domestic scene (the space of the living room) and a space where such triangulated desires and fantasy scenes as both characters indulge in can be openly acknowledged and played out (the darkroom). They are stuck in a tertiary space, somewhere in between the two, where the fantasies are clearly present and even dominate and shape their interactions but still need to remain oblique and be disavowed.

As my analysis has shown, the triangular relationship between Jonathan, Isabel and Alec remain essentially the same in both play and movie; at the same time, the larger canvas of the feature film, and the addition of a number of characters, allows the playwright to explore her main characters in greater depth, especially Jonathan's coming to terms with – and self-recognition of – his emerging bisexual subjectivity. The film thus revisits and rereads the central conflict of the play. A slight alteration of focus also occurs in the movie compared to the play as regards structures of queer sexuality and kinship. Diana's relationships, for instance, in a way stand in for a different heterosexual kinship arrangement than the one favoured by Isabel and, presumably, Jonathan at the beginning of the movie: In the movie, Diana's husband is currently having an affair with Diana's understudy for the Broadway play both she and her husband are starring in. This affair clearly makes her uncomfortable first and foremost because it is happening too close to home for her comfort zone; but Diana is afraid of addressing the issue directly with her husband and of renegotiating the terms of their relationship for fear of losing him to her rival. Also, several more gay characters are added to the cast, among them Henry, Diana's current director and gay male best friend, her most nurturing relationship in the movie. The topic of polyamorous vs. monogamous relationships is thus reworked over the characters of Diana and Benjamin Stone. But maybe more radically, the movie in the end and in its climactic scenes surprisingly turns its focus away from bonds of sexual and romantic love, foregrounding instead other forms of kinship relations which serve to nurture the characters, offering them a sense of community and connection and thus furthering their resilience. These are: (i) bonds of friendship such as the one between Diana and Henry, opening up Michel Foucault's notion of alternative queer kinship models in "Friendship as a Way of Life" to include friendships between (straight) women and queer men – in this interview, Foucault claims that what ultimately scares straight culture the most about queer people is not the specter of deviant or transgressive sexual acts queer people might or might not engage in, but the alternative kinship models they might invent, which (as per Foucault) have the potential to pose a much greater fundamental threat to the existing hegemonic social order; and (ii) intergenerational bonds such as the one between Diana and Isabel, whose troubles with their respective partners serve to strengthen their mother/daughter bond as the closing scenes of the movie indicate, which see Diana holding and comforting a distraught Isabel. Both of these relationships (Diana's with Henry and Isabel's with Diana) feature moments of mutual recognition as theorized by Benjamin over the course of the movie. Turn-of-the-century New York City emerges thus in both *Heights* the movie and the play as a queer time and place, where cultural representations of queer lifestyles can become visible as that "open mesh of possibilities, gaps, overlaps, dissonances and resonances, lapses and excesses of meaning" that emerges, as Sedgwick described, "when the constituent elements [...] of anyone's sexuality aren't made (or *can't be* made) to signify monolithically" (*Tendencies* 8).

When Readers Become Writers: The Case of Queer Fan Fiction

But spectators can also themselves become creators of queer cultural narratives. In the following I want to present the hypertextual genre of fan fiction writing as another narrative strategy of resilience for queer consumers of mass-media cultural productions. Extensions of queer reading practices, reception processes have here become processes of cultural production where readers have become active, creative participators in the creation of textual worlds.

The term 'fan fiction' commonly refers to a genre of fiction that employs characters from popular movies and television series (and to a lesser extent also from books and graphic novels). Originally produced in 'zine' (i.e. magazine) form and circulated privately and at conventions, the stories and the subculture of writers and readers around them have become much more visible since fandom's move to the internet during the 1990s. Operating in a legal grey area, fan fiction writers have been celebrated as modern day Robin Hoods, refusing to remain passive consumers of mass-media products who have, in a form of creative reader response, taken to producing their own, 'poached' versions of mass-media narratives (cf. Jenkins, *Textual Poachers* and Penley, *NASA/TREK*).[47]

Fan fiction has traditionally been discussed as a literary genre. Abigail Derecho places it in the context of an entire genre of explicitly intertextual writing that, she maintains, has historically been produced by subjects belonging to cultures of the subordinate, including women and ethnic minorities, and that has existed since the early seventeenth century, its most prominent example probably being a much later text, Jean Rhys' novel *Wide Saragossa Sea*; Derecho terms this genre 'archontic literature'. When one reads archontic literature, "one is really reading two texts at once. The prior text is available and remains in the mind even as one reads the new version" (73). In the case of fan fiction, this archive contains not only the originary text and the fan fiction story one is currently reading, but the whole fan text; all of the stories currently in the archive. Thus, the extratextual knowledge a fannish reader is drawing on – pertaining for instance to a character's past or future, to their looks and habits, likes and dislikes, to the design of their living room and workplace – comprises knowledge derived from the originary text as well as knowledge derived from previously consumed fan texts. This kind of reading practice is mostly foreign to the modern prose reader, but it is not at all foreign to the premodern reader and to the audience of mythopoeic texts. Mafalda Stasi has drawn both of these parallels, likening fan fiction texts to the medieval palimpsest and fan writing and reading practices to medieval systems of allegory. The intertextual links between originary text and fan texts allow fan writers to use a number of shortcuts and allusion techniques: Fan writers and readers share a common set of associations, much like an allegorical code, and most fan texts make use of this possibility for rich symbolism, for evoking a whole range of associations in the fannish reader by for instance implicitly or explicitly referencing the originary text or other fan texts, or by careful choice of highly symbolic imagery or metaphor; it could even be argued that some of the pleasures of reading fan fiction thus come closer to aesthetic pleasures typically derived from reading poetry than from reading modern prose (cf. Stasi). At the genre level, Stasi suggests, the intertextuality at work in fan fiction functions like a mythological discourse. Fan fiction thus takes the form of myth making or mythopoeia, "a way of making and transmitting meaning through collective narrative creation" (124).

As a genre, fan fiction favours an immersive reading experience (cf. Coppa 240). The majority of fan fiction writers use a transparent prose style that quite often relies heavily on dialogue. First person and limited third person narratives

---

47 For an excellent overview of more recent debates around fan and fan fiction studies cf. Busse and Hellekson, "Introduction: Work in Progress". An overview of seminal texts of the last twenty years of fan and fan fiction studies can be found in Hellekson and Busse, *The Fan Fiction Studies Reader*.

predominate, allowing readers to directly access the characters' thoughts and feelings; they are thus drawn into empathizing and/or identifying with the characters. However, as both Francesca Coppa and Jane Mailander have pointed out, unlike in any other literary genre, the fan fiction reader enters the virtual reality of the story world 'primed', bringing extratextual knowledge of the characters' relationships, of their physical bodies and voices to bear on the text. As Coppa puts it, "we know who these characters are because we know the actors who play them, and we bring our memories of their physicality to the text" (235-236). There are some writers and readers who appreciate a prose style that draws attention to the materiality of language as such and for whom the texture of the text then becomes an additional layer of writerly/readerly *jouissance*. Those writers and readers might gain a certain kind of bliss or ecstatic enjoyment out of the materiality of the text itself.[48] However, for the majority of fan fiction readers and writers the pleasures derived from experiencing the narrative world is first and foremost one of immersion in the virtual reality of the story. This has led Coppa to propose that fan fiction may be better understood as ultimately a dramatic art form. To the non-fannish reader, fan fiction's emphasis on character, bodies, relationships as well as its repetitive nature may appear odd; all of these are, however, intrinsically theatrical or performative values, for "in theatre, bodies are the storytelling medium, the carriers of symbolic action" (236). Coppa therefore concludes:

> "If traditional theatre takes a script and makes it three-dimensional in a potentially infinite number of productions, modern fandom takes something three-dimensional and then produces an infinite number of scripts. This is not authoring texts, but making productions – relying on the audience's shared extratextual knowledge of sets and wardrobes, of the actors' bodies and their smiles and movements – to direct a living theatre in the mind." (243)

Coppa casts her fan fiction writers mainly in the role of directors in this "living theatre in the mind". However, the nature of fantasy seems to allow for an occupation of a number of roles on the part of both writers and readers: They may equally

---

48   Roland Barthes meditates on this kind of writerly/readerly bliss in *The Pleasure of the Text* – and it is pertinent that the French term *jouissance* employed by him to describe this kind of pleasure carries erotic overtones. The text itself, Barthes suggests, can become a figure, a tissue, possibly a fetish, an erotic site; a physics of bliss can be at work for instance at the level of a text's words and phrases. "[T]he word", says Barthes, "can be erotic on two opposing conditions [...]: if it is extravagantly repeated, or on the contrary, if it is unexpected, succulent in its newness", adding that "in certain texts, words *glisten*, they are distracting, incongruous apparitions" (42) – fetishism being just one example of textual bliss in his "typology of the pleasures of reading – or of the readers of pleasure" (63).

well perform the roles of actors, spectators and/or directors in this imaginary theatre.[49]

A subgenre of fanfiction stories, termed 'slash' fiction, refers to stories exploring relationships between same-sex characters, mostly between men. Slash fiction takes the original characters' emotional and/or sexual relationships where the source writers did not think – or dare – to go. Slash fan fiction originated with Kirk/Spock fan fiction in the 1970s; the term slash derives from the '/' employed to denote a specific romantic pairing (cf. Jenkins 186-187). Statistics are notoriously hard to come by, but there is tentative agreement both within fandom and among scholars that the subgenre of slash forms a major part of the fan fiction archive – in some fandoms it is the dominant genre produced – that within the slash genre, sexually explicit stories make up a large part of the stories written, and that the overwhelming majority of slash fiction is written by (both straight and queer) women. This clear bias towards stories focusing on male characters and male-male relationships has been the focus of much critical attention. Henry Jenkins, drawing on the work of Sedgwick, regards male-male slash as an exploration of utopian versions of male friendship, as "the conscious construction of a male homosocial-homosexual continuum"; slash can then take on the form of ideological critique (206). For Constance Penley, slash operates in a utopian fantasy space where one can both 'have' and 'be' the characters; the traditional poles of fantasy – identification or objectification – are thus superceded by a structure that allows for fluctuating identifications and desires (cf. Jenkins 198). In fact, any instance of cross-gender identification with the male slash characters on the part of the female writer/reader does not automatically have to be the performing of an 'other' masculinity, nor does it have to result in a feminization of the characters; it can also be a performing of *one's own* masculinity as a female (whatever that may mean) slash writer/reader. Eden Lackner, Barbara Lynn Lucas and Robin Ann Reid take on the shared nature of this fantasy space, proposing fandom as a queer female space where fan interactions over slash texts can both express and foster queer desires between writers and readers (cf. "Cunning Linguists"). This has led for instance science fiction writer Joanna Russ to celebrate slash fiction in the 1980s already as a form of "pornography by women, for women, with love" (cf. Penley 103). The question of whether slash fan fiction can be understood to constitute a kind of feminist or queer pornography has subsequently been the subject of lengthy debate among both fans and scholars alike (cf. Penley). I posit that slash fiction, as a narrative strategy of queer resilience, enables readers to fill

---

49 Already Sigmund Freud has linked the activity of creative writing to daydreaming or *Phantasieren* (cf. "Der Dichter und das Phantasieren"). In fantasy, one is both the one who fantasizes and a participant in the fantasy scenario, where one can occupy a number of changing roles (cf. Laplanche and Pontalis 393).

in subject positions that were lacking in the original cultural archive by rewriting the archive to include LGBTQ subjectivities and lives. It is thus both a communal and grass roots critique of popular cultural narratives and also at the same time of heteronormative notions of gender and sexuality.

How is this refashioning of the storyworld and its characters achieved? A few textual examples may illustrate the range of techniques employed. Fan fiction writer shalott's short story "Limestone" employs the settings and characters of the television series *Stargate Atlantis*, which is set in the present day but follows the adventures of a team of intergalactic explorers led by Air Force Major John Sheppard and head scientist Rodney McKay. In the story, both characters become trapped in an underground cavern which leads to a change in the nature of their relationship.

> "'Okay, this is not so great.' Rodney was pretty impressed with how calm he sounded. He struggled up to his feet, wiping stone dust from his eyes; not that it mattered, seeing how they were in pitch darkness under something like, oh, *a million tons of rock*, and they were going to die horribly, either by starvation or asphyxiation, assuming the rest of the cave didn't come down on top of them first.
>
> Then he noticed there hadn't been any answer. 'Major?' he said. He groped for the wall, fumbling, heart pounding now. 'Major!'
>
> He stumbled over something and fell hard, hissing in pain as his hands came down on gravel and sharp rocks. And forgot the pain immediately as the rock he'd stumbled over groaned and shifted. 'Major?' he said, and felt over John's body, trying to see if he was pinned under anything.
>
> 'You're getting a little friendly there, McKay,' John said groggily, and groaned, his legs shifting as he sat up. 'What happened?'"

John experiences here Rodney's touching him in a state of panic, in order to try to establish the state of his health, as intrusive and inappropriate considering their status as co-workers and John's presumed heterosexual masculinity. After first squabbling over who is to blame for them ending up in their current predicament, John and Rodney deliberate on how to proceed. As Rodney points out, the limestone underground hall they find themselves in may prove instable if their teammates try to set up an explosion in an effort to get through to them. Hence, a different strategy becomes necessary.

> "'Maybe we could move farther in,' Rodney said after a minute. 'If this chamber comes down, the cave system might restabilize again, and there's a chance there would be an opening left then.'
>
> 'It's a plan,' John said. 'Which way is farther in?'"

'Away from the cave-in is good,' Rodney said. He groped for John's arm and together they got to their feet. They walked along the curving, moisture-slick wall, Rodney's hand running along the surface their only guide. Beyond the sound of their footsteps, there was only the irregular drip-drip-drip of trickling stalactites. Rodney found his breath coming quick, fluttering, noisy. John shifted, and his hand, dry and warm and firm, slipped into Rodney's free hand. Their fingers silently interlaced.

They went on deeper into the dark."

John's move to take Rodney's hand and interlace their fingers in an effort to reassure his companion (Rodney's holding onto his arm would have sufficed to establish proximity and contact in the dark) is read by the fan reader as John taking the step to cross the dividing line between homosocial and homosexual, as the numerous online comments to the story attest, after his having previously insisted verbally on the demarcation of this line. Thus the characters are drawn into a continuum of homosocial and homosexual desire, which Sedgwick, in *Between Men*, had proposed exists for women but not for men in contemporary Western culture. John's and Rodney's moving further into the darkness of the unknown, potentially unstable cave is thus at the same time a moving into the foreign waters of a more intimate relationship than is explored in the original text of the television series.

Another fan fiction story makes use of alien technology as a plot device to queer the characters and propose alternative kinship arrangements. In shalott's "A Beautiful Lifetime Event", John and Rodney accidentally touch a piece of ancient alien technology which turns out to be an artificial womb.

"'Well, how was I supposed to know?' Rodney yelled, wide-eyed and panicky. 'You're the one who activated it!'

'You're the one who told me to touch it!' John yelled back.

'Oh, like you didn't want to!' Rodney said.

'I didn't know what the hell it was going to do!'

'Will the both of you please shut up and get out of the bloody way so I can make out the readings?' Beckett yelled at both of them, pointing them to opposite corners of the room.

John backed up against the wall and folded his arms, shooting another dark look at Rodney across the room, and telling himself not to freak out. Maybe it was a mistake. Beckett had just gotten here and taken a first look – he might have misread the screen. It could just be some *other* kind of medical equipment. Maybe it just did DNA analysis – compatibility scans –

The oval canister in the middle of the device started to glow faintly, a kind of translucent reddish-orange light filtering through the milky interior. 'Oh my,' Beckett said."

After accidentally conceiving a child together, John and Rodney first squabble about whether or not the device should be allowed to continue its work of fabricating a human baby. When the device releases the newborn baby, the fight continues over the act of naming her. Here it becomes apparent that from the start and despite their differences in opinion, both John and Rodney have already grown attached to the child. The constellation of the newly formed, alternate family unit forces them into a closer emotional proximity than their previous working relationship entailed. The naming of the baby becomes the scene where the newly formed family unit establishes itself.

> "'Hypatia!' Rodney stared at John in sudden wide-eyed delight. 'That's it, oh my god, that's just *perfect* –'
>
> 'You know what, Marie has been kind of growing on me,' John said.
>
> 'No, seriously, listen to me,' Rodney said. 'She taught at the library in Alexandria, she was one of the top scientists of her time, she wrote books on astronomy and mathematics, she invented the freaking astrolabe – that's *perfect*, we have to go with that –'
>
> 'Okay, look,' John said, desperate; he had to save her. 'One of us should get to pick the first name, the other one gets the last name.' He felt that was pretty heroic; he really wanted her to have his name, but Rodney was clearly on a rampage here and had to be stopped.
>
> 'Yeah, okay, that's fair,' Rodney said. 'Anyway, it'll be good for her not to be in my shadow when she starts publishing.'
>
> 'What?' John said.
>
> 'Hypatia McKay Sheppard!' Rodney said, and he picked her up out of the crib and held her up, beaming.
>
> The baby opened her mouth and screamed."

In the end, it is the baby who in this rendering of the scene makes herself heard and understood, announcing herself as her own, separate individual being and not the prize in a tug of war between Rodney and John. In shalott's novella-length story, the domestic scene of cohabitating with the precocious Hyp, as she comes to be called, as well as the attachment both have to the child, leads the characters over the following years into an increasing emotional intimacy and a realizing, finally, that they have somewhere along the line fallen in love. Domesticity serves in this fan revisioning of the world of the television series as the precipitator for non-heteronormative desires and lives.

A very different kind of queering occurs in the following poem by Brighid, which derives its title from Algernon Charles Swinburne's poem "The Garden of Proserpine". Whereas in Swinburne's poem, dead men never rise up, Brighid's poem describes the act of rising, or rather of being resurrected, of one previously dead man, the television series *Supernatural*'s protagonist Dean Winchester. Dean had previously, in the originary source text, sacrificed his life for the life of his deceased brother Sam by making a deal with a demon that ensured that Sam would be brought back to life in exchange for Dean's continuing to live for another year before his soul would be collected and he would spend the rest of eternity in hell. The beginning of the fourth season of the television series sees a very much alive Dean climbing out of his own grave; he was resurrected, as he later learns, by Castiel, an angel of the Lord. The actual scene of resurrection is never shown in the originary source text. Brighid expands on the scene of resurrection in her poem, whose speaker is the angel Castiel; the addressee of the poem is Dean.

"That Dead Men Rise Up (Never)

This time there was no chariot,
No gaping maw in ravished earth,
Just the silent grave,
Your pieced and piercéd flesh and
The lamentation of the boy who called you
Brother.

Below, there was none of
The simplicity of storybook apples.
They offered, instead, a fruit far older.
It stained your fingers, your teeth,
Rooted itself into your soul
To bind you to Hell's heart itself,
To open you from the inside out
Until you were nothing but meat and malice,
A creature halfway to their making.

We stormed the heat and hatred,
Sword-bright and sharp and found
You smeared and bleared in sin but still,
Even still I could see your soul-light shining.
I held you close and found each seed
Beneath your bloodied tongue,
Sucked and sipped their
Bitter weight from the corners
Of your pomegranate mouth
Until all that was left

Was the taste of a man broken
But yet beautiful.

I held you close and raised your rooted soul
Through fire and night to lay you down again
Into the hollows of your shattered bones,
Bade you bloom again with only
The taste of clear skies,
    Cool waters,
And the sharp, bright bite of apples,
Whose seeds you could spit into
Your broken grave and then
    Leave behind."

In Brighid's rendering, the scene of resurrection carries decidedly homoerotic overtones. The first stanza sets up the narrative scene with Dean dead and his brother Sam in mourning. The second stanza describes Dean's introduction into Hell as a scene of seduction that has him eat the fruit offered to Persephone, or Prosperina, in the Greek and Roman underworld: a pomegranate, the ingestion of which will tie him to Hell forever just as it tied Persephone to Hades; in the Greek myth which Swinburne takes up, the ingestion of pomegranate seeds ensured that Persephone had to remain in Hades for several months of the year. In Brighid's poem, eating the pomegranate fruit is supposed to "bind" Dean "to Hell's heart itself", to taint his soul and break him until he is "nothing but meat and malice", a "creature halfway to their making". The third stanza describes Castiel and his fellow angels entering Hell in order to save Dean. Here already, homoerotic desire enters the picture as Castiel is described as being drawn to Dean's as yet untarnished soul. Castiel's removal of the pomegranate seeds from Dean's mouth takes the form of an embrace and a kiss: he holds him close, removes the seeds from inside Dean's mouth and "suck[s] and sipp[s] their bitter weight from the corners" of his mouth, removing the traces of Hell until all that is left is "the taste of a man broken but yet beautiful". Castiel's desiring of Dean becomes evident in the metaphorical language employed: the removal of the pomegranate seeds and juices as a sucking and sipping as if the bitter fruit were a divine nectar, and the apprehension, finally, of Dean as a broken, but beautiful man. The final stanza sees Castiel carrying Dean out of Hell; the love and care Castiel takes is conveyed in the description of his holding Dean close to shield him from Hell's fires, and his depositing him finally in his mortal body in his grave. He bids Dean "bloom again" with only the taste of earthly delights, sunlight, water, apples; this performative act, a kind of blessing, is the final resurrection of Dean as a human being. It is

Castiel's love and caretaking of Dean that saves Dean from Hell in this fan reimagining of the originary source text.

Another work by Brighid, "The Bitten Peach", makes use of a short narrative form, a prose vignette consisting of 100 words. The focalizer of this short short story is Jayne Cobb, a character from the television series *Firefly*, a space Western set in the twenty-sixth century. The science fiction setting presents a culture that unites elements of a North American and pan-Asian background from the 'Earth that was'. *Firefly* is the name of a spaceship inhabited by, among others, Jayne, a seemingly rough and uneducated macho mercenary though the television series leaves it open whether this is really all there is to Jayne; and Simon Tam, a higher class former trauma surgeon who throughout the series appears fashionably well-dressed.

"The Bitten Peach

Doc had a sweet, sweet mouth on him. Said things, poetry, against his thighs in between warm, wet kisses. Contrary to all reason he pulled the man up and kissed him hard, licked the taste of peach wine from his mouth.

'Would you cut off that fine silk sleeve for me, boy?' he asked, rough and breathless, and when the Doc's eyes got wide in surprise he whispered something about nine springtimes of joy a whore had taught him once.

When the Doc was arched over his body, eyes closed and mouth wide he shuddered and it was damn fine."

In her story, Brighid rewrites Jayne's butch masculinity to include queer desires. But this is not what surprises the reader, or on the level of story the character of Simon, the most in this vignette. (The reader already gathers which characters will be portrayed in a romantic and/or sexual relationship from the extratextual information provided by the author in the form of the indicated pairing, here Jayne Cobb/Simon Tam.) The surprise is evoked by Jayne revealing himself, in his direct speech, not only as not averse to same-sex sexual encounters but also as versed in allusions to ancient homosexual Earth cultures. The cut-off silk sleeve, as well as the peach referenced earlier, both refer to ancient Chinese stories of same-sex desiring couples, a prince and his male courtesan who shared a particularly sweet peach, and an Emperor who cut off the silk sleeve of his gown so as not to disturb his sleeping male lover (cf. Woods 60). The seemingly uneducated Jayne reveals himself to be rather well educated, at least on the topic of same-sex sexual love and companionship and the cultural references that allude to this topic. In this story, Brighid rewrites not only normative masculinity to include same-sex desire but also weaves in references to a queer cultural archive on the level of the story's title and the characters' thoughts and direct speech.

The fan fiction stories and poems discussed here have served as examples of fan writers actively engaging with mainstream cultural texts which lacked LGBTQ content by rewriting, in the form of a creative reader response, the source texts to include LGBTQ subjectivities and lives. Fan writers thus redress the elision of queer content (up until very recently) from much of the archive of popular cultural narratives and also extend the queer cultural archive, which is essentially, as I argue, a reparative and a resilient move.

It is thus, finally, not only acts of writing – ourselves and our pasts – but also acts of reading, and as the example of queer fan fiction has shown, acts of writing derived from acts of reading, that can be subsumed under the heading of narrative resilience strategies; that is, strategies that can, when employed, further the resilience of queer subjects. For to narrate – one's story, the story of one's community and one's past to oneself and others, or to actively engage as a reader with cultural texts and archives – can be a form of agency, a doing, and a resilient method of (re)writing the self. By being the ones who assign meaning to their own subjectivities, queer subjects can thus (partially or fully) evade societal ascriptions. Furthermore, an extending of queer textual and cultural archives will further the creation of sites which in turn may serve as sites of individual and collective queer cultural memory.

The Art of Queer Emptiness

In the following chapter I want to present what I term the art of queer emptiness as one further resilience strategy that might prove useful for queer subjects. Following Louis Althusser's notion that an individual becomes a subject by being hailed into an ideological subject position, thus becoming recognized as a subject (in the case of a queer subject in a heteronormative social order this amounts to a position of abjection), I pose the question whether queer artists might have discovered ways by which one might disregard ideology's interpellating call. The art of queer emptiness is one form of 'doing' subjectivity in an other way while still being recognizable to oneself as a subject. What I term the art of emptiness is basically a way of letting go of the need to be recognized as a subject. This is a stance towards human subjectivity that is best known from Buddhist epistemologies, but I suggest that the same gesture can be found in the queer subjectivities of e.g. a number of characters in novels by Sylvia Townsend Warner (among them Lolly Willowes from the novel of the same name, as well as Sophia Willoughby and Minna Lemuel from *Summer Will Show*), and in the poetry of Mary Oliver.

As a set of philosophies and practices, the art of queer emptiness may pertain to a non-attachment to self and thus also to an employment of 'indifference' as an affective strategy engaged in momentarily by a queer subject who finds him- or herself faced with an act of homophobic violence or insult. This comprises a form of emptying oneself out, an act of refusal, an engaging in an attitude of non-caring, which is finally an activity that does not strive to change the status quo but that may serve as a form of affective self-care for the individual in question. The art of queer emptiness might thus be understood to represent an example of what Eve Kosofsky Sedgwick calls a *reparative* practice of queer subjectivity in that it is both non-anticipatory and non-paranoid but favours instead open-endedness and an openness to elements of surprise. Already Sedgwick herself became increasingly interested in her later work in Buddhist conceptions of emptiness and nonself, as well as in practices of realizing such states in both life and art.[1] This chapter aims at showing ways queer artists have found of stepping outside of discourse, of

---

1 Cf. Sedgwick, "Paranoid Reading and Reparative Reading" from *Touching Feeling*. The essays dealing most directly with Buddhist thought are "Pedagogy of Buddhism", also from *Touching Feeling*,

'doing' subjectivity in another way that may help towards furthering their resilience. I close with a postscript outlining Michel Foucault's notion of self technologies with which he offers another way of doing subjectivity differently that he gathers from authors of late antiquity. Here, taking care of the self becomes more important than a knowing of the self, once again a move towards greater resiliency for the subject.

Why Queer Emptiness?

The following is how, as Louis Althusser posits in his essay on the functioning of ideology and ideological state apparatuses, individuals become subjects: they are interpellated into the social order particular to their specific time and culture by an act of recognition which takes place inside the individuals themselves. Only by this act of recognition can they fully attain the status of the subject:

> "[I]deology 'acts' or 'functions' in such a way that it 'recruits' subjects among the individuals (it recruits them all), or 'transforms' the individuals into subjects (it transforms them all) by that very precise operation which I have called interpellation or hailing, and which can be imagined along the lines of the most commonplace everyday police (or other) hailing: 'Hey, you there!'
>
> Assuming that the theoretical scene I have imagined takes place in the street, the hailed individual will turn round. By this mere one-hundred-and-eighty-degree physical conversion, he becomes a *subject*. Why? Because he has recognized that the hail was 'really' addressed to him, and that 'it was *really him* who was hailed' (and not someone else). [...] Naturally for the convenience and clarity of my little theoretical theatre I have had to present things in the form of a sequence, with a before and an after, and thus in the form of a temporal succession. There are individuals walking along. Somewhere (usually behind them) the hail rings out: 'Hey, you there!' One individual (nine times out of ten it is the right one) turns round, believing/suspecting/knowing that it is for him, i.e. recognizing that 'it really is he' who is meant by the hailing. But in reality these things happen without any succession. The existence of ideology and the hailing or interpellation of individuals as subjects are one and the same thing."

For Althusser, it is primarily the ideological state apparatuses – such as the school, the church, the family – who interpellate individuals into the specific subject

---

and the posthumously published "Making Things, Practicing Emptiness" and "Reality and Realization", both from *The Weather in Proust*.

positions offered by the dominant ideology or social order of their specific time and culture.

If one follows Althusser's line of reasoning, as Foucault and other queer theorists such as Gayle Rubin, Judith Butler and Eve Kosofsky Sedgwick have done, one must regard our contemporary heteronormative sex/gender system as one such ideology specific to our time and culture, which offers to its subjects certain subject positions organised around a set of binaries of sexes and genders which is organized in hierarchical terms: male vs. female, and heterosexual vs. homosexual or queer. One is then, as a queer subject, in our current sex/gender system necessarily always already interpellated into a minoritarian subject position of sexual abjection. Queer theorist Gayle Rubin provides a whole list of examples of these contemporary 'bad' sexual subjects in her groundbreaking essay "Thinking Sex", and Eve Kosofsky Sedgwick even goes so far as to suggest, in her book *Epistemology of the Closet*, that "many of the major nodes of thought and knowledge in twentieth-century Western culture as a whole are structured – indeed, fractured – by a chronic, now endemic crisis of homo/heterosexual definition, indicatively male, dating from the end of the nineteenth century" (1), a crisis of definition which, according to Sedgwick, has infused a whole set of binarisms underlying our modern thinking.

One might be inclined to ask, is there any way out of this quandary for the queer subject? Do queer subjects have no choice, in the matter of attaining subjecthood, but to respond to the interpellating call of the current dominant social order, to the hailing of Althusser's ideological policeman? "[N]ine times out of ten it is the right [individual]" who responds to the policeman's hailing, writes Althusser. What about the one subject out of ten who, in Althusser's "little theoretical theatre" refuses to acknowledge ideology's interpellating call? Is this subject still thinkable as a subject? And under what terms might this individual's subjectivity be understood? In the following chapter I want to showcase a strategy of queer resilience which undertakes, I propose, just such a rethinking of the notion of queer subjectivity. I want to present one possible solution to this quandary of queer subjectivity, an example of a reparative and redemptive understanding of queer sexual subjectivity: what I term the art of queer emptiness.

What exactly happens in that precise moment when a hypothetical queer subject simply disregards, ignores, refuses to answer or respond to ideology's interpellating call? This subject, I propose, momentarily engages in a practice of non-engagement with the machinery by which an individual is transformed, ideologically, into a subject. This subject displays an attitude of non-attachment towards being recognized by the dominant social order as a subject. It thus remains empty – of signification, of self. The notion of an empty subject has been best explored, and popularized, by the epistemologies found in Eastern, and modern Western Buddhism. In Buddhist epistemology, being dependent on the need for recognition by a social order which abjects the subject, is what potentially causes suffering for the queer subject. However, queer subjects can free themselves of this dependency by engaging in an attitude of non-attachment towards that need (cf. Keown, *Buddhism* 44-56). How can this state of subjectivity be accomplished? By practicing and cultivating, among other things, mindfulness, that is a constant state of awareness of all things without assigning meaning or judgment, even indeed signification to them – Buddhist philosphers furthermore contend that the world itself is indeed empty (cf. Keown, *Buddhism* 66-68); it is human perception of the world that causes human suffering – and by engaging in practices of meditative absorption such as for instance *zazen*, or sitting medi-tation, or 'just sitting', or as Sam Hamill phrases it, paraphrasing seventh-century Chinese writer Hui Neng's *Platform Sutra*, "a meditative state in which perception is utterly free of discrimination between mind and matter, self and object; where the only permanence is impermanence; and where change, whether subtle or vio-lent, remains the essence of being" (Hamill and Seaton 2). This stance towards an ideal state of an experientially empty notion of subjecthood is exemplified for instance by the following poem by the eighth-century Chinese poet Li Po:

"Zazen on Ching-t'ing Mountain

The birds have vanished from the sky.
Now the last cloud drains away.

We sit together, the mountain and me,
Until only the mountain remains."

To further elaborate on the concepts of non-attachment and emptiness as they appear in Buddhist epistemologies: Non-attachment, as *arāga*, figures in Bud-dhist ethics as one of the three "roots of good" (Keown, *Dictionary* 151), where *arāga* denotes a stance of non-desire or non-greed and is seen as one of the central Bud-dhist virtues (cf. Keown, "Ethics"). Importantly, desire itself is not regarded as problematic in Buddhism per se. As regards what we term desire, Buddhist phi-losophy differentiates between, on the one hand, *chanda* (which denotes desire in the sense of intention or motivation) which can be good, bad or neutral depending on what it is directed at; and on the other hand, *tṛṣṇā* (craving) which is regarded as the underlying cause of human suffering in one of the foundational texts of Buddhism, the Four Noble Truths.[2] According to the third noble truth, the truth of cessation (*nirodha*), it is the cessation of craving which equals the cessation of

---

2 Cf. Keown, *Dictionary* 52, 72, 310-11. The Four Noble Truths are a set of insights into human exis-tence that form part of the first sermon delivered by the Buddha after he had reached enlighten-

suffering: "This, O Monks, is the Truth of the Cessation of Suffering. It is the utter cessation of that craving (*taṇhā*), the withdrawal from it, the renouncing of it, the rejection of it, liberation from it, non-attachment to it" (Keown, *Buddhism* 52).[3]

How, then, does one practice this cessation, this letting go of – in our case for instance the need to be recognized? The fourth noble truth proposes an Eight-fold Path, that is a set of eight practices or principles which, if followed, will help the practitioner to achieve just that goal.[4] Without going into further detail into these practices, let us just note that among them are a set of meditation practices, a set of ethical principles and a set of knowledge/wisdom practices. Among the knowledge/wisdom practices, I want to single out 'right understanding', which entails, as Damien Keown points out, "the acceptance of Buddhist teachings and later their experiential confirmation" (Keown, *Buddhism* 55). Among such teach-ings are concepts such as, for instance, *anitya*, or the truth of impermanence, that is the notion that things in the world are always changing, either due to the influ-ence of time or, as Carol S. Anderson points out, due to things being "influenced by other elements of the world, and thus all existence is contingent upon some-thing else" (Anderson 23); and the concept of *anātman*, or non-self, which follows out of the truth of impermanence: Buddhist epistemologies reject the notion of an essentialist or transcendental self, for as K.T.S. Sarao has it, "what we expe-rience to be a person is not a thing but a process; there is no human being, there is only becoming" (Sarao 18).[5] Philosophers of the Mahāyāna school of Buddhism took this idea one step further by claiming that, not only did an individual human being lack an intrinsic, essential self, but this condition of ultimate 'emptiness' (*śūnyatā*) extended to all objects and ideas as well. The realization of this truth can potentially for the practitioner provide a shortcut to the cessation of craving,

---

ment; specifically, they deal with the arising and ending of human suffering (cf. Keown, *Buddhism* 44-56).

3 *Taṇhā* is here the Pali equivalent of the Sanskrit term *tṛṣṇā*. Note, however, that there exists in Tantric traditions of Buddhism also the notion of reaching enlightenment not through a cessation of craving but instead through a transmutation of craving/desire into an experience of luminous awareness which results, as Francesca Fremantle puts it, in "an uncovering of the hidden order that dwells at the heart of chaos and confusion" (Fremantle 116). Cf. Keown, *Buddhism* 82 and Fre-mantle 114-16.

4 These consist of right understanding, right resolve, right speech, right action, right livelihood, right effort, right mindfulness and right meditation (cf. Keown, *Buddhism* 55).

5 Sarao contends that at "the level of 'conventional truth' [...], Buddhism accepts that in the dai-ly transactional world, humans can be named and recognized as more or less stable persons. However, at the level of the 'ultimate truth' [...], this unity and stability of personhood is only a sense-based construction of our productive imagination. What the Buddha encouraged is not the annihilation of the feeling of self, but the elimination of the belief in a permanent and eternal 'ghost in the machine'" (19).

for as Keown puts it, "the realization that things are empty destroys the fear – or craving – we have for them" (Keown, *Buddhism* 68).

Here are some definitions various scholars and writers have provided for the term and the concept of emptiness: Donald Lopez describes it as "the absence of substantial nature or intrinsic existence in any phenomenon in the universe" (*Buddhism* 267). Roger Jackson says that "the term *śūnyatā* has been glossed as 'openness,' 'inconceivability,' or 'unlimitedness,' but is best translated as 'emptiness' or 'voidness.' It refers to what dharmas (elements of reality) really are through what they are not: not as they appear, not conceptualizable, not distinguishable, and, above all, lacking permanent, independent intrinsic existence" (809). As Ralph Flores points out in his discussion of one famous Buddhist text dealing with emptiness, the *Heart Sutra*, the notion of things being empty does not imply that they are empty of existence but that they are empty of "inherent self-existence or *'own-being'*" (105). "Emptiness", says Flores, "functions much as does Derrida's *différance*, in dismantling presumptions about independent or self-present entities" (107). Indeed, the concept of emptiness seems to insist that there is no transcendental signified, merely a chain of interdependent, arbitrary signification fabricated by the human mind. Or, as Jacques Derrida would famously put it, *Il n'y a pas de hors-texte*. It would, however, be wrong to claim that Buddhist philosophers 'discovered' deconstruction *avant la lettre*. 'Sign' and 'signifier' are terms and ideas firmly entrenched in twentieth-century Western philosophy; they do not translate directly into Buddhist cultural and/or linguistic concepts. Yet there is undoubtedly a similar movement of thought going on here.[6] And just as the proponents of deconstruction point to a potentiality of textual or semiotic freedom or bliss which the application of their method may bring about for the practitioner, Buddhist thinkers point to the openness and potentiality inherent in the concept of emptiness. "Empty of a separate self means full of everything", says for instance Thich Nhat Hanh (Flores 114). And Peter Conradi, also a practicing Buddhist, writes:

> "Emptiness, properly understood, is not negation but, rather, openness. [...] Indeed 'shu' within the Sanskrit word for emptiness (*shunyata*) – carries the connotation of

---

6 For a lucid discussion of the cultural (un)translatability of emptiness in terms of concepts of the Western philosophical tradition see for instance Lopez, *Elaborations* 239-60. Sedgwick also addresses the problems inherent in Western adaptations of Buddhist thought in her essay "Pedagogy of Buddhism" (*Touching Feeling*, esp. 154-57 and 164-68). Crucially, however, she comes to the interesting conclusion that a Western reader can apprehend Buddhism "just to the degree that she can apprehend it through a Buddhist sense of knowing rather than a Western one. Conversely, from within the framework of the Buddhist respect for realization as both dense process and active practice, a theorized scholarly skepticism as to whether Buddhism can be known by Westerners may reveal its own dependence on an eerily thin Western phenomenology of 'knowing'" (168).

being 'pregnant with possibilities' – open – as well as empty. Beyond the protective survival mentality of 'this' and 'that', 'I' and 'other', lies an experience of the world's wealth 'just as it is', empty of self-clinging. Thus the encounter with 'emptiness' is said to involve, properly speaking, not throwing everything out so that all that is left is a blank kind of nothing, but rather an experience of bursting into an openness that is rich, unbounded, powerful, creative." (126-127)

It seems to me important to note that, whereas deconstruction offers 'only' a philosophical tradition for its practitioners to fully grasp the nature of *différance*, Buddhism offers both a philosophical and an experiential, practical path to fully understanding the concept of emptiness.[7] The various Buddhist schools differ somewhat in the practices they advocate for realizing states of emptiness. The Mahāyāna school advocates both meditation and the study of Buddhist sutras, whereas the Chinese Chan and Japanese Zen schools favour meditation practices such as the aforementioned practice of *zazen*, and practices which enable moments of sudden realization and insight, brought about for instance by the study of *kōans* (short anecdotes featuring a Zen master and a disciple) or by writing or reading a poem such as the aforementioned "Zazen on Ching-t'ing Mountain", which not only depicts but also performs practices of emptiness. For according to Jacob Kinnard, at "the heart of Zen Buddhism is the attempt to actualize emptiness, *śūnyatā*. This is most typically realized through intense meditation, exemplified by Dogen's *zazen*, 'just sitting,' technique, whereby the practitioner develops a mode of being without thinking, a way of being in the world as the world is happening, in flux – this is, in essence, experiencing the world [...] as it is, impermanent. The art of Zen is fundamentally an extension of the basic goal of Zen" (Kinnard 58). Speaking of the art of painting, Kinnard writes that, like "a *kōan*, a Zen painting is intended to provide a means for the artist and the viewer to enter into the reality of emptiness" (58). Surely the same principle can be said to apply to Zen poetry as well.[8]

Going back to Althusser's 'little theoretical theatre' (and the usefulness of the concept of emptiness to theories of queer subjectivity): Following the logic of emptiness, letting go of the need to be recognized can open up a space of possibility for the Althusserian subject. If needing to be recognized entails following the policeman's hailing and turning around – essentially a paranoid move, then *not* turning around, letting go of the need to be recognized by the dominant social

---

7 Sedgwick is also quite aware of this when she describes her late interest in non-dualism: "My shorthand for this relation at the time was 'Deconstruction is the theory, Buddhism is the practice'" (*The Weather in Proust* 75). Quite literally, Sedgwick's practice ended up being the creation of Japanese textile art that involves marbling and dyeing. Examples of her *suminagashi* (marbling) and *shibori* (shaped resist dyeing) art works are reprinted in *The Weather in Proust*.

8 Cf. Kinnard in "Art and Zen" and David L. McMahan in "Meditation (Chan/Zen)".

order will be an essentially reparative move for the Althusserian subject. Emptying oneself out means surrendering oneself to surprised openness, letting oneself become, not-knowing in advance what this becoming will eventually entail. The willingness to let oneself be surprised is incidentally one of the qualities Sedgwick singles out in her theory of reparative practices. A position of paranoia leads us to anxiously anticipate certain (mostly bad) outcomes, she maintains, whereas a reparative, non-anticipatory position will allow for surprising (and potentially good) things to happen (cf. *Touching Feeling* 146).

Queer Emptiness in the Poetry of Mary Oliver

The poet Mary Oliver never came to embrace either the confessional or the activist mode of poetry favoured by many of her U.S. American lesbian contemporaries. As Sue Russell puts it, "Oliver will never be a balladeer of contemporary lesbian life in the vein of Marilyn Hacker, or an important political thinker like Adrienne Rich; but the fact that she chooses not to write from a similar political or narrative stance makes her all the more valuable to our collective culture" (22). What is this value that Oliver brings to literary representations of queer subjectivity? Critic Rose Lucas makes out a different, non-teleological (and therefore queer, I would argue) temporality in Oliver's oeuvre, what she refers to as an "aesthetic of the drift": "To drift is thus to pay attention to different cues – ones which may not register in trajectories of the rational and of the classificatory. It is to read different markers in what Oliver views as the meditative and non-linear journeying of life, thus reconsidering notions of goal and arrival and success" (Lucas). Janet McNew finds in Oliver's nature poetry an epistemology based on notions of a dissolution of human subjectivity that "enables [Oliver] to be truer to the original intentions of romanticism than were the great male poets [i.e. Wordsworth, Coleridge and Keats, S.J.] who found themselves tugged toward solipsism and away from their original desires for a reconnection to nature" (67-68). Taking up McNew, Laird Christensen attributes to Oliver's nature writing a strategic construction of "a subject position based on ecological interdependence [which] will obviously influence how we see the world and how we engage it" (144).[9]

The following reading of her poem "Wilde Geese" may serve as an example of how Oliver treats the notion of contemporary (queer) sexual subjectivity, employing a stance of queer emptiness towards notions of abjection and shame, or – as a

---

9 Christensen draws on Martin Buber's concept of *I-You* (instead of *I-It*) relations as a theoretical
model to explain how Oliver's subjects relate to their natural surroundings and thus arrive at being "fully present in a world of presences", which Christensen says is "the most spiritual of acts to Oliver" (149).

reaction formation – pride, that might otherwise surround queer sexual subjectivity under the regimes of a heteronormative social order.

The poem, I suggest, contains three movements of thought.[10] The first five lines serve to clarify the speaker's sense of her own self, her attitude towards her own, queer sexual subjectivity, which she invites the reader to share. The speaker rejects being interpellated into a position of 'good' or 'bad' sexual subjectivity and also rejects the notion of any experiences of shame, the affective response connected to a 'bad' sexual subjectivity under current regimes of the normal. There is no need, in Oliver's epistemology of queer emptiness, for repenting – "You only have to let the soft animal of your body / love what it loves" (*New and Selected Poems* 110).[11] An invitation for a conversation between speaker and reader follows. The speaker offers to the reader an act of recognition that can take the place of the harmful recognition into a subject position of abjection offered by the existing heteronormative social order.

The speaker then goes on to perform her epistemology of queer emptiness, which I take at the same time again to be an invitation extended to the reader to perform her own subjectivity in a manner similar to the performance of subjectivity exemplified by the speaker of Oliver's poem in lines seven to thirteen. This is the second of the three movements of thought. "Meanwhile the sun and the clear pebbles of the rain / are moving across the landscapes" (110). Mindfully aware, the speaker offers us a meditation on goings-on in the natural world, human perception and description filtered through language but without any notions of evaluation or judgement, a performance of the kind of meditative absorption recommended by Buddhist treatises as exercises to be undertaken by the individual who wishes to attain subjectivity states of emptiness.[12]

Movement of thought number three contains, however, a return towards notions of recognition. In the closing lines of the poem it is the (natural) world which offers recognition to the speaker's – and reader's – queer subjectivity, a recognition which can take the place of recognition by the existing heteronormative social order and its concurrent interpellation of queer subjects into subject positions of abjection. The queer subject, in "Wild Geese", is then finally not required

---

10 You can listen to Mary Oliver read the entire poem of "Wild Geese" in her interview with Krista Tippett online at https://onbeing.org.

11 I read the second person pronoun ("you") in the first five lines of this poem as the speaker talking about herself, i.e. referring to her *own* subjectivity, and generalizing from there. This is a point that must, however, remain ambiguous, as the "you" can be understood either to be referring to the speaker or as a form of direct reader address. The poem allows for both readings.

12 See Gisela Ullyatt's essay "'The Only Chance to Love This World': Buddhist Mindfulness in Mary Oliver's Poetry" for a more in-depth discussion on Oliver's poetry and how it relates to Buddhist concepts of mindfulness, especially the concepts of Beginner's Mind, Mindful Awareness and Nowness.

to completely let go of the last vestiges of attachment to an individual subjectivity and self, or permanently relinquish her need for recognition by any kind of order, be it the natural or the social.

The seeking out and acceptance of a 'real' (queer) subjectivity of emptiness is a movement of thought contained, finally, in another of Mary Oliver's poems, "In Blackwater Woods". Again it is the contemplation of the natural world which leads the speaker of this poem to meditate on the nature of attachment and loss in human life, and to come, finally, to a position of not only understanding but acceptance of the loss premeditated in any form of human recognition and attachment. Here, the speaker does, in the end, come to perform, and embody, a subjectivity of emptiness, and here the speaker is trying to teach herself the art of unbecoming.

"In Blackwater Woods

Look the trees
are turning
their own bodies
into pillars

of light,
are giving off the rich
fragrance of cinnamon
and fulfillment,

the long tapes
of cattails
are bursting and floating away over
the blue shoulders

of the ponds,
and every pond,
no matter what its
name is, is

nameless now.
Every year
everything
I have ever learned

in my lifetime
leads back to this: the fires

and the black river of loss
whose other side

is salvation,
whose meaning
none of us will ever know.
To live in this world

you must be able
to do three things:
to love what is mortal;
to hold it

against your bones knowing
your own life depends on it;
and, when the time comes to let it go,
to let it go." (177)

To love already implicates loss here, and loss implicates past (and enduring) love. Human beings are presented as part of the natural world; their existence is based on the same law of change, of impermanence that governs the comings and goings of the seasons. But this is not presented as something threatening by the speaker. Rather, it is presented as a universal constant in both the human and the natural world. Letting go, the work of mourning, is as much a natural part of this life as the leaves turning their colours in the fall. The metaphor of the "black river" of loss hints at the fact that the speaker is well aware of the fact that letting go, here the work of mourning, is no easy task. But "salvation", "the other side" of that river hints at the possibility of a transformative gain if the natural process is allowed to fully run its course. As Jeffrey Thomson writes of Oliver's nature poetry, here "grief exists not to torment or so that rapture can transpire; loss exists so gain can follow" (160).[13]

---

13 Janet McNew comes to a similar conclusion when she writes that "[i]nstead of forsaking the natural for supernatural eternity, [Oliver's] poems follow the cycles of the seasons to image loss and the possibility for renewal. These vast natural cycles, which usually symbolize traps and prison houses for the romantic visionary, are strangely consoling for Oliver. Wedding herself to them holds her close to the deepest mysteries she knows, those of natural transformation" (70).

Queer Emptiness in Sylvia Townsend Warner's *Lolly Willowes* and *Summer Will Show*

Sylvia Townsend Warner's career as a writer spans five decades. Originally trained as a musicologist, she turned to writing poetry, novels and short stories from the mid 1920s onwards. A contemporary of Virginia Woolf's, she never rose to the latter's fame. Critics generally attribute this either to her personal life (she was both a lesbian and a Communist) or to her rather conventional narrative style, conventional that is compared to the narrative styles of high modernists like Woolf, Djuna Barnes or James Joyce.[14] But first impressions about narrative style are deceptive with Warner. As Jane Garrity points out, "in larger narrative structure Warner's fiction, far from conventional or conservative, frequently melds satirical fantasy, social realism, allegory, and literary allusion – always with a convoluted eye toward subversiveness. The cumulative effect of her individually accessible sentences is never one of transparency" (*Step-Daughters of England* 148).

Published in 1926, *Lolly Willowes* is Warner's first novel. It tells the story of an unmarried woman at the beginning of the twentieth century who engages in an act of refusal by taking herself outside of the options her world has to offer her, choosing instead to embrace a life of radical emptiness. Laura, or Lolly, as she has been nicknamed by her nieces and nephew, grows up at her family's home in Somerset, where she stays on after her mother's untimely death, continuing to live with her father. Laura, the reader is told, does not see the necessity of getting married: "her upbringing had only furthered a temperamental indifference to the need of getting married – or, indeed, of doing anything positive – and this indifference was reinforced by the circumstances which had made her so closely her father's companion" (*Lolly Willowes* 26). *Lolly Willowes* does not contain a same-sex relationship of any kind. I still read Laura as queer for two reasons: (i) her rejection of marriage during the first part of the novel and her rejection of any kind of social existence towards the novel's close allow for a reading of Laura as non-heteronormative; and (ii), the only moment Laura is portrayed as showing any signs of other-directed desire is during a scene featuring her dancing with Emily, a young woman at Great Mop, which she quite enjoys (the reader has previously learned that Laura abhors dancing).[15]

---

14 See Garrity, *Step-Daughters of England* 147-53. For Warner's personal life and her relationship with the poet Valentine Ackland, which lasted for several decades, see e.g. Terry Castle's essay "The Will to Whimsy".

15 "Laura liked dancing with Emily; the pasty-faced and anemic young slattern whom she had seen dawdling about the village danced with a fervor that annihilated every misgiving. They whirled faster and faster, fused together like two suns that whirl and blaze in a single destruction. A strand of the red hair came undone and brushed across Laura's face. The contact made her tingle

After her father's death, Laura moves in with her older brother Henry and his wife Caroline at Apsley Terrace in London, helping raise their two daughters Fancy and Marion. It is in her late forties that Laura finds herself regularly getting anxious during the autumn months; she is haunted by visions of living not in London but somewhere in the country:

"At these times she was subject to a peculiar kind of day-dreaming, so vivid as to be almost a hallucination: that she was in the country, at dusk, and alone, and strangely at peace. She did not recall the places which she had visited in holiday-time, these reproached her like opportunities neglected. But while her body sat before the first fires and was cosy with Henry and Caroline, her mind walked by lonely seaboards, in marshes and fens, or came at nightfall to the edge of a wood. She never imagined herself in these places by daylight. She never thought of them as being in any way beautiful. It was not beauty at all that she wanted [...]. Her mind was groping after something that eluded her experience, a something that was shadowy and menacing, and yet in some way congenial; a something that lurked in waste places, that was hinted at by the sound of water gurgling through deep channels and by the voices of birds of ill omen. Loneliness, dreariness, aptness for arousing a sense of fear, a kind of ungodly hallowedness – these were the things that called her thoughts away from the comfortable fireside." (73-74)

Laura is longing not only to move out of the city but also yearns for escaping her London life and the place society has assigned to her. What she is drawn to is not a picturesque setting, but an existence that includes "darkness", "a something that [is] shadowy and menacing", "a kind of an ungodly hallowedness". Prompted by her visions, she decides to move to Buckinghamshire, to a little village called Great Mop, where she proceeds to spend as much time in the outdoors as she can. It is in a field near Great Mop that she experiences a moment of transformative insight and bliss, an awakening prompted by her opening herself up to letting herself be affected by the sensory experience of her natural environment:

"When she walked into the meadow it was bloomed over with cowslips, powdering the grass in variable plenty, here scattered, there clustered, innumerable as the stars in the Milky Way.
    She knelt down among them and laid her face close to their fragrance. The weight of all her unhappy years seemed for a moment to weigh her bosom down to the earth; she trembled, understanding for the first time how miserable she had been; and in another moment she was released. [...] She was changed, and she

---

from head to foot. She shut her eyes and dived into obliviousness – with Emily for a partner she could dance until the gun-powder ran out of the heels of her boots" (*Lolly Willowes* 175).

knew it. She was humbler, and more simple. She ceased to triumph mentally over her tyrants, and rallied herself no longer with the consciousness that she had out-raged them by coming to live at Great Mop. [...] There was no question of forgiving them. [...] If she were to start forgiving she must needs forgive Society, the Law, the Church, the History of Europe, the Old Testament, great-great-aunt Salome and her prayer-book, the Bank of England, Prostitution, the Architect of Apsley Terrace, and half a dozen other useful props of civilization. All she could do was to go on forgetting them. But now she was able to forget them without flouting them by her forgetfulness." (135-36)

Laura understands that it is not Henry or Caroline or the rest of her family who had until then imprisoned her in an existence that had made her feel miserable; it is the ideological subject position inscribed into her by the institutions of "Society" that has made her suffer – she has up to this point in the novel allowed herself to be interpellated by Althusser's ideological state apparatuses – "the Law, the Church, [...] the Old Testament [...] and half a dozen other useful props of civili-zation" – into a position of abjection. Lying in a field of cowslips, undergoing a moment of dissolution of her human subjectivity not unlike the subjectivity states portrayed in Mary Oliver's nature poetry, she is able to engage in an attitude of non-caring towards being hailed by these institutions of society into any kind of subject position. Renouncing recognition takes the form of forgetting for Laura: "All she could do was to go on forgetting them".

But Laura's new-found freedom does not last. When her nephew Titus decides to join her in Great Mop, Laura finds herself once again interpellated into her role of Aunt Lolly. On one of her walks in the countryside, she calls out for help and finds her call answered by the appearance of a kitten in her home on her return. Laura comes to the conclusion that it is Satan who has answered her call and that "[s]he, Laura Willowes, in England, in the year 1922, had entered into a compact with the Devil" (155). As Laura finds out, all the other inhabitants of Great Mop turn out to be witches and warlocks as well. Her landlady Mrs Leak takes Laura to the celebration of a local Witches' Sabbath, and the devil's playful ploys cause Titus to leave Great Mop and return to London. Laura encounters the devil twice in the novel, once in the form of a gamekeeper and once as a gardener. Both occa-sions offer her opportunities to make enquiries into the purpose of witches and witchcraft. Warner's move into the fantastical offers a number of reading possi-bilities.[16] I read the novel's theme of witchcraft as a metaphor for non-conformity

---

16 I concur with Barbara Brothers who argues that "Warner [...] has Lolly reject the whole value sys-tem of the patriarchal society and decide that if God is on the side of female servility and propri-ety, male pomposity and tradition, and the institutionalism that is civilization, then her calling is to be a servant of the devil, a witch" (200). John Lucas regards Warner's move from realism into

and Warner's devil as embodying the bad Althusserian subject *par excellence*.[17] By becoming his followers, the characters in the novel are set free from the obligation to adhere to societal norms. For Laura, this opens up whole new ways of being, especially for women. "One doesn't become a witch to run round being harmful, or to run round being helpful either, a district visitor on a broomstick", she remarks in an impassioned monologue towards the novel's end. "It's to escape all that – to have a life of one's own, not an existence doled out to you by others, charitable refuse of their thoughts, so many ounces of stale bread of life a day, the workhouse dietary is scientifically calculated to support life. As for the witches who can only express themselves by pins and bed-blighting, they have been warped into that shape by the dismal lives they've led" (215).

The novel's final scene, however, sees Laura even leaving behind her newfound community of witches and transcending her new identity as a witch. Setting out, at night, to walk from the local train station back to Great Mop, Laura envisions herself falling asleep in "a suitable dry ditch" or "burrow herself a bed" in a local wood.

> "Lovely to be with people who prefer their thoughts to yours, lovely to live at your own sweet will, lovely to sleep out all night! She had quite decided, now, to do so. It was an adventure, she had never done such a thing before, and yet it seemed most natural. She would not sleep here: Wickendon was too close. But presently, later on, when she felt inclined to, she would wander off in search of a suitable dry ditch or an accommodating loosened haystack; or wading through last year's leaves and this year's fern she would penetrate into a wood and burrow herself a bed." (222)

Yearning to shed her human identity by merging with the natural world, Laura longs to enter a subjectivity state of emptiness not unlike the ones portrayed by the speakers of Mary Oliver's nature poetry. As for the devil, Laura feels certain

---

the realm of fantasy as having an even further-reaching political agenda, claiming that *Lolly Willowes'* "formal radicalism is *intrinsically political*. The novel moves through a succession of deftly presented narrative stages which are also historical, social moments: from pre-war England via the war itself to the post-war period and on into the near future. As it does so realism loosens its apparently 'natural' and unyielding grip and the fantastic and visionary increasingly take control. And as they take control so the sense of capital's four-square bricky presence – its claim to be the 'real' world – is first disputed and then replaced by liberated and liberating glimpses of alternative possibilities, other ways of living" (209).

17 With a slightly different emphasis, Jane Garrity reads witchcraft in *Lolly Willowes* as a cipher for lesbianism (cf. *Step-Daughters of England* 150). Satan, for Garrity, functions as "Lolly's double to the extent that he represents her repressed lesbianism, for from the outset it is he who has been her stimulus, guiding her away from her role as London spinster and [...] easing her into her subversive calling as a witch" (175).

that he will not care either way, his authority being of an "indifferent" and therefore also empty nature. "A closer darkness upon her slumber, a deeper voice in the murmuring leaves overhead – that would be all she would know of his undesiring and unjudging gaze, his satisfied but profoundly indifferent ownership" (222).

Unlike *Lolly Willowes*, Warner's 1936 novel *Summer Will Show* very prominently features a same-sex relationship between its female protagonists Sophia Willoughby and Minna Lemuel. However, Warner sidesteps any terminologies of sexuality on the level of both narration and character speech, leaving the novel's central 'lesbian' relationship essentially unmarked and undefined. Both the novel itself and its characters thus refuse to be interpellated in terms of a contemporary system of classification into specific sexual subject positions, sexological or otherwise.[18] This is quite in contrast to Radclyffe Hall's 1928 novel *The Well of Loneliness*, which frames its female same-sex relationships in terms of sexological discourses of inversion. The characters in *Summer Will Show* are furthermore not portrayed as regarding their desire as abject, problematic or a 'truth' to be anxiously sought or known; instead, the novel features moments of emptiness and surprised openness that carry the potential of transformation for the characters. Sophia Willoughby especially, the heroine of *Summer Will Show*, is someone willing to let herself be surprised.

The novel is set in 1848 and starts out in rural Dorset, where Sophia, part of the landed gentry, lives with her two children on her estate at Blandamer House. She feels herself to be, like the chestnut trees growing on her estate, past their bloom: "I am done with blossoming", she says at the novel's outset, "done with ornament and admiration. I live for my children – a good life, the life my heart would have chosen" (*Summer Will Show* 12). Her mother and father have died, and it falls on her to take care of Blandamer House, a task she is happy to comply with: "She was a landowner, and a mother, and every day there was more to do, more to oversee the doing of. Duties came out of thought, and after another, swift as bees coming out of a hive. She was a mother, and a landowner; but fortunately she need no longer be counted among the wives" (21). For she is estranged, as the reader learns, from her husband Frederick, who has run off to Paris to join the entourage of his latest

---

18 The downside to Warner's deliberate choice to leave Sophia and Minna's relationship as unmarked is that it can be misread as platonic friendship by the (ignorant) reader. Or rather, such a misreading is not completely foreclosed by the text. Whether this constitutes a problem or not depends on whether one regards lesbian (in)visibility as such as a problem or not. For an important early exploration of the novel as primarily a lesbian text see Terry Castle, *The Apparitional Lesbian*. Castle also impressively makes out various nineteenth-century French and English novels as important intertexts for Warner's *Summer Will Show*. On the other end of the critical spectrum, for a lucid discussion of *Summer Will Show* as a primarily Marxist novel see Janet Montefiore's *Men and Women Writers of the 1930s* (esp. 168-77).

mistress, the actress and bohemian Minna Lemuel. Normally indifferent towards her husband's extramarital affairs, his choice of a mistress this time around fills Sophia with a certain fury:

> "For even to Dorset the name of Minna Lemuel had made its way. Had the husband of Mrs. Willoughby chosen with no other end than to be scandalous, he could not have chosen better. A byword, half actress, half strumpet; a Jewess; a nonsensical creature bedizened with airs of prophecy, who trailed across Europe with a tag-rag of poets, revolutionaries, musicians and circus-riders snuffing at her heels, like an escaped bitch with a procession of mongrels after her; and ugly; and old, as old as Frederick or older – this was the woman whom Frederick had elected to fall in love with, joining in the tag-rag procession, and not even king in that outrageous court, not even able to dismiss the mongrels, and take the creature into keeping." (29)

It is the death of her two small children from small-pox, which comes as quite a shock to Sophia, which sets off a chain of events that leads to Sophia's travelling to Paris, originally with the intention to convince Frederick to give her another child. However, Frederick is not to be found in his Paris apartment, and Sophia sets out for Minna Lemuel's apartment in order to confront him. Once there she stumbles upon a party going on in full swing, with Minna, as it turns out an accomplished storyteller, as the main attraction. With great apprehension, Sophia hears – and sees – her presumed rival for the first time. Minna turns out not to be what Sophia expected her to be – this is where the element of surprise comes in – and Sophia cannot help to be affected, or rather *allows herself to be affected* by Minna's performance, by entering a state of deep listening, a state of mindful attention and present openness:

> "'Most beautiful Minna, we are here to be enchanted. Will you not wave your wand, will you not tell us one of your beautiful *Maerchen*?' [...]
> The fulsome voice was lost among other voices making the same request. That's Frederick! her mind cried out, and forgot him in the next instant [...].
> 'No, not a fairy-tale. I have told so many. This shall be a true story.'
> See her she must. And in the jostle of rearrangement which had followed the requesting voices, Sophia shifted her place till she could see from the ante-room into the room beyond. When she could hear again, Minna was already speaking, leaning forward with her elbows on her knees, her face propped between her hands – the attitude of one crouched over a sleepy fire, watching the embers waste and brighten and waste again." (96)

The narrator's description of Minna's pose is striking here: "leaning forward with her elbows on her knees, her face propped between her hands – the attitude of one crouched over a sleepy fire, watching the embers waste and brighten and waste again". The imagery conjured is one of meditative absorption, of a state of stillness and presence, of being present in the flow of the present moment, empty, open, mindful. The description is meant to convey to the reader both the state into which Minna lets herself fall, as well as the state into which she draws her audience, including Sophia. This passage is the end of Part One of the novel. Part Two opens directly with Minna's story. No framing narrative is provided, which has the effect of casting the reader in the role of Minna's attentive audience, and narration fades into character speech via the shared image of a burning candle/fire:

> "'But the first thing I can remember is the lighting of a candle.
>
> It is the middle of the night it seems to me […]. My father is there, moving softly in the dusky room. He speaks to himself in a language which I have never heard before, and coming to the hearth he takes up an ember with the tongs, and breathes on it, as though he were praying to it. At his breath it wakens and glows, and I see his face, and his lips moving amid his beard. […]
>
> But that was in summer, an endless lifetime, when the sky was as blue as a cornflower […]. But best of all I remember the first spring. […]
>
> In the night, the wind changed. I woke up, and heard a different voice, loud like the coming of an army, and yet thick and gentle, as though it wrapped one in velvet. I pinched my mother, and said, 'What's that?' She woke with a start, and lay still, listening and trembling. 'It is the thaw-wind,' she said […].
>
> The wind brought rain, a soft brushing rain like tassels of silk. […] Day after day the wind blew warm, and the snow melted, and the ground appeared, and thawed, and clucked like a hen, drinking the snow-water. Blades of new grass came up, and small bright flowers, flocks of birds came flying, and settled on the patches of cleared ground, or pecked at the glistening tree-trunks. […]'" (99-100)

Minna's seduction, of both Sophia and her audience, is by way of storytelling. She tells a story of childhood memories in her native Lithuania which ends in the child witnessing a pogrom and being orphaned, and yet these opening paragraphs are striking in their minute descriptions of the sensory experiences of her domestic life and of the natural world and the comings and goings of the seasons – a first Sabbath celebration, a first summer, a first spring, a first thaw-wind, a first witnessing of the ice bursting, melting on a frozen river. With mindful or Zen-like attention to minute details of her child self's observations and sensory experiences, Minna evokes for her listeners a Zen-like state of emptiness that forms the underpinning of her own (queer) subjectivity of emptiness. One gets the impression that, horrific as her experience has been, she has not been traumatized by it. There is a vast, open, empty space inside her which the pogrom was not able to touch. There is a moment during the telling of the tale that Minna's and Sophia's

gazes meet, and after the telling of the tale has been interrupted by the 1848 revolution that is about to start outside, Minna confides in Sophia that it was her she
had been speaking to: "I wish you had not been interrupted." / "I was sorry to lose
such listening as yours. Yes, as yours. Did you not know that I was speaking to
you?" (116).[19]

Sophia ends up spending the night at Minna's apartment and, over the course
of the following weeks, a romance starts to bloom between the two women, with
Frederick increasingly getting sidelined by both women. In due course Sophia
moves in with Minna and is increasingly drawn into the activities of Minna's
friends, the bohemian artists and Socialist and Communist revolutionaries. Ideological interpellations occur for Sophia in the form of Frederick's and her aunt
Léocadie's interventions. Frederick tries to make his wife comply by cutting her
off financially, and Léocadie tries to appeal to Sophia's standing as a member of
a social class far removed from her revolutionary friends. But to no avail. Sophia
will not let herself be hailed: "I have changed my ideas", she will tell Léocadie
towards the end of the novel. "I do not think as I did" (327). But this is the scene
with Frederick:

> "'He has cut off my supplies. As he is entitled to do, being my husband. He has told
> the bank not to honour my signature, he has removed the gold fittings from my
> dressing-case. So you see, Minna, I am penniless, or soon shall be. I have what is
> left over from my ring, that will last a while. I have my clothes for what they are
> worth. And my hair, I believe one can always sell one's hair. After that, unless I com-
> ply with Frederick's wishes, nothing.'
> 'You will stay? You must, if only to gall him.'
> 'I don't think that much of a reason.'
> 'But you will stay?'
> 'I will stay if you wish it.'
> It seemed to her that the words fell cold and glum as ice-pellets. Only
> beneath the crust of thought did her being assent as by right to that flush of plea-
> sure, that triumphant cry.

---

19   For Janet Montefiore, too, this scene proves to be pivotal for the transformation of Sophia's consciousness: "A central passage of *Summer Will Show* is the long scene, charged with political and
erotic energies, in which a relationship is set up between two women, strangers to each other: a
speaker and a listener on the periphery of her audience, through whose consciousness the story
is told. [...] The experience of listening to Minna inaugurates Sophia's complete transformation
of her own life and identity; the hardheaded, apolitical materfamilias abandons her own class, is
recruited as a messenger by the Communists, and fights alongside Minna on the revolutionary
side of the barricades in June 1848" (168). Montefiore sees Minna's "spoken words" liberating "the
listening Sophia both emotionally and politically" (172). As Sophia "listens to Minna, her judging,
stereotyping habits of mind dissolve" (173).

'But of course,' said Minna a few hours later, thoughtfully licking the last oyster shell, 'we must be practical.'" (224)

Indeed, Frederick's interpellation prompts a declaration of love and a promise between Minna and Sophia ("I will stay if you wish it"), and results in a deepening of their budding relationship – even if the sex scene between the characters is here merely hinted at. The 'bad' Althusserian subject will not let herself be interpellated into a position of abjection, as for instance Radclyffe Hall's Stephen Gordon in *The Well of Loneliness*, published eight years earlier than *Summer Will Show*, constantly does.[20]

However, a happy ending is withheld for Minna and Sophia. The 1848 revolution, as we know, failed. The reader last sees Minna as Sophia sees her, fighting on the barricades, stabbed with a bayonet. Sophia is taken prisoner but eventually released. The novel ends with Sophia returning to Minna's apartment and starting to read a pamphlet written by her friend Ingelbrecht, which turns out to be Marx and Engels' *Communist Manifesto*. Literary critics differ in the way they read the ending of the novel. Terry Castle, for instance, insists that there is yet a chance that Minna is alive, as her dead body has not been found at the novel's close (*The Apparitional Lesbian* 87). Others, like Heather Love, read Minna's death at being implied in the bayonette-stabbing scene.[21] Whether one reads the ending as Sophia being still in denial about Minna's certain death, or whether one shares her hope of her lover's survival; it is definitely a strange choice to end the novel with this shift of focus away from the characters' fates. I read this as another emptying out. The characters' fates ultimately do not matter, in the sense that their eventual fate is not the point of the novel. What matters is the way Sophia has changed by meeting Minna, opening her *self* up to a larger existence, realizing her wish from the novel's beginning to "extend" her "shade, [...] unquestioned as a tree" (22). What matters is maybe also how the *reader* has been changed by the reading the novel. Finally, a further emptying out will even suspend the question of life and death itself. To paraphrase the novel's very Zen epigraph: For Sophia and for us, Summer *will* show, whether we live – or die.

---

20   In fact, Gay Wachman convincingly argues that in *Summer Will Show*, Warner deliberately satirizes Hall's *The Well of Loneliness* (cf. Wachman 171-79).

21   Cf. Love 144-145. Wachman sees Minna's death as unrelated to her or Sophia's lesbian sexual identity. According to her, "Minna dies as a result of the class war and of Sophia's arrogant, racist refusal to take [her West Indian nephew, S.J.] Caspar's infatuation seriously. Caspar kills Minna because Sophia loves her and neglects him and because he has absorbed the values of the patriarchal imperialism that brought him into the world" (214).

A Postscript: Michel Foucault's Technologies of the Self

What other option is there besides learning to embody a queer subjectivity of emptiness if one whishes, as a queer subject, to arrive at a mode of 'doing' a kind of contemporary subjectivity that allows one to disregard ideology's interpellating call? Queer theorist and historian Michel Foucault finds in the alterity of history the model for an other subjectivity. Recurring to Greek and Roman authors of late antiquity, Foucault makes out certain technologies of the self, what he calls "aesthetic practices", or "practices of freedom", "an exercise of the self on the self by which one attempts to develop and transform oneself, and to attain to a certain mode of being" in his essay "The Ethics of the Concern of the Self as a Practice of Freedom" (282). This mode of subjectivity, of 'doing' the self according to a set of ethical principles, where *ethos* is understood to be "a way of being and of behavior" (286), is based around the notion of the care of the self. It is a mode of self-mastery, of "governmentality", of governing oneself, and by extension, governing others since "a person who took proper care of himself would, by the same token, be able to conduct himself properly in relation to others and for others" (287). Foucault points out that Greco-Roman philosophers were much more concerned with the proper care of the self than with the knowledge, or discovery, of certain 'truths' of the self – and the Althusserian model of the functioning of ideology would certainly fall under the notion of a model of subjectivity concerned with installing certain 'truths' in the subject, in our case sexual identity as one 'truth' around which a subject comes to understand, and conceive of, itself as a subject. As Foucault argues, these kinds of truth games have only entered the picture and been able to develop fully in Early Christianity, where confession played a major role in putting the emphasis for subjects on a knowing of their 'true' selves.[22]

This is what for Greco-Roman philosophers is entailed in the notion of *epimeleisthai sautou*, or the taking care of the self, a concept that was to them as important as, if not more important than, the often quoted Delphic principle of *gnothi seauton*, or 'know thyself': the performing of a number of "technologies of the self, which permit individuals to effect by their own means, or with the help of others,

---

22 Cf. Foucault, "Technologies of the Self". It bears saying in light of the preceding chapter that an exchange of ideas (limited though it may have been) took place in classical antiquity between Greek and Indian philosophers. Ancient Greek historians and philosophers displayed an interest in Indian (both Hindu and Buddhist) philosophies, most notably from the times of Alexander the Great. Whether the Greco-Roman practices of self-care that Foucault is drawn to can be regarded as being directly originating from these cross-cultural contacts, must remain mostly speculative. Admittedly, critics such as Thomas McEvilley make out some surprising similarities in Ancient Greek and Buddhist thought. For an in-depth discussion of these cross-cultural encounters see Wilhelm Halbfass's *India and Europe* (esp. 2-23) and Thomas McEvilley's *The Shape of Ancient Thought*.

a certain number of operations on their own bodies and souls, thoughts, conduct, and way of being, so as to transform themselves in order to attain a certain state of happiness, purity, wisdom, perfection, or immortality" (Foucault, "Technologies of the Self" 225). For Socrates it "involves various things: taking pains with one's holdings and one's health. It is always a real activity and not just an attitude" (230). For the Stoics it is a form of attention to the self; one must "retire into the self and stay there" (232). This can take the form of a self-examination of one's thoughts and actions in the form of a notebook or letters to friends, or possibly a rural retreat. Marcus Aurelius, for example, relates in a letter what kinds of books he read, what he ate for lunch, how he took care of his sore throat by gargling with honey water ("Technologies of the Self" 233). One becomes one's own doctor. Also, one is never to stop taking care of one's self, and one is never to stop learning and to stop listening to the voice of a master, a counselor, a friend: a certain complete achievement of life is only reached in old age (cf. 235). Self-writing, for Marcus Aurelius as for Seneca as well, becomes a form of administrative practice: a taking stock of one's daily life and activities, thoughts and conduct; a comparison of what one wanted to accomplish and what one managed to accomplish during the day. While still concerned with his thoughts throughout the day, with a disclosure of self and an examination of self and conscience, the emphasis of contemplation, for Seneca, lies still on (past, present and future) actions. He is an administrator, not a judge, of his own life (cf. "Technologies of the Self" 237). Subjectivity becomes about a 'doing', not a 'being'. For the Stoics, a "retreat into the country becomes a spiritual retreat into oneself. It is a general attitude and also a precise act every day; you retire into the self to discover – but not to discover faults and deep feelings, only to remember rules of action, the main laws of behavior. It is a mnemotechnical formula" (238).

For Michel Foucault, this alternative historical model of an ethical self, a self that is based on principles of what he calls "governmentality", or an administrative view of managing the self, proves interesting insofar as Foucault is concerned, throughout his oeuvre, with questions of truth, subjectivity and power. His own theories around sexuality, subjectivity and truth – that modern power is dispersed, that sexuality is a historical construct, that the subject is a product of the formation of certain historical discourses – builds on his teacher Louis Althusser's model of the functioning of ideological power, of the interpellation of subjects via ideological state apparatuses into certain ideological subject positions. Foucault's model of the care of the self, borrowed from late antiquity, provides an alternative view of 'doing' subjectivity, of managing both oneself and "the space of power that exists in all relationships [...] in a nonauthoritarian manner" ("The Ethics of the Concern of the Self" 287). Eluding "states of domination", "the concept of governmentality makes it possible to bring out the freedom of the subject and its relationship to others" (300). If modern subjectivity, as theorized by Althusser and others, is based around epistemological foundations organized around the Delphic principle of 'Know thyself', Foucault here invites us to rethink and redo subjectivity in a different manner, following an older philosophical tradition and employing an other epistemological foundation based around the "Socratic injunction 'Take care of yourself,' in other words, 'Make freedom your foundation, through the mastery of yourself'" (301). Foucault's move into the performative mode, his shift from 'being' to 'doing' a self, crucially decentres questions of sexuality and self-identity – another form of emptying out. Instead, Foucault offers us with his self-care practices a more holistic, less identity-focused conception of the self.

Performative Strategies

In the fall of 2004, a young gay man made me the unsuspecting witness of a spectacle, a public performance of his queer sexuality, in a part of downtown San Francisco known as Yerba Buena Gardens, a carefully designed public space near the Museum of Modern Art which houses, among other attractions, a monument to civil rights movement leader Martin Luther King. Inscribed on the walls of a public fountain featuring a one-storey high cascading waterfall is a quote from one of his speeches: "No. No, we are not satisfied, and we will not be satisfied until justice rolls down like water and righteousness like a mighty stream." I tried to capture the poetic essence of the exchange which took place between the young man, his friend, and me in the following poem.

Yerba Buena Gardens

You've got to admit the kid has a sense
of drama, approaching you on the walkway
below the MLK Jr. Memorial, pressing a camera
into your hand. He doesn't say a word and you
might not be able to hear him over the thundering
water anyway, but from his facial expression, half
asking, half demanding, it's quite clear what
he expects you to do. Next he drags his friend
to stand with him on a stone in the spray, water
dripping on their upturned faces, drenching their
brightly coloured shirts. Selectig the right angle
in the viewer, you realize what's been missing
from your life, when you take their picture; in front
of the waterfall, two seventeen-year old boys, kissing.

To this day I am not quite sure what function I had for this young man's public performance, whether I served for him primarily as audience, witness, or photographer. I also do not know whether he read me as gay or straight, or whether he at all cared about the sexual orientation of his audience/photographer. But I recognized the signs of his artistry: he was undoubtedly projecting, reaching out with his focus of attention both towards his boyfriend and towards me and the camera; he was also quite obviously familiar with the art of positioning both one's own body and one's partner's body at such an angle so they appear fully present to the observing eye – whether that eye was meant to be me, a fellow tourist incidentally wandering by, or his own camera, in which case the finished product of his art was meant to be a picture, not a theatrical performance in and of itself. Nevertheless, he had chosen his stage quite carefully, with obvious intent, a public memorial to a civil rights leader. He was not just kissing his boyfriend for the family album; he was quite obviously, with his performative act, making a public statement about his queer sexuality and positioning both his performance of the kiss and himself in the context of a civil rights discourse.

On the other side of the equation I, the witness/observer/photographer, was caught by surprise by this performance because I had not read either him or his friend as gay previous to the moment of the enactment of the kiss. His performance had also had its transformative effect on me, the momentary audience member, in that it made me realize in a moment of epiphanic clarity that I was simply not used to seeing teenage boys kiss in public, anywhere, that it was indeed not an everyday occurrence I was witnessing, and it made me ponder the reasons why that might be so, from all the obvious ones – that most gay teenage boys, whether in the U.S. or in Europe, experience fear and do not feel safe enough in public spaces to perform such an act of public displays of affection; and at the same time it made me realize how much I yearned for a future that might include public displays of affections of queer teenage boys, with no one minding or feeling offended or threatened or provoked into acts of homophobic violence or insults.

This fear, which I had long regarded as a form of weakness that must needs be overcome by the queer subject in his or her developmental narrative of a heroic struggle of successfully coming out of the closet, can however give rise to another, in certain contexts equally successful performative strategy: the strategic non-disclosure of one's sexuality as a preemptive move on the part of a queer subject to prevent oneself from being harmed by acts of homophobic violence or insults. Witnessing, a few years later, a close friend, another queer young man, use secrecy quite intentionally, for a prolonged period of time, as one of his performative strategies of successfully managing his affective life as a contemporary queer subject, made me reevaluate the notions of both secrecy and closetedness as possibly, in certain contexts and for certain subjects and for certain time periods, quite useful strategic devices, a line of thought I tried to capture in another, the following poem.

The Secret

Two boys I loved who both loved other men,
One openly; the other kept it secret,
Close to his heart, and guarded it as if
It were the rarest and most treasured gift
The heavens could bestow upon him:
To love another boy, be close to him
And share not just his body but his heart,
To open up completely and to yield
To feelings, wants, desires of the flesh
And mind was dangerous, potent stuff for him.
He was an alchemist, a farrier
Of souls. The rules of gravity did not
Apply to him. Mercurial, he worked
An ancient stardust magic on the world.

This young man experienced his secret as something that was both too precious and too fragile and thus in need of protection; risking exposure meant risking destruction – of both secret and self. As the two previous examples have shown, both disclosure and non-disclosure of one's queer sexuality may thus serve as viable modes of engaging with one's surroundings as a queer subject.

But what exactly is a performance, and what do I mean by the notion of performative strategies as possible strategies of resilience for queer subjects? In his book *The Presentation of Self in Everyday Life*, the sociologist Erving Goffman describes as a 'performance' the following:

"A 'performance' may be defined as all the activity of a given participant on a given occasion which serves to influence in any way any of the other participants. Taking a particular participant and his performance as a basic point of reference, we may refer to those who contribute to the other performances as the audience, observers, or co-participants. The pre-established pattern of action which is unfolded during a performance and which may be presented or played through on other occasions may be called a 'part' or a 'routine.' These situational terms can easily be related to conventional structural ones. When an individual or performer plays the same part to the same audience on different occasions, a social relationship is likely to arise. Defining social role as the enactment of rights and duties attached to a given status, we can say that a social role will involve one or more parts and that each of these different parts may be presented by the performer on a series of occasions to the same kinds of audiences or to an audience of the same persons." (15-16)

The notion of performance may thus be understood to include both theatrical performances and everyday social interactions. I understand the adjective 'performative' as meaning, on the one hand, relating to the notion of performance as defined above. However, I regard as 'performative' also, in the tradition of J.L. Austin's speech act theory, the uttering of words that is at the same time the performance of an action (cf. Austin 6-8). Thirdly, following the work of Judith Butler, I regard gender as ultimately performative (cf. *Gender Trouble*).

This chapter will look at ways in which queer subjects employ performance and performativity as strategies of queer resilience. I will firstly look at contemporary queer cultural icons and the public performance of their sexuality, specifically looking at their strategic uses of patterns of disclosure and non-disclosure of their sexuality, as well as analysing the performance and publication of a song in terms of an act of creative sexual citizenship and finding an instance of periperformativity in a comedic stand-up performance. I will draw on interviews and art by the actors Ian McKellen and Zachary Quinto, musician Melissa Etheridge and writer, musician and performance artist Lynnee Breedlove. I will then analyse how George, the protagonist of Christopher Isherwood's novel *A Single Man* employs the strategic non-disclosure of his queer sexuality as a performative resilience strategy in early 1960s California. I will finally present a close reading of contemporary British actor and playwright DeObia Oparei's play *Crazyblackmuthafuckin'self*, analysing how its protagonist Femi, played in the original staging of the play by Oparei himself, employs camp as a performative resilience strategy that helps destabilize normative notions of gender and sexuality and uses performing, performativity and ritual as resilience strategies for his many, queer selves.

Queer Cultural Icons and the Performance of Sexuality: Patterns of Disclosure and Non-Disclosure, Acts of Creative Sexual Citizenship and the Periperformative

"Where there is power, there is resistance", Michel Foucault famously wrote in his *History of Sexuality Vol. 1* (92). With his activism around the passing of Section 28 of the Local Government Act into law by the British Parliament in 1988, the actor Ian McKellen is living testament to this, one of Foucault's central, claims. Section 28, only repealed as late as 2003, was a legal measure introduced by the Thatcher government which was to 'prohibit the promotion of homosexuality' in schools, government and the arts, preventing for example teachers from so much as even addressing the topic of homosexuality in higher education, and also effectually cutting public funding of queer themed art – theatre, exhibitions, etc. (cf. Local Government Act). McKellen's public coming out as a gay man, a public performance of his queer sexual subjectivity prompted by the passing of restrictive measures into law, forms part of a counterdiscourse narrative to the dominant discursive legal narrative of queer sexuality as sexual deviancy (cf. McKellen, "How I Came Out").

This is how McKellen dramatically retells the story of his public coming out on the BBC's Radio 3.

> "Enter into Broadcasting House, Peregrine Worsthorne, editor of The Sunday Telegraph. Week after week last winter, he was viciously parading his ignorance of homosexuality on the leader page. On air, we debated the new law and, riled by the bland pomposity of his homophobia, and, honestly, without thinking, I mentioned to those few thousands who tune into Radio 3, that I opposed Section 28 because I was gay." ("How I Came Out")

McKellen presents the performance of his coming out as accidental, a performance by an actor in the truest sense of the word: acting as reacting in the moment, as has for example been advocated by theories of acting following the approach to acting advocated by Sanford Meisner (cf. Moseley); McKellen being 'in the moment' and reacting to his adversary "without thinking". Of course McKellen would be the first to examine, and present to the reader, his own insightful analysis of how his own truthful reaction in that very moment came about, providing his own subtextual 'intention' or 'motivation' (speaking in Stanislavskian terms, cf. Carnicke) to this public performance of his queer sexuality. He relates an incidence which took place six months earlier when he had met up with openly gay writer Armistead Maupin and his partner in California.

> "Armistead and Terry had asked me why I wasn't out: and then, in part, answered their own question by noting that there wasn't a single leading actor in the world who was. [...] Good acting is so dependent on projecting sexuality, that American film producers don't risk confusing an audience's fantasies by allowing their stars publicly to be anything but straight as Hollywood Boulevard. And in the British theatre too, even 40 years after Gielgud was named, we are not allowed to declare which half of our best actors here are privately lesbian or gay. [...] In San Francisco, I learnt that coming-out was crucial to self esteem – why hadn't any British friend helped me understand that? And I accepted the argument, that people who thrived in society's mainstream and had access to the media, could, by telling the truth, help others in the backwaters, whose views were never sought and whom society either ignored or abused. An actor is protected more than most. These days, I daily make this point to anyone who will listen, because when I eventually accepted it on the BBC, it changed my life forever for the better." ("How I Came Out")

Being out as an actor, the continued public performance of his queer sexuality, is necessary for McKellen for two reasons: one, it is in his opinion "crucial to self esteem" – by remaining closeted the actor publicly presents a self to the world that is incongruous with the self he presents as in private, and this incongruency, a game of disguises he has not willingly chosen to enter but which has been thrust upon him by the dominant sexual order, can be experienced, in the long run, as undermining the actor's – or anyone's – sense of self worth or self esteem; and two, as a public figure who has "access to the media", McKellen can, "by telling the truth", actively shape media discourses about homosexuality, thus becoming part of a media-facilitated reverse discourse to the dominant legal discourse of heterosexual hegemony. In true artistic fashion, McKellen, together with his activist friends from The Arts Lobby, follows up his public coming out on Radio 3 with "a momentous news conference, which was the best show of the year" ("How I Came Out"); a march through Manchester with 20,000 "friends" wearing an "'Out and Proud' t-shirt"; he meets up with and talks to politicians and ministers in Westminster, and is "in the public gallery when the abseilers landed and, to quote Jenny Wilson, brought the camp back into campaigning", thus creating a spectacle, his final big, public performance, together with other activists, to try to prevent homophobic laws from being passed and help further social transformation: The stage actor has left the West End theatres and has momentarily become a political performer, making the British Parliament at Westminster his, and his fellow actors/protesters' stage. McKellen was, in 1988, a founding member of Stonewall UK, a non-profit organization working towards legal and social equality for LGBTQ people in the UK (cf. McKellen, "Stonewall UK"). To this day, he continues to act as both actor and activist, by for instance visiting secondary schools, in an effort to promote tolerance and tackle homophobic bullying (cf. McKellen, "Visiting UK Schools With Stonewall").

Witness twenty-three years later another up-and-coming actor's long and winding path through navigating the waters of public disclosure and non-disclosure of his queer sexuality. Ian McKellen's claim, uttered in 1988, about "American film producers" being unwilling to "risk confusing an audience's fantasies by allowing their stars publicly to be anything but straight as Hollywood Boulevard" does not hold true any longer; still, the issue of whether or not to come out arguably remains a contentious one for actors with Hollywood aspirations, and some will still choose, for career purposes, to remain either closeted or to be at the very least publicly rather vague about their sexual orientation. Zachary Quinto, star of the recent *Star Trek* remakes, as Mr. Spock, followed, at the beginning of his career, exactly this performative resilience strategy: the public non-disclosure of his sexual orientation. To quote from an interview in the *New York Times* from October 2010:

"Despite Mr. Quinto's efforts to keep his private life private, the blogosphere is rife with speculation about his sexuality, no doubt fueled by his support for gay rights and organizations like the *It gets better* campaign. He prefers not to feed that rumor mill with either substantiation or dismissal. [...] 'The fact that these things are such hot-button issues right now, socially and politically, I would much rather talk about that than talk about who I sleep with,' Mr. Quinto said. 'I would love to be a voice in this maelstrom of chaos and obsessive celebrity infatuation that says, 'Let's talk about something that matters.'"" (Rooney)

Nevertheless, a year later, in October 2011, Quinto came out publicly in print in an interview in *New York Magazine* and on his personal online blog. What had made him change his mind towards favouring public disclosure over public non-disclosure of his queer sexuality as his preferred performative resilience strategy? He credits two events as catalysts for this change of mind: one, the suicide of gay teenager Jamey Rodemeyer, and two, playing the for him obviously transformative role of Louis Ironson in a Broadway production of Tony Kushner's *Angels in America*. This is Quinto in his blog in his own words:

"when i found out that jamey rodemeyer killed himself – i felt deeply troubled. but when i found out that jamey rodemeyer had made an *it gets better* video only months before taking his own life – i felt indescribable despair. i also made an *it gets better* video last year – in the wake of the senseless and tragic gay teen suicides that were sweeping the nation at the time. but in light of jamey's death – it became clear to me in an instant that living a gay life without publicly acknowledging it – is simply not enough to make any significant contribution to the immense work that lies ahead on the road to complete equality. [...] i believe in the power of intention to change the landscape of our society – and it is my intention to live an authentic life of compassion and integrity and action." ("10.16.11. nyc...")[1]

Quinto's change of mind from evading definitive answers to journalists' and fans' questions about his sexual orientation to publicly coming out mirrors Louis Ironson's character development in Tony Kushner's *Angels in America*, the Broadway role Quinto had been playing for eight months previous to his public coming out. By his own admission, playing Louis was both "the most challenging thing [he] had] ever done as an actor and the most rewarding" (qtd. in Rooney). Set in 1980s

---

1 *It Gets Better* is an online project founded by gay journalist Dan Savage in 2010, featuring video messages by LGBTQ adults and their straight allies. The videos present an effort to prevent queer teenage suicides and are meant to convey to troubled queer teenagers the message that they should not let homophobic bullying get to them, and that things will eventually get better, presumably once they are out of high school.

New York City in the middle of the AIDS crisis, *Angels in America* deals with the lives of several gay men. Louis, unable to deal with his boyfriend's illness and with the way AIDS is culturally constructed as a gay plague in Reaganite America, abandons him. In act 3 scene 2, Louis finally stops trying to evade seeing what is happening all around him and tries, instead, to address the question of civil liberties and human rights issues around AIDS and gay male sexuality in 1980s America:

> "You have Bush talking about human rights, and so what are these people talking about, they might as well be talking about the mating habits of Venusians, these people don't begin to know what, ontologically, freedom is or human rights [...]. That's just liberalism, the worst kind of liberalism, really, bourgeois tolerance, and what I think is that what AIDS shows us is the limits of tolerance, that it's not enough to be tolerated, because when the shit hits the fan you find out how much tolerance is worth. Nothing. And underneath all the tolerance is intense, passionate hatred. [...] *Power* is the object, not being tolerated. Fuck assimilation." (Kushner 95-96)

Louis finds he finally needs to take a stand. Pretending the problem does not exist only makes him part of the problem, instead of working towards being part of the solution. Concluding its Broadway run, Quinto, Louis' actor, comes to the conclusion that "[d]oing that play made me realize how lucky I was to be born when I was born and to not have to witness the decimation of an entire generation of amazingly talented and otherwise vital men"; and also, publicly stating for the first time that in his case, it was a gay actor playing the role of Louis, "at the same time, *as a gay man* [my emphasis], it made me feel like there's still so much work to be done, and there's still so many things that need to be looked at and addressed" (qtd. in Wallace). It is the actor who has played – and been transformed by playing – the character of Louis Ironson who comes to the conclusion that "it is my intention to live an authentic life of compassion and integrity and action" ("10.16.11. nyc…"), which for Quinto as of October 2011 includes publicly performing his queer sexuality, being out as a gay male actor despite his Hollywood career aspirations.

Performance studies theorist Richard Schechner tries to capture the theatre's potential for transformative experiences by borrowing anthropologist Victor Turner's concept of the liminal, or in the context of modern Western art, the liminoid. While for the audience, attending a play can be a liminoid, and thus transformational, experience, for the actor the theatrical performance constitutes an experience of transportation, not transformation, for Schechner. However, it is for Schechner the rehearsal process preceding the actual performance run of a play which holds the potential of personal transformation for the actor. During this time period, the actor works at building a character, finding the right body language and patterns of speech (which may be different from his own, seemingly natural but of course actually culturally determined ones), tracing the character's interior journey and finding a character's intention underlying his lines and stage actions for every scene (which again may be closer or further removed from the actor's own set of typical behaviours and intentions in similar circumstances). It is this continued process which – much like learning a new kind of sport – involves a lot of repetition of speech, movement and action, which eventually leads the actor to a finished performance of a part. For the time of being on stage during the performance of the character, the actor is then present as both himself and the character, which Schechner describes as the "not-me, not-not-me of acting" (72). Depending on the actor and the part, the actor may emerge from this process having experienced a fictional version of reality as someone using a different type of speech, action, movement and intention to his previous range of expression, a potentially transformative experience.

"My point of entry for a lot of characters tends to be their shadow", Quinto states in another interview. "I'm a big believer in the notion that our greatest potential lies in our darkest parts. To a certain extent it's only in facing those parts of ourselves that we can truly grow, and I think that's true of all of the characters I've played, certainly in the past few years" (qtd. in Rooney). It is probably no coincidence that Quinto, in his blog entry, uses acting metaphors to describe what has for him been the ultimate reason for publicly coming out as a gay man. Having undergone the transformative experience of creating the character of Louis Ironson from Tony Kushner's performance text, and having publicly performed him for an extended period of time on stage, he states that "i believe in the power of *intention* [a Stanislavskian term, cf. Carnicke; my emphasis] to change the landscape of our society – and it is my *intention* [my emphasis] to live an authentic life of compassion and integrity and action" ("10.16.11. nyc..."). The performance of a queer fictional character on Broadway in a play created by Tony Kushner and set in 1980s New York City changes the actor's strategic use of disclosure and non-disclosure, the performance of his queer sexuality in the real world in 2011.

But what could such an 'authentic life of compassion and integrity and action' look like for a contemporary queer artist in a Western European or North American cultural context? Openly lesbian musician Melissa Etheridge provides one such example. To put her song "Miss California" in its historical and cultural context: The song was released after the passing of Proposition 8 into Californian state legislation in 2008, which had annulled all lesbian and gay marriages that had previously been sealed in California. This state legislation was again repealed by the U.S. Supreme Court in 2013 and has also by now been overruled by the U.S. Supreme Court's decision in 2015 in *Obergefell v. Hodges* which ruled all state legislation banning same-sex marriage to be unconstitutional, thus in effect paving the way for making same-sex marriage legal in all states of the U.S.[2] In her song "Miss California" from 2010, Etheridge casts 'Miss California', a personification of the state as such, in the role of an abusive lover. The speaker expresses in both lyrics and the accompanying rock music her anger at the treatment of gay and lesbian unions by the State of California: The state is here presented as abusing its power to bestow recognition to the unions of gay and lesbian couples. Of course, by seemingly arbitrarily bestowing state recognition to the union of some of its citizens, and then taking said recognition away again, the state itself, through its actions, could be argued to be deconstructing the institution of marriage as a state sanctified union, whether heterosexual or homosexual. Etheridge's song, however, does not necessarily follow that trajectory of thought but takes as its theme the affective resonance of Proposition 8 for California's queer citizens.

But the writing and release of "Miss California" in 2010 can be read as much more than just an artistic expression of feelings of anger of a lesbian musician at being discriminated against by the State of California and consequently as a bearing witness to that insult. It can also be understood to constitute an act of creative sexual citizenship on the part of a lesbian musician, which one might term a performative strategy of queer resilience. 'Act of citizenship' is a concept developed by Engin Isin and Greg Nielsen, who understand the notion of citizenship as processual rather than static, a doing not a being (cf. Isin and Nielsen; Tan 11-12). Citizenship, for Isin and Nielsen, is not a legal status conferred upon, or a social practice performed upon, any individual subject by the state. Rather, it is a series of acts which, performatively, produce the subject *as* citizen.[3] And these acts can be carried out by both state and subject, thus conferring agency not just to the state but also to the subject in the relational process of determining citizenship, in the case of the release of "Miss California", sexual citizenship. The artist as citizen performs a creative act of citizenship, inscribing herself as agent in the ongoing negotiation with the state about notions of queer legal citizenship.

Finally, the following short excerpt of a comedy performance by queer writer, musician and performance artist Lynnee Breedlove[4] may serve as an example for a perfomative resilience strategy utilizing what Eve Kosofsky Sedgwick has come to call periperformative speech acts, that is speech acts uttered in the vicinity of,

---

2   For the Supreme Court's ruling on Proposition 8 see *Hollingsworth v. Perry*.

3   I am indebted to Kathy-Ann Tan for introducing me to the concept of acts of creative sexual citizenship.

4   Breedlove is the author of the novel *Godspeed*, but is more familiar to queer audiences as a member of one of the most influential queercore bands, *Tribe 8*.

or around a performative speech act.[5] In his *One Freak Show*, Breedlove employs periperformativity as a performative strategy of queer resilience. Importantly, Breedlove self-identifies as transgender, and presents as genderqueer. Making himself the centre of his performance piece, Breedlove, in one stand-up routine, tells the audience that "[p]eople are always asking if I'm a man or a woman" (22). However, instead of letting herself be interpellated into categorically one gender or the other by uttering the performative speech act 'I am a man', or 'I am a woman', Breedlove's follow-up, "What are they asking *me* for. Do I look like I know?" cleverly evades the fixitiy of the performative and routinely draws laughter from the audience. S/he employs a mix of both periperformative strategies and performative strategies by (i) answering the question with another question, "What are they asking *me* for", thus evading any definitive answer and throwing the question back at those who have found themselves prompted to ask it in the first place; and (ii), Breedlove follows up his own refusal of committing, in a performative speech act, to one gender or the other, with his own attempt at interpellating the audience of his *One Freak Show*: "Do I look like I know?" Breedlove performs, on stage, her own gender, or rather his own gender indeterminacy, asking the audience to please look, really look, and then try to make up their own minds from the signifiers they perceive about his supposed gender identity. Yes, s/he seems to be implying, look here, gender is indeed both theatrical and performative, but I'm leaving what kind of gender *I am*, up to *your* imagination and judgement, dear spectator. In the postmodern age, there are no definitive answers any more. I can live with my own gender indeterminacy. But crucially, can you?

In her groundbreaking book *Gender Trouble*, Judith Butler boldly proposed among other things the ultimately performative nature of gender. Gender, the cultural meanings attached to sexed bodies, i.e. what we refer to as masculinity and femininity, she argues, is not something that one is, but something that one does; it is being produced through a repetition of stylised acts; this is not a conscious performance, exactly, for there is no "subject who might be said to preexist the deed" (25), but the acts appear naturalized to us because they are constantly being repeated by all of us. They accrue their validity through constantly being reiterated and recited everywhere in our culture. Through his comedy performance, Breedlove asks his audience to allow themselves to let their notions about fixed gender identities, about men, women, masculinity and femininity to be transformed. S/he employs performative resilience strategies to put herself, her

---

5 J.L. Austin's most famous example for a performative speech act, that is a speech act that is not just a saying but at the same time a doing, is the marriage vow 'I do'. Sedgwick's periperformative utterances include utterances that are made in the vicinity of such performative utterances, which however undermine, or question, the performative nature of the utterance in question. Cf. Sedgwick, *Touching Feeling* 67-69.

own indeterminate gender identity and the gender identities of others like him, on the map of genders intelligible to his audience; for, those audience members who let themselves be affected by his performance may find that they will have to endure their own sense of reality and their understanding of who they think they are to be turned upside down, a potentially threatening but ultimately transformative experience.

Butler addresses the – to some individuals potentially threatening – experience of being confronted with a world in which all individuals, be they transsexual, transgendered or possibly intersexed, can attain the status of the human and become intelligible and thus recognized, in her book *Undoing Gender*. Butler asks:

> "What might it mean to learn to live in the anxiety of that challenge, to feel the surety of one's epistemological and ontological anchor go, but to be willing, in the name of the human, to allow the human to become something other than what it is traditionally assumed to be? This means that we must learn to live and to embrace the destruction and rearticulation of the human in the name of a more capacious and finally, less violent world, not knowing in advance what precise form our humanness does and will take." (35)

A non-violent response to a confrontation with the Other opens itself up to the possibility of transformation. It "lives with its unknowingness about the Other in the face of the Other, since sustaining the bond that the question opens is finally more valuable than knowing in advance what holds us in common, as if we already have all the resources we need to know what defines the human, what its future life might be" (*Undoing Gender* 35). With his performance, Breedlove acts thus as both artist and social activist, presenting us with his own queer version of an artistic 'life of integrity and action'.

Navigating the Closet in Christopher Isherwood's *A Single Man*

Christopher Isherwood's novel *A Single Man* was published in 1964. Originally a British writer and part of the so-called Auden Group, a group of British writers around the poet W.H. Auden which had published extensively during the 1930s, Isherwood is best known for his two novels portraying the demi-monde of the last days of the Weimar Republic in Berlin, *Mr Norris Changes Trains* and *Goodbye to Berlin* (cf. Berg and Freeman, "Introduction: The Isherwood Century"). W.H. Auden and Christopher Isherwood both emigrated to the United States in 1939, where Auden settled on the East Coast and Isherwood on the West Coast. Both were pacifists and both were homosexual. The 1960s saw Isherwood living in Santa Monica with his long-time partner Don Bachardy, while earning his living primarily with the writing of Hollywood screenplays; he also wrote a number of novels, worked on translations of Sanskrit texts into English and taught a number of lectures and classes at Los Angeles State College and the University of California at Santa Barbara (cf. Berg and Freeman, "Introduction: An American Outsider" and "A Real Diamond"). Both Isherwood and his novel *A Single Man* left a lasting impression on a future generation of American gay male writers. Armistead Maupin cites Isherwood as a role model and notes that he "spoke out more fearlessly – and more often – than any of his queer contemporaries; certainly more than Truman Capote, who once equated his gayness to his alcoholism, or even Gore Vidal, who wrote brilliantly about our oppression but remained cagey about his own life while he still had a shot at the Senate" (xiii). And David Garnes relates that if he were "to make a list of the books that have mattered most to me, Christopher Isherwood's *A Single Man* would figure near the top. When I first read the novel [in 1965], its influence on me was enormous because of the matter-of-fact, positive presentation of the main character's homosexuality" (196). Similar quotes can be found by writers such as Edmund White and others (cf. Bergman, "Isherwood and the Violet Quill"). The early 1960s, the period Isherwood's novel is set in, were marked by a conservative social climate and an on-going legal prosecution of homosexuality. Patricia Juliana Smith outlines the political and social situation of queer people in both Britain and the U.S. in her introduction to *The Queer Sixties*.[6] In Britain, up until the late 1960s, sexual acts between consenting adult men were punishable by a two-year prison sentence, with or without hard labour. Legal change was to occur finally in 1967:

> "The 1967 Sexual Offences Act decriminalized homosexual acts between consenting adult men (a full ten years after the government-commissioned Wolfenden Committee's report first proposed this change) and, in effect, repealed the repressive Labouchère Amendment to the Criminal Law Amendment Act of 1885, the very law that had resulted in the imprisonment of Oscar Wilde.
>
> In the United States, however, prohibitions against homosexual activities were a matter of state and local, rather than national, law. Thus, no such national legal reform was possible [...]." (xiii)

In California, the state Isherwood's novel is set in, homosexual acts between consenting adults in private became only officially legal as late as 1975. A turning point in the social history of homosexuals in the U.S. occurred when at the end of the 1960s, on the "evening of Friday, June 27, 1969, the New York Police Depart-

---

6 For further details on the situation of gays and lesbians in post-War America see John D'Emilio, *Sexual Politics, Sexual Communities*. On the situation in Britain see Jeffrey Weeks, *Sex, Politics and Society*.

ment raided the Stonewall Inn, a gay bar on Christopher Street in New York City's Greenwich Village" and, for the first time, "drag queens, butch lesbian, and queers of all varieties fought back, and the rioting continued over the entire weekend" (Smith xiii). This historic moment is regarded, Smith relates, as "the flashpoint – the originary moment – of the American Gay Liberation movement of the 1970s" (xiii). Smith maintains, however, that the "deeds that brought about Stonewall in the United States and the decriminalization of male homosexuality in Great Britain were, in reality, the actions of the brave and the few" (xiv), painting a much bleaker picture for the lives of ordinary LGBTQ people. "For most ordinary queers, the 1960s were spent in the closet – in isolation, fear, and repression – and, accordingly, in the fragmented, and often not completely coherent, half-life of 'all the sad young men' and 'odd girls out,' to use the code words of pulp fictions" (xiv).

The closeted life of Isherwood's protagonist in *A Single Man* differs from what Smith describes as prototypical for the lives of most ordinary queers in the 1960s. Shame, fear and repression are markedly absent from his experience. Isherwood's novel tells the story of a day in the life in 1962 of George, an Englishman in his fifties, currently living in Los Angeles and teaching at the fictional San Tomas State College. It recounts his activities from waking up in the house he used to share with his recently deceased partner Jim, having breakfast, teaching a literature class on Aldous Huxley, visiting a dying friend in hospital, going to the gym and the supermarket, having dinner with his best friend Charlotte, another British expatriate, and finally going to a bar where he runs into Kenny, a student of his class with whom he goes for a nighttime swim before taking him back to his house where they spend the rest of the night drinking and talking. He falls asleep, finds on waking Kenny gone, and dies, eventually, supposedly, of a heart attack in his sleep. The novel traces George's working through his grief over Jim's death. What is remarkably absent from George's memories of his life with Jim and from the way he experiences and expresses his queer sexuality and his desire for men in general, is any notion of the shame generally associated with a closeted queer life. George performs his queer sexuality depending on the spaces he moves in and the people he interacts with. He takes charge of the way he wants to be perceived by others, successfully navigating the queer closet to evade discrimination.

Tellingly, the novel's opening paragraphs provide a meditation on waking up, on the body (which might be any body) slowly becoming conscious of itself, of its surroundings and obligations – to wash and shave itself, to dress – and to become conscious of itself, finally, as a person called George:

> "Its nakedness has to be covered. It must be dressed up in clothes because it is going outside, into the world of the other people; and these others must be able to identify it. Its behaviour must be acceptable to them.

Obediently, it washes, shaves, brushes its hair; for it accepts its responsibilities to the others. It is even glad that it has its place among them. It knows what is expected of it.

It knows its name. It is called George." (2-3)

The performative aspect of everyday social interactions that Erving Goffman outlines in *The Presentation of Self in Everyday Life* is stressed here: George's only half-conscious body knows that certain types of behaviour are expected of it if he wants to be part of "the world of the other people", which he obviously does. It "accepts its responsibilities to the others" and is "even glad that it has its place among them". This performance of self extends to a performance of the sexual self. It, too, must be framed in terms of being intelligible and acceptable (within reason) to "the world of the other people". What is intelligible and acceptable, however, depends on the intersubjective spaces and contexts George moves in: George is thus out to his friend Charlotte, suspects that his neighbours know about his queer sexuality, but keeps his sexuality hidden in the workplace and with his students. Being in his home space, his house, which is still suffused with the memories of his life with Jim, and being with Charlotte, with whom he can be open about his sexuality, thus keep George sane. Here he does not have to hide parts of himself and his subjectivity. Here he can fully be himself:

"This is a tightly planned little house. He often feels protected by its smallness; there is hardly room enough here to feel lonely. [...]

Think of two people, living together day after day, year after year, in this small space, standing elbow to elbow cooking at the same small stove, squeezing past each other on the narrow stairs, shaving in front of the same small bathroom mirror, constantly jogging, jostling, bumping against each other's bodies by mistake or on purpose, sensually, aggressively, awkwardly, impatiently, in rage or in love – think what deep though invisible tracks they must leave, everywhere, behind them!" (3-4)

By moving through the space of his house which is also the space of his relationship with Jim, George is moving through a space where he can fully be George, including his queer sexual self. But with Jim's recent death in a car accident in Ohio, George's fragile stability, it turns out, is on breaking point:

"[I]t is here, nearly every morning, that George, having reached the bottom of the stairs, has this sensation of suddenly finding himself on an abrupt, brutally broken-off, jagged edge – as though the track had disappeared down a landslide. It is here that he stops short and knows, with a sick newness, almost as though it were for the first time: Jim is dead. Is dead." (4)[7]

Grief is always isolating, but George's grief over Jim's death is even more isolating since he cannot mourn him in public. The world does not see his grief, and George does not want it any other way either. He has told the neighbours that "Jim's folks, who are getting along in years, have been trying to persuade him to come back home and live with them; and that now, as the result of his recent visit to them, he will be remaining in the East indefinitely" (16-17). George will move through his grief over the course of the day, helped along by conversations with Charlotte, the hospital visit with his dying friend Doris and his meeting with Kenny. He will come out at the other end accepting the finality of Jim's death ("Jim is in the Past, now", 148), and deciding that he will look for another Jim. "[W]hy will George stay here?" a part of his deep subconscious mind will ask itself. "This is where he found Jim", another part will answer. "He believes he will find another Jim here. He doesn't know it, but he has started looking already" (149).[8]

It is Charlotte he runs to upon hearing the news of Jim's death. And Charlotte continues to take care of him in the aftermath as well, "cooking his meals and bringing them down to the house while he was out [...]; leaving him notes urging him to call her at any hour he felt the need" (101). With Charlotte he can reminisce about his time with Jim. Indeed, she has been a good and helpful friend to both of them. "Dear old Charley", George muses (in what constitutes a somewhat under-handed compliment). "How many times, when Jim and I had been quarrelling and came to visit you [...] did you somehow bring us together again by the sheer power of your unawareness that anything was wrong?" (98). Charley causes him to feel "this utterly mysterious unsensational thing – not bliss, not ecstasy, not joy – just plain happiness [...]. Charley creates it astonishingly often; this doubtless is some-

---

7   For the reader 'in the know', it becomes obvious at this point that George has previously been in a same-sex relationship and has lost his long-time partner only recently. For the reader 'not in the know', the status of George's and Jim's previous relationship and George's queer sexuality are maybe less obvious and reveal themselves only as the novel goes on.

8   Carola M. Kaplan sees Isherwood as working through with Jim's death his feelings of abandonment and grief over the potential break-up with his partner Don. "During a particularly turbulent period in his relationship with Don Bachardy, in which a breakup seemed imminent, Christopher Isherwood wrote multiple drafts of the novel that was to become A Single Man. In these drafts, he recounts a journey from shock to resignation, as he contemplates the loss of his beloved life partner" (37). She comes to the conclusion that the novel, in its finished form, was both an artistic and a personal triumph for Isherwood. "It records and works through Isherwood's deepest fears – of losing his beloved partner, of remaining an exile, of dying alone in a foreign land. As a result, Isherwood emerged from his crisis with Don more confident as a man and as a writer and more hopeful that he and Don could forge a future together – a future that was in fact to last two more decades to the end of Isherwood's life" (47).

thing else she isn't aware of, since she can do it even when she herself is miserable" (98-99). In a dinner conversation with George at her house, Charley maintains that Jim, in a momentary premonition of his death, instructed her that George and Charley should take care of each other after his death. George is not quite convinced, but he also comes to the somewhat similar conclusion that if "I'd been the one the truck hit [...], Jim would be right here, this very evening, walking through this doorway, carrying these two glasses. Things are as simple as that" (103).

George's performance of his everyday self in his workplace is markedly different from the self he performs with Charley. For George accepts, more or less grudgingly, that being evasive about his queer sexuality is part of the appropriate performance of the social role of college professor in early 1960s California. The preparation for the performance of this role already starts in his car on his way to campus: "In ten minutes they will have arrived on campus. In ten minutes, George will have to be George; the George they have named and will recognise. So now he consciously applies himself to thinking their thoughts, getting into their mood. With the skill of a veteran, he rapidly puts on the psychological makeup for this role he must play" (27). And indeed, this preparation is followed by George's first performance as college professor of the day, the entry of the Department Office:

> "So now George has arrived. He is not nervous in the least. As he gets out of his car, he feels an upsurge of energy, of eagerness for the play to begin. And he walks eagerly, with a springy step, along the gravel path past the Music Building towards the Department Office. He is all actor now; an actor on his way up from the dressing-room, hastening through the backstage world of props and lamps and stagehands to make his entrance. A veteran, calm and assured, he pauses for a well-measured moment in the doorways of the office and then, boldly, clearly, with the subtly modulated British intonation which his public demands of him, speaks his opening line, 'Good morning!'" (30)

Isherwood frames his protagonist's entry into his workplace in extended theatrical metaphors. George is "all actor now", leaving the dressing-room, preparing his entrance on the stage of the Department Office, where the three secretaries, "each of them a charming and accomplished actress in her own chosen style [...] reply 'Good morning!' to him" as well (30). George's entry into the classroom is phrased in similarly theatrical terms: "His entrance is undramatic, according to conventional standards. Nevertheless, this is a subtly contrived, outrageously theatrical effect" (40). George waits until the class falls silent, refusing to "give some sign, no matter how slight, that the class is to begin". Instead, "[s]lowly, deliberately, like a magician, he takes a single book out of his briefcase and places it on the reading-desk. As he does this, his eyes move over the faces of the class. His lips curve in a faint but bold smile. Some of them smile back at him" (40). This is, for George, "one of the peak moments of the day. He feels brilliant, vital, challenging, slightly mysterious and, above all, *foreign*. His neat dark clothes, his white dress shirt and tie (the only tie in the room) are uncompromisingly alien from the aggressively virile informality of the young male students" (40). George evidently enjoys the performative aspects of his teaching activity, even before the activity itself has properly started. The performance of the role of college professor is not a burden to him, but instead a delight. George revels in the role of "magician", the simile conjuring up an aura of suspension, mystery, and of a world of make-believe, which the students, at the same time his audience and his co-actors, are about to enter. He also revels in being different from them, "*foreign*", not only because of his being British and because his clothes are "uncompromisingly alien" from those of his students. The difference in dress is as much a result of the different requirements of the role of student and teacher as it stands symbolically for George's being markedly different as regards his sexuality from, presumably, the majority of the student body. Being alien or foreign becomes here a metaphor for being sexually other; an otherness, that is, however, not in itself a cause of shame or concern for George. Indeed, George revels in this mysterious otherness.

But how does George's queer sexuality fit into the performance of the role of college professor in direct one on one contact with his students? On his way to teaching his class, George runs into one of his advanced students, Russ Dreyer. The ensuing conversation prompts George to wonder what, exactly, his students do or do not know about his queer sexuality: "Does he know about me, George wonders; do any of them? Oh yes, probably. It wouldn't interest them. They don't want to know about my feelings or my glands or anything below my neck. I could just as well be a severed head, carried into the classroom to lecture to them from a dish" (35). By restricting focalization to George, the novel withholds the thoughts and feelings of George's actual students. The reader thus never learns whether George's estimation of his students' attitude towards his queer sexuality is entirely accurate or merely a projection. George assumes that at least some of his students probably know about his queer sexuality, but that they would probably regard this information as entirely irrelevant, since they conceive of their professors as not having any kind of sexuality at all. In this conception, the performance of the professional self is one from which any kind of sexual self is excised, a dehumanizing scenario for which George's mind conjures up the image of the professor reduced to a severed, talking head "carried into the classroom to lecture to them from a dish", casting the students in the role of Salome and himself in the role of John the Baptist, an image that is quite violent and cruel.

If George complies with his students' presumed wishes of performing his role appearing to have no sexual self and remaining rather circumspect regarding his sexuality, this does not stop him from openly appreciating athletic male bodies on campus. Two tennis players provide him with the subtly homoerotic vision of a competitive tennis match on campus in which the two players are "stripped nearly naked":

> "They have nothing on their bodies but rubber gym-boots and knit shorts of the kind cyclists wear, very short and close-fitting, moulding themselves to the buttocks and the loins. [...] Their nakedness makes them seem close to each other and directly opposed, body to body, like fighters. [...] This game is cruel; but its cruelty is sensual and stirs George into hot excitement. [...] From his heart, he thanks these young animals for their beauty. And they will never know what they have done to make this moment marvellous to him, and life itself less hateful—" (37-38)

Indeed, George's appreciation of the beautiful, semi-naked tennis players and their competitive game which appears to George like the precursor to a sexual act takes place during the aforementioned conversation with his student Russ Dreyer that had prompted the vision of the lecturing head on a plate. George's sexuality and sensuality vividly reassert themselves here in the extended dwelling on the sensual perception of his surroundings and the depiction of the effect this has on George's vivid imagination.

George does not shy away from addressing homoerotic content in his class on a novel by Aldous Huxley, addressing for example an allusion to a Greek myth which sees Zeus falling in love with Ganymede. He also makes a point of trying to subtly encourage students who he suspects might be gay. Relating the myth about Ganymede has him looking "at Wally Bryant – about whom he couldn't be more certain – and sure enough Wally is wriggling with delight" (47). Without addressing his own minority status directly, he delivers a lecture on minorities in general, fully aware of the fact that his class also consists of African American, Asian American and Latino students, outlining ideas which are shaped not in the least by his own minority status as a gay man. He maintains that "a minority is only thought of as a minority when it constitutes some kind of a threat to the majority, real or imaginary. And no threat is ever *quite* imaginary" (53). He addresses false liberalism, claiming somewhat contentiously, that "it's *better* if [as a majority] we admit to disliking and hating [minorities], than if we try to smear our feelings over with pseudo-liberal sentimentality. If we're frank about our feelings, we have a safety-valve; and if we have a safety-valve, we're actually less likely to start persecuting" (53). He outlines psychological double binds inherent in the positionality of the minority versus the majority: "[S]uppose this minority does get persecuted – never mind why – political, economic, psychological reasons – there always *is* a reason [...] that's my point [...] we now run into another liberal heresy. *Because* the persecuting majority is vile, says the liberal, *therefore* the persecuted minority must be stainlessly pure" (54). His final point is then his contention that the minority status itself may cause minoritarian subjects to experience feelings of anger and hatred:

> "A minority has its own kind of aggression. It absolutely dares the majority to attack it. It hates the majority – not without a cause, I grant you. [...] Do you think it makes people nasty to be loved? You know it doesn't! Then why should it make them nice to be loathed? While you're being persecuted, you hate what's happening to you, you hate the people who are making it happen; you're in a world of hate. Why, you wouldn't recognise love if you met it! You'd suspect love! You'd think there was something behind it – some motive – some trick—" (54)

The reader knows from a previous interior monologue that George himself is at times prone to these feelings of intense hatred of the heterosexual majority. This monologue included, among other things, a quite graphic revenge fantasy featuring a "newspaper editor [who had] started a campaign against sex deviates (by which he means people like George). They are everywhere", the newspaper editor claimed; "you can't go into a bar any more, or a men's room, or a public library, without seeing hideous sights" (23). But George dislikes not only the homophobic newspaper editor but also for instance his neighbours, whom he suspects of harbouring variously feelings of fear, condescension or pity for him: "Among many other kinds of monster", George thinks, "they are afraid of little me" (15). It remains doubtful that George's assessment of his neighbours' feelings is entirely accurate. In a rare occasion, the novel presents another focalizer apart from George in a short passage featuring George's neighbour Mrs Strunk. Mrs Strunk's reaction to seeing George leave his house and drive away in his car is not one of hatred, but still shows a certain disconnect and estrangement between her and George. "As he makes the half-turn on to the street, she waves to him. He waves to her. Poor man, she thinks, living there all alone. He has a kind face" (19). This disconnect, and the feelings of anger George experiences, may be a consequence merely of his outsider and minority status, as George assumes. They may, however, also be the cost of the closeted life George leads. They can be argued to constitute the psychic cost of the performance of a sexual self that tries to remain within the limits of intelligibility and acceptability of 'the world of the other people' at all times and in all contexts.

The novel singles out one of George's students in particular, Kenny Potter, for a number of lengthy interactions. Kenny is "what's nowadays called crazy, meaning only that he tends to do the opposite of what most people do: not on principle, however, and certainly not out of aggressiveness. Probably he's too vague to notice the manners and customs of the tribe, and too lazy to follow them, anyway" (43). George feels himself drawn to Kenny. He suspects "Kenny of understanding the innermost meaning of life; of being in fact, some sort of a genius [...]. And then again, maybe Kenny is just very young for his age, and misleadingly charming, and silly" (44). Kenny lets George know in a conversation on campus that other students and he himself experience George as cagey. They sense that there is something left out of the conversation, that George is hiding something. "I'm not saying you don't teach us a lot of interesting stuff", Kenny says; "you do – but you never tell us all you know about something—" (60). It remains unclear whether Kenny does in fact know about George's sexuality. George suspects or rather hopes so, but still does not come out and say so. Instead, his oblique answer is that "[s]omeone has to ask you a question [...] before you can answer it. But it's so seldom you find anyone who'll ask the right questions" (61). He continues to, in a roundabout way, try to explain that he is bound by the standards of intelligibility and acceptability that come with the performance of the role of college professor in California during the times of the Cuban missile crisis.

> "'It's not that I *want* to be cagey,' he says, keeping his eyes on the ground and making this as impersonal as he can. 'You know, Kenny, so often I feel I want to *tell* things, *discuss* things, absolutely frankly. I don't mean in class, of course – that wouldn't work. Someone would be sure to misunderstand—'
> Silence. [...] Perhaps [Kenny] hasn't even been listening. It's impossible to tell." (61)

George insists that he does not feel at liberty to discuss what remains unnamed – among other things surely his queer sexuality – in class and on campus. It is unclear, both to George and to the reader, what Kenny makes of this conversation. He does apparently remain intrigued by the mystery that is George, though. Later in the evening, he waits in George's favourite bar on the off-chance that George will drop by. As it happens, George does, and they continue their conversation during which it emerges that Kenny needs George as someone who can advise him about life and the future, a mentor and an authority figure of sorts. He insists on continuing to call George 'Sir', even after George quizzes him about it. Kenny's most pressing question, it turns out, concerns the notion of experience. "They keep telling you", he says, "when you're older, you'll have experience – and that's supposed to be so great. What would you say about that, Sir? Is it really any use, would you say?" (130). George, who is flattered by the attention and the rapport he feels building between them – and also somewhat attracted to Kenny even though he refrains, even in his by now quite drunk state, from acting on it, answers without circumspection this time. In George's view, experience does not necessarily make you wise; in fact, he claims that it has made him only sillier. It is not something you can use. It functions more like a treasure trove. If you do not try to use it, "if you just realise it's there and you've got it – then it can be kind of marvellous –" (130). Kenny decides to test him on this, daring George to go for a nighttime swim with him at the nearby beach. George, who has by now left the performance of the college professor and all the requirements of that role behind, casting himself and Kenny instead in the roles of partners in a platonic dialogue, an encounter of "symbolic figures – like, in this case, Youth and Age" (125), takes him up on his dare and they go for a naked swim in the nearby ocean. They continue their conversation at George's house, where their encounter is "getting positively flirty, on both sides. Kenny's blanket, under the relaxing influence of the talk and beer, has slipped, baring an arm and a shoulder and turning itself into a classical Greek garment, the chlamys worn by a young disciple – the favourite, surely – of some philosopher. At this moment, he is utterly, dangerously charming" (138). The erotically charged atmosphere does not, however, lead to a sexual encounter; instead, George who has decided that they have arrived at a "person-to-person" encounter by now (142), doing away with the performative roles of teacher and student, though perhaps taking seriously the role of philosopher-mentor Kenny has assigned to him, performs a monologue before drifting off to sleep. Waking up, he finds Kenny, who has undressed him and put him to bed, gone. Due to his attempt to finally speak the unmitigated truth as he knows it in spite of his state of inebriation, George's monologue is both muddled and lucid at the same time. He is not a fan of identity categories, George reveals. They stand in the way of truly communicating with one another.

> "I mean, what is this life of ours supposed to be *for*? Are we to spend it identify-ing each other with catalogues, like tourists in an art gallery? Or are we to try to exchange *some* kind of a signal, however garbled, before it's too late? [...]
>
> It's all very fine and easy for you young things to come to me on campus and tell me I'm cagey. [...] Don't you have a glimmering of how I must feel – longing to *speak*?
>
> You asked me about experience. So I told you. Experience isn't any *use*. And yet, in quite another way, it *might* be. If only we weren't all such miserable fools and prudes and cowards. [...] Oh God, don't you *see*? That bed – what that bed *means* – that's what experience is—!" (142-143)

Knowledge is here understood in terms of sexual knowledge, and the secret – that which cannot be articulated – is of course George's queer sexuality. This is in line with Eve Kosofsky Sedgwick's argument in *Epistemology of the Closet* that, since the end of the nineteenth century, (male) homosexuality is constituted as the secret *par excellence* and that at the heart of the closet lies sexual deviancy. I would argue, however, that Isherwood takes things one step further by making George's mono-logue first and foremost about experience and only in a second instance about knowledge.

> "Why are you here in this room at this moment? *Because you want me to tell you some-thing!* That's the true reason you came all the way across town tonight. [...] You want me to tell you what I *know*—

Oh Kenneth, Kenneth, believe me – there's nothing I'd rather do! I want *like hell* to tell you. But I can't. I quite literally can't. Because, don't you see, *what I know is what I am?* And I can't tell you that. You have to find it out for yourself. I'm like a book you have to read. [...]

You could know what I'm about. You could. But you can't be bothered to. [...] Instead of trying to know you commit the inexcusable triviality of saying *he's a dirty old man*, and turning this evening [...] into a *flirtation*! [...] It's the enormous tragedy of everything nowadays. Flirtation. Flirtation instead of fucking, if you'll pardon my coarseness. All any of you ever do is flirt [...]. And miss the one thing that might really – and, Kenneth, I do not say this casually – *transform your entire life*—"
(143-144)

What George arrives at in his monologue is an emphasis on personal experience. He privileges experience over putting on a performance for the sake of a social role. This includes sexual experience, which may serve as an epistemological tool, a mode of acquiring knowledge and also self-knowledge, but also as a means of personal transformation. George furthermore stresses the importance of hermeneutics, that is acts of reading, necessarily to be performed by someone who is not George if that someone truly wants to understand and know George. Performative strategies reach their limit when truly transformational person-to-person encounters and self-encounters are the aim of (social) interactions. Kenny will discover the value of experience by undergoing transformative experiences. And George cannot disclose himself (including his queer sexual self) unless the person willing to know him is also capable of reading him. And a Kenny who has not, via experience, found out who he is sexually, but continues to skirt around the issue (or flirt his way around the issue) has no chance of reading George accurately. And George does want to be read – and known – accurately, that is in a way that includes understanding of his queer sexuality and what that means and entails, and also in a way that is congruent with his own understanding of himself. He longs to be recognized. He longs for a connection like the one he shared with Jim, and it is very doubtful, George realizes, that Kenny would be able to fill this particular gap in George's life.

As this chapter has argued, George successfully navigates the closeted existence that comes with the territory of living in California in 1962 and working as a college professor. He takes charge of his experience and successfully performs his self, including his sexual self, in everyday life according to the requirements of his time and place and the various contexts that make up his life. There are psychic costs attached to some of those requirements for George, among them feelings of anger and disconnection, but notably, for George, feelings of shame are not on that list. Furthermore, as George's interactions with Kenny make clear, there are limits to making the terms of his life understandable to an other who does not share George's experiences of his sexual self, his time and his place. Still, with the memories of his life with Jim and in his friendship with Charlotte, intersubjective spaces remain available to him where he can perform his sexual self without circumspection, where he can 'truly' be himself.

Theatrical Performance, Camp Performativity and Ritual in DeObia Oparei's *Crazyblackmuthafuckin'self*

In his first full-length theatrical play *Crazyblackmuthafuckin'self* from 2002, British actor and playwright DeObia Oparei presents, with the creation of his protagonist Femi, a fictionalized version of one black British queer actor's struggle with patterns of disclosure and non-disclosure of his queer sexuality and the performance of the many different roles that make up his life. Over the course of the play, Femi can furthermore be found to be employing two additional, distinctive performative strategies of queer resilience. One, employing the art of improvisation and making use of the aesthetics of camp, he playfully deconstructs notions of fixed racial, sexual and gender identities. And two, with the help of the performative strategy of ritual he manages to incorporate abjected self-parts, alleviating the suffering of his own split subjectivity, and the suffering of others. Femi was played in the original staging at the London Royal Court Theatre, the only staging of the play to date, by Oparei himself. My analysis is informed by both my reading of the play text as well as by my attending the original staging of the play at the Royal Court Theatre and witnessing both the original staging of the play text as well as Oparei's performance of Femi. Asked whether his play contains any autobiographical references, Oparei states in an interview the following:

> "The play is autobiographical in the context that writing it was born of a need to see myself reflected in the mainstream. Living in the white heterosexual hegemony that is western culture I'm identified by my color first and the threat level of my blackness second; 'The big black guy' – my humanity comes a poor third!
> And as a successful working actor celluloid success is pre-determined by how well I assume the role of a stereotype: big black guy, the nigger or the nigga – the nigger is feared and the nigga (post hip hop) is revered, then there's the friendly, benevolent, uncle tom type black who is usually a sexually impotent authoritarian figure or best friend to the white hero who sacrifices himself to the white cause and dies or is killed by the end of the third act...
> So you can see that writing 'crazyblackmuthafuckinself' was a cathartic experience and process where I got to be powerfully imaginative from an authentic and truthful place. Because just like Femi Olutuje, as a black gay man to survive and thrive in this world I have had to learn to juggle plural identities and masquerade in mul-

tiple personalities. So, in my play the main character whom the world revolves around is not a white, blue eyed, blonde, heterosexual but a big, black, gay man. He's not the comic relief nor is he some sexually impotent benevolent figure. He's a complex hero who is unapologetically and unashamedly sexually aggressive and expressive and he doesn't end up sacrificing himself at the altar of white life and caucasian love!" (*Personal Interview*)[9]

Addressing the role of performing in his own life, Oparei thus deems performative resilience strategies as central to the contemporary Black queer experience: "[J]ust like Femi Olutuje, as a black gay man to survive and thrive in this world", he had, he states, "to learn to juggle plural identities and masquerade in multiple personalities".

The fictional Femi Olutuje's many identities include 'Laurence', a Shakesperean actor, but also 'Big Black Jungle Nigga', a macho rent boy, and 'Shaneequa', a transsexual call girl. Depending on who he is interacting with, in what role, in which context, Femi performs his queer sexuality in quite different ways. The actor 'Laurence' is not out to his fellow actors or his director, pretending to be straight. As a leading actor in the Royal National Classical Heritage Company's rendition of *Othello*, he denies the existence of his male lover; it is the smarter career move to make, as an up-and-coming actor, to pretend to be straight, as in the following exchange taking place at a theatre rehearsal in act 2 scene 5:

"Laurence: What the fuck j'u want, Colin?
Colin: Last night you had your cock up my arse, now it's 'What the fuck j'u want, Colin!'
Laurence: (*for all to hear*) Look, I'm really sorry, man, but I'm not into you in that way, yeah?
Colin: What way?
Laurence: I'm not gay, man!
Colin: Oh! I see. I get it.
Laurence: I'm really sorry, man. I'm just into girls.
Colin: No, I'm the one who's sorry. (*Colin exits.*)
Laurence: Sorry, my man. Peace, yeah! Take it easy." (64-65)

Femi himself is out to both his friends and his brother but not to his Nigerian mother, pretending to be in a relationship with his best female friend Kareema (cf. act 1 scene 1); and with the creation of his sex worker identities 'Big Black Jungle Nigga' and 'Shaneequa', Femi deliberately plays into the sexual fantasies of his

---

9   I am indebted to students of Ingrid Hotz-Davies' and Franziska Bergmann's class on queer theatre for providing me with a copy of their email interview with DeObia Oparei.

white, male upper-middle class clientele of closeted lawyers, police commissioners and judges.

Femi and Colin meet 'on the job' in act 2, performing as two drag queens, 'Shaneequa' and 'Buffy', for Cyril, a white retired judge who pays them for having sex and for roleplaying sexually and racially charged encounters between various characters. The final touches of the transformation of Femi into 'Shaneequa' occurs in act 2 scene 1.

> *"Femi's bedroom. Colin and Femi are in full drag. Femi lies across the bed. Colin is on top of him, doing Femi's make-up.*
> Femi: Aah!
> Colin: Keep still.
> Femi: Aah! Yer hurting me.
> Colin: You keep on moving, what d'u expect?
> Femi: Yer poking me right in my eye.
> Colin: Keep still.
> Femi: Aaah! You're doing it on purpose.
> Colin: No, I'm not.
> Femi: Yes, you are." (31)

Gender is revealed as performative here; the construction of femininity is not withheld from the audience. Colin's and Femi's light banter at some point turns into flirtation and a sharing of previous sexual encounters. It ends with Colin's relating a recent encounter with a Nigerian cab driver.

> "Femi: Thought you weren't into black?
> Colin: I said, I don't do queens! I like my man to be a man. (*The doorbell rings.*)
>   Grab ya tiara, our carriage is waiting!" (33)

Drag performances usually, and *Crazyblackmuthafuckin'self* is no exception in this regard, tend to be characterized by an exaggerated, highly theatrical and oftentimes ironic display of either femininity or masculinity. In their theatrical manner, they perfectly embody camp, a sensibility that, as per Susan Sontag in her seminal essay on the subject, "among other things, converts the serious into the frivolous" ("Notes on 'Camp'" 276). Camp may also refer to an object that aesthetically blurs the line between art and kitsch – Femi's/Shaneequa's non-existent tiara, for instance – or denote a mode of perception; one finds something hilariously over the top which had been intended quite seriously. It has its very useful role as a playful, ironic strategy of resistance for marginalized subjects, upsetting conservative value and belief systems and denaturalizing all fictions of stable identities (cf. Sontag).[10] Judith Butler proposes gender parody, the hyperbolic performance of genders that can be found, for instance, in drag performances, as a subversive strategy to expose the ultimately performative nature of gender (cf. *Gender Trouble*). During the course of act 2 scene 2, which has Colin and Femi performing as Buffy and Shaneequa for Cyril, the retired judge, Colin and Femi interact as Buffy/Shaneequa, but also as Little Red Riding Hood/Wolf (as per the judge's request) and Iago/Othello (their own idea of a sexually and racially charged roleplay within a roleplay; they quote at length lines from Shakespeare's *Othello*'s act 3 scene 3 at each other while performing sexual acts on each other).[11] It does not get much more camp than two drag queens, one of whom going by the name of Buffy (as in Joss Whedon's Buffy the Vampire Slayer, a petite powerful blonde), roleplaying Othello and Iago. Thus, while the judge directs them, giving them a staging and various prompts, Colin and Femi make it their own encounter. Out of his given circumstances, they improvise a scene in which they still retain agency.[12] By using the judge's interpellations as prompts to improvise around rather than as instructions to simply follow, they end up enjoying their encounter, making it about their own interaction, less about a performance for the white judge, and, as an unintended side effect, they fall in love.

---

10   For an extended discussion of camp, both its aesthetic and its subversive potential for queer subjects, see David Bergman, "Introduction" and Fabio Cleto, "Introduction: Queering the Camp". In the original stage production, Oparei employed a somewhat over-the-top, exaggeratedly feminine style for his performance of 'Shaneequa', what one might term with Sontag deliberate camp, while Paul Ready's more subtly understated, innocent femininity rendered his performance of 'Buffy' closer to what Sontag describes as naïve camp.

11   Oparei's extended citation of Shakespeare's *Othello* can be read as an act of disidentification with one of the few canonical theatrical texts that feature non-white characters (cf. Muñoz, *Disidentifications*). Franziska Bergmann also finds that the intertexts the play draws on function in this way. "Im Zusammenspiel mit den zahlreich eingearbeiteten Dialogpassagen aus Shakespeares Tragödie *Othello* bilden diese [popkulturellen] Fragmente ein breiteres diskursives Feld ab, das wesentlichen Anteil an der Produktion schwarzer Identität hat, denn alle Prätexte behandeln in irgendeiner Form die Themen Schwarzsein und/oder Alterität. Insofern dokumentiert *Crazyblack* gesellschaftlich zirkulierende, mitunter vom Nachleben des *Othello*-Narrativs geprägte Phantasmen des Schwarzseins und stellt sie in einen neuen Zusammenhang, der essentialistische Identitätsmodelle suspendiert" (209-210).

12   As per the stage directions, the retired judge moves about the stage "*[s]upported by his Zimmer frame*" wearing "*a white judge's wig and a long red cloak*" (41). His opening lines of "Order! Order! Silence in court! (*Gavel in hand, Cyril bangs on the Zimmer frame)*" already reveal that he is portrayed as a flat character of high comedy, in contrast to Colin and Femi who are portrayed as fully rounded characters (41). This already undermines Cyril's authority in this scene and confers agency to Colin and Femi, exposing the judge to ridicule and laughter from the audience.

"Othello: Damn her, damn. O damn her!
            They cum together.
Iago: I am your own forever.
            Panting, Colin and Femi stare into each other's eyes.
Cyril: (*claps*) Bravo, bravo! Totally believable! (*They stare into each other's eyes.*)
            Love the filthy language. (*They stare into each other's eyes.*) You must
            come again. Bravo, bravo! I'll just go get your money. I'll pay you extra
            for that.
            *They stare into each other's eyes. Cyril, with his Zimmer frame, trundles off
            to get the cash. Colin and Femi look awkwardly at each other. Silence. They
            change into their boy clothes.*
Femi: What is it about this play, man?
Colin: We did it at college. Tamed wild savage passionately falls in love with
            prim 'n' proper white chick. [...]
Femi: Excuse me.
Colin: You heard.
Femi: What?
Colin: You made me cum when you savaged me! When you became wild,
            yourself! You! You don't have to be anything else, for anyone else, not if
            you don't want to.
Femi: You telling me or Laurence?
Colin: I've never met Laurence, just heard about him. I like you, Femi O'la-
            tah'jee. [...]" (45)

The end of *Othello* act 3 scene 3 reaches, in this rendition, its climactic end in
Femi's and Colin's sexual encounter. By the end of the scene, the stage directions
have Femi and Colin staring into each other's eyes, the judge who is supposedly
running this scene by now completely forgotten.[13] Oparei's use of a performance

---

13 With its use of sexually explicit scenes, the play can be read as influenced by the genre of In-Yer-
    Face Theatre (the original stage production, it must be said, refrained from employing full nu-
    dity). Aleks Sierz characterizes In-Yer-Face Theatre as "a type of drama that uses explicit scenes
    of sex and violence to explore the extremes of human emotion"; it "usually involves the break-
    ing of taboos", while its "basic aesthetics is that of experiential theatre" (110). The comparison,
    however, goes only so far. *Crazyblackmuthafuckin'self* is clearly geared towards entertainment,
    comedy, laughter. It may want to provoke at times, but it does not display the violence, cruel-
    ty or shock value of a Sarah Kane or Mark Ravenhill play. Similarly, the sexually explicit scenes
    are hardly ever employed to show a disconnection between the characters, but instead serve
    as vehicles for connection and transformation for the main characters involved. A sensibility of
    bleakness and disconnection is, for Sierz, a prerequisite for In-Yer-Face Theatre. He maintains
    that "[i]t's worth emphasising that In-Yer-Face Theatre is a question of sensibility rather than of
    showing any specific acts. It's crucial that while such plays might contain shocking scenes, the
    really disturbing thing about them is the bleakness, nihilism or despair of the emotions of their

within a performance within a performance, or a play within a play within a play, successfully deconstructs any notions of the fixity and stability of roles and identities and the function of canonical cultural texts as master narratives.

However, when too many of his personas collide, and when he can no longer disentangle the contexts in which he is open about his queer sexuality from the contexts in which, for strategic reasons, he remains closeted, Femi's sense of self collapses. Confronted in act 3 scene 4 with the arrival of a barrage of people on his doorstep who know him from different contexts, as one or the other of his many alter egos, Femi tries to escape the inevitable collision of the many personas he has created and the many worlds they move in by locking himself up in his bathroom and significantly falling silent.[14] In her book *Touching, Feeling*, Sedgwick links twentieth-century experiences of closetedness and queer sexual subjectivity with affective experiences of abjection and shame. In this final, climactic scene of *Crazyblackmuthafuckin'self*, the bathroom represents the metaphorical and physical space of the closet, which is, however, in Femi's case both a sexual and a racial closet.[15] Unable to acknowledge either his queer sexual self or a version of his black self which does not try to concede to culturally acceptable versions of normative cultural otherness, the experience of revealing himself to his fellow actors and acquaintances (who know him variously as 'Laurence' and 'Shaneequa') as 'Femi' proves too shameful for Femi; he has successfully abjected these sexual and racial selves. Neither properly self nor other, the abject, according to Julia Kristeva, is that which the subject desires, which is part of the subject but which cannot be acknowledged, which is forbidden, which has to be disavowed and excluded, which threatens and disrupts, if acknowledged, the stability and coherence of self and subject, "repelling, rejecting, repelling itself, rejecting itself. Ab-jecting" (13). In *Crazyblackmuthafuckin'self*, the term 'nigga' comes to stand in for Femi's, and the other characters', abjected self-parts. It is only through the intervention of his brother Olunde and his lover Colin that Femi is able to be persuaded to leave the

characters. In-Yer-Face Theatre is about human emotions, not just shock tactics" (110). This sensibility, I maintain, cannot be found in *Crazyblackmuthafuckin'self*. Bergmann argues in a similar vein that the play does away with the nihilism of In-Yer-Face Theatre by its employment of comic elements and its happy ending (cf. Bergmann 208-209). "Auf diese Weise wendet sich das Stück vom Nihilismus des *In-Yer-Face Theatre* ab. [...] Den expliziten Umgang des *In-Yer-Face Theatre* mit Sexualität nutzt *Crazyblack* als emanzipative Strategie, um erotische Praktiken, die nicht den Mustern der heterosexuellen Ordnung entsprechen, öffentlich sichtbar werden zu lassen" (209).

14 I realize that there is also an element of farce in this climactic scene, but I maintain that the reality depicted in the play is still a plausible, if maybe heightened, version of the reality outside the theatre, and that the play and its characters can therefore be analysed in terms of psychological realism. All the relevant characters in this scene are furthermore depicted as three-dimensional or round characters.

15 Cf. also Bergmann 217-219 on Femi's trying to pass as white as 'Laurence'.

confines of his closeted space and rejoin the other characters on stage. His inter-actions with Olunde and Colin provide Femi with a moment of intersubjective rec-ognition and affirmation of self that is able to counter the effects of abjection and shame around his queer, black self.

> "Femi: I don't know who my nigga is.
> Colin: Your nigga is …
> Olunde: (to Colin) Hol' up, Barry White! Pass on de microphone! (He bangs on the door.) Nigga whaa'? You don't know who you is! Bwoi, you is a bluck man, dread! Your nigga is bluck! Your nigga is free! Your nigga is choice! To be who da fuck you is, brodder-man! And whaa't eva' da fuck you wanna be! […]
> Colin: Femi ola'tah'jee.
> Femi: Olu …
> Colin: Sssh! He's many things, and I love them all. (Colin takes Femi's face in his hands.) He's a rent boy called Big Black Jungle Nigga!
> Femi: Yeah, but …
> Colin: (kissing him) And I love him!
> Femi: But Colin …
> Colin: He's a drag queen called Shaneequa … (Kissing Femi.) and I love her.
> Femi: But my name …
> Colin: He's an actor called Laurence … (Kissing Femi.) And I love him. I love all of them, because our nigga is all of that! And then some!
> Femi: But Colin, my name is …
> Colin: Just shut it, and kiss me! (They kiss passionately.)" (87-88)

Psychoanalyst Jessica Benjamin provides a framework through which one may grasp the process of intersubjective recognition and come to understand love as a healing, nurturing space. In the words of Judith Butler, "Benjamin's work relies on the presumption that recognition is possible, and that it is the condition under which the human subject achieves psychic self-understanding and acceptance" (Undoing Gender 131). Butler elaborates some of Benjamin's central claims:

> "It is not the simple presentation of a subject for another that facilitates the recog-nition of that self-presenting subject by the Other. [Recognition] is rather, a process that is engaged when subject and Other understand themselves to be reflected in one another, but where this reflection does not result in a collapse of the one into the Other (through an incorporative identification, for instance) or a projection that annihilates the alterity of the Other. […] Recognition is neither an act that one performs nor is it literalized as the event in which we each 'see' one another and are 'seen.' It takes place through communication, primarily but not exclusively ver-

bal, in which subjects are transformed by virtue of the communicative practice in which they are engaged." (*Undoing Gender* 131-132)

Colin's and Femi's exchange provides such a moment of intersubjective recognition. And if misrecognition of the Other, an instance where "the relation to the Other relapses into the relation to the object" is always par for the course for this process of mutual recognition, as is exemplified here with Colin's constantly getting Femi's actual name wrong, misrecognition is still "occasional, but not a constitutive or insurpassble feature of psychic reality [...]. [R]ecognition, conceived as free of misrecognition, not only ought to triumph", for Benjamin, "but can" (Butler, *Undoing Gender* 132).

Fully affirmed and recognized by his lover, his brother and the community of other characters on stage, and directly addressing the audience and thus breaking, in the final moments of the play, the 'fourth wall' separating the world of the characters from the world of the audience, Femi goes on to perform a ritual of affirmation of all our selves. (This is the way the original stage production performed this particular, and particularly moving, scene from the play text; the stage directions, too, have Femi deliver his speech from downstage and thus to the audience.)

"*The djembe plays, as Femi comes downstage.*

Femi: Like a slave caught in the middle passage, I have yearned for home. So many of my people are caught up in the bite of schizophrenia and, like them, I have wandered around not knowing who I am. The truth is, I am all of you! I call out the names of my ancestors.

Full Company: My people!

Femi: Those that came before, and those that shall follow.

Full Company: My people!

Femi: I ask them to integrate my soul as only they have the power to do. I call out their names, and ask that they step forward and represent in all a' me in all a' you, words that I speak from my forefathers passed on to them from slaves who like me, yearned for home in the middle passage.

Full Company: My people!

Femi: That in my calling, with their passing, are set free as I am free now!

Full Company: My people!

Femi: [...] The names of my crazy black mutha fuckas! The names of my niggas, that dance with Ogun in disco heaven!" (88-89)[16]

---

16 Bergmann convincingly reads Femi's subjectivity at the beginning of this passage "als ein nomadisches, das keinen heimatlichen Ruhepunkt kennt, aber auf der beständigen Suche nach einem solchen ist" (214); indeed as a subject, even, "[in] das sich das historische Motiv der 'middle pas-

Only for a black, gay man who has successfully integrated his abjected self-parts can "heaven" ever be a "disco" which at the same time contains the Nigerian deity Ogun, who in the traditional Yoruba belief system presides, among other things, over the areas of politics and war. Femi's final performative resilience strategy includes a reaching out towards others by extending an invitation to the audience to join him in his performance of ritual; to undergo with him a transformational experience that goes beyond the usual theatrical experience experienced by the regular theatregoer. With his invocation of his Nigerian forefathers – his incantations of, "I call out their names, and ask that they step forward and represent in all a' me *in all a' you* [my emphasis; this was addressed in the original staging directly to the audience], words that I speak from my forefathers passed on to them from slaves who like me, yearned for home in the middle passage" – he comes, in the final moments of the play, to address the audience directly, together with the other actors, as 'company' not as individual characters, inviting the audience members to participate in his ritual of integration of abjected self-parts.[17] Richard Schechner describes rituals as "collective memories encoded into actions. Rituals also help people [...] deal with difficult transitions, ambivalent relationships, hierarchies, and desires that trouble, exceed, or violate the norms of daily life" (52). Drawing on concepts developed by anthropologist Victor Turner, Schechner states:

> "Performing rituals helps people get through difficult periods of transition and move from one life status to another. Ritual is also a way for people to connect to a collective, to remember or construct a mythic past, to build social solidarity, and to form or maintain a community. Some rituals are liminal, existing between or outside daily social life; other rituals are knitted into ordinary living. During their liminal phase, ritual performances produce communitas, a feeling among participants that they are part of something greater than or outside of their individual selves. On a larger scale, ritual plays an essential role in social dramas, helping to resolve crises by bringing about either the reintegration needed to heal or allowing

---

sage' als unauslöschliche Spur in seine Psyche eingeschrieben habe und sich dort in Form eines Gefühls der Entwurzelung und radikalen Unsicherheit manifestiere" (214).

17 This is the way the original stage production performed this scene in a, to me, convincing and moving manner. Femi's "in all a' you", marked by italics above, was addressed directly to the audience. The full company of actors' chorus ("My people") was also addressed directly to the audience in a manner that meant to convey that the pronoun "my" included or referred to both Femi and the company of actors on stage as well as the people sitting in the audience, similar, perhaps, to a gospel choir addressing, with the call and response of soloist and choir, a church congregation, where the church congregation is as much part of the experience of 'communitas' created by the gospel choir's performance as the members of the gospel choir themselves.

a schism needed to form a new community. In either case, ritual is necessary for closure." (87)

Using the space of the stage and auditorium to create what Victor Turner terms 'communitas', an experience of a shared common humanity among actors and audience, Femi / Oparei tries to bring theatre back to its anthropological roots here as an, in the terminology of Turner, liminal and thus potentially transformational, communal performance space.[18] As Oparei himself puts it, "Crazyblackmutha-fuckin'self is not the absence of white or heterosexuality. It is the exact opposite. It's the inclusion of all of that from a gay, black, and, in the form of transsexual call girl Shaneequa, transgendered perspective" (*Personal Interview*). And it is, in these final moments of the play, not only an inclusion, but also an integration, I would argue, that is at stake for Oparei, of both Femi's, and all the other characters' – and the audience members' – many, disparate selves.

---

18 Cf. Schechner, *Performance Studies* for a detailed exploration of the characteristics of ritual, the-atre and performance, and a more detailed application of Turner's concept of the liminal and liminoid to the space of the theatre (66-72).

Spatial Strategies

"The present age may be the age of space", Michel Foucault declared in 1967 ("Different Spaces" 175). But what, exactly, is space, and what could strategies of queer resilience that make use of space and place potentially look like? Recent cultural geographers, such as Doreen Massey, Edward Soja and David Harvey, drawing on the work of Henri Lefebvre, understand space not as a natural, static given but as socially constructed, suffused always with a web of power relations, indeed as performatively produced and maintained (cf. for instance Massey, *Space, Place and Gender*).[1] Michel Foucault's lecture on "Different Spaces" is an early example of the same kind of approach to the notion of space. Foucault, too, regards space as a set of relations:

> "The space in which we are living, by which we are drawn outside ourselves, in which, as a matter of fact, the erosion of our life, our time, and our history takes place, this space that eats and scrapes away at us, is also heterogeneous space in itself. In other words, we do not live in a void, within which individuals and things might be located. We do not live in a void that would be tinged with shimmering colors, we live inside an ensemble of relations that define emplacements that are irreducible to each other and absolutely nonsuperposable." (177-178)

Following the notion of space as a set of power relations, as socially constructed, the predominant cultural geographical model of space can be assumed in our contemporary Western cultural context to be heteronormative space. Queer space, on the other hand, can then be assumed to be a form of utopian space. However,

---

1 Judith Halberstam makes out a lacuna in Soja's and Harvey's theories on space: the category of sexuality is markedly absent from their analysis "precisely because desire has been cast by neo-Marxists as part of a ludic body politics that obstructs the 'real' work of activism. This foundational exclusion, which assigned sexuality to body/local/personal and took class/global/political as its proper frame of reference, has made it difficult to introduce questions of sexuality and space into the more general conversations about globalization and transnational capitalism" (*In a Queer Time and Place* 5). The category of sexuality is also strangely absent from Doris Bachmann-Medick's otherwise excellent overview of spatial theorizations in recent cultural studies (cf. *Cultural Turns* 285-329).

as Foucault rightly points out, "[u]topias are emplacements having no real place" ("Different Spaces" 178). For actual places existing in the real world that exhibit utopian qualities, Foucault coins the term 'heterotopias'. The following is how Foucault describes what he means by the notion of heterotopic space.

> "There are also, and probably in every culture, in every civilization, real places, actual places, places that are designed into the very institution of society, which are sorts of actually realized utopias in which the real emplacements, all the other real emplacements that can be found within the culture are, at the same time, represented, contested, and reversed, sorts of places that are outside all places, although they are actually localizable. Because they are utterly different from all the emplacements that they reflect or refer to, I shall call these places 'heteroto-pias,' as opposed to utopias[.]" (178-179)

In the Foucauldian conception of different kinds of spaces, queer space can then be understood to be one form of heterotopic space. Indeed, the connection has already been made by a number of queer writers and theorists, most notably by Samuel R. Delany in his book *Times Square Red, Times Square Blue* (cf. Chisholm 27).

I concur with Jane Garrity, who understands queer space as referring to "nonnormative locales that are physical, social, and constituted by and through social relations, as well as nonexclusionary and nonhomogenous locations that are largely or exclusively theoretical constructs [...]. To examine the complexity of queer space is to show how spaces that appear asexual are actually inflected by a range of consequences attendant upon heteronormative ideologies" ("Mapping Queer Space" 1-2). An analysis of space attendant to the category of sexuality can thus be based on conceptual as well as material understandings of space; it can include the "geographical, discursive, virtual" as well as the metaphoric and the symbolic ("Mapping Queer Space" 3).[2] Space is also indelibly linked to (self-)conceptions of identity, sexual or otherwise. As Eveline Kilian and Hope Wolf point out in their introduction to *Life Writing and Space*, "[w]ho we are, and how we narrate ourselves, depends on our ability, our desire or failure, to locate our identities within space and with respect to certain places" (1). Queer subjects, I argue, can employ spatial strategies to help further their resilience and balance out vulnerabilities. This chapter aims at looking at how fictional queer characters and actual queer cultural workers and authors make conscious use of the spaces they travel to, construct or inhabit, places both metaphoric and real, in the search for

---

2 Similarly, for Halberstam who analyses queer space in the context of a postmodernist critique, queer space "refers to the place-making practices within postmodernism in which queer people engage and it also describes the new understandings of space enabled by the production of queer counterpublics" (*In a Queer Time and Place* 6).

pockets of non-heteronormative space. By creating, searching out and maintaining these cultural spaces – which happen to be sometimes spaces that Foucault already marked as potential heterotopias – twentieth and twenty-first century queer subjects can be understood, I suggest, to be employing spatial strategies of queer resilience.

I analyse in the first instance two short stories by Katherine Mansfield and Elizabeth Bowen, "Leves Amores" and "The Jungle" (both dating from the early decades of the twentieth century) and Maureen Duffy's poem "Mulberries", which all utilize the trope of the garden as a queer heterotopia, a space where female same-sex desire can be felt and sometimes realized. The speaker of Robert Duncan's poem "Often I am Permitted to Return to a Meadow" (written in the late 1950s), I then argue, finds in the imaginary space of the meadow an internal heterotopia, a place of first permission. Finally, I trace the emergence of queer space in the city of San Francisco from the beginning of the twentieth century to the late 1970s. The decade of the 1970s saw the development of a new phenomenon, whole residential neighbourhoods with openly gay and lesbian residents which drew increasing numbers of LGBTQ visitors and saw many moving there permanently or stay for longer or shorter periods of time. The emerging LGBTQ communities helped foster a sense of connection among LGBTQ people and provided both a safe space and a space to belong. I furthermore trace how a political movement could develop from the openly gay space of the Castro. The figure of the first openly gay elected official, Harvey Milk, the 'unofficial mayor of Castro Street', emerges in the late 1970s as a community leader arguing not only for civil rights for LGBTQ U.S. citizens, but also, crucially, for the importance of engendering hope in (especially) queer youth. I conclude by tracing the resilience of hope through Wendy O'Brien and José Esteban Muñoz' utilizations of, variously, Hannah Arendt and Ernst Bloch's conceptualizations around hope. Hope emerges here as a structure of feeling that can not only counter despair but is actually the first step an individual can take towards imagining an otherwise and an elsewhere, once again (routed this time through Bloch instead of through Foucault) a utopian feeling.

The Garden as Queer Heterotopia in Katherine Mansfield's "Leves Amores", Elizabeth Bowen's "The Jungle" and Maureen Duffy's "Mulberries"

In his lecture "Different Spaces", Michel Foucault points to the garden as one potentially heterotopic space. The trope of the garden in Western art and literature can be linked on the one hand to the medieval *hortus conclusus*, the enclosed garden denoting both the paradisiacally innocent and enchanting (and at the same time unbreachably virginal) space of the Virgin Mary in Christian iconography, though its origin in the form of a space of the beloved in the Bible's *Song of Songs* already marks it also as a space of both (holy) love and desire; and on the other hand to the *locus amoenus* of Roman antiquity, the beautiful place in nature that provides its visitor with rest and tranquillity. Foucault points to an even older tradition of symbolic meanings attached to the trope of the garden, which he traces back to the traditional gardens of ancient Persia:

> "One should bear in mind that in the East the garden, an amazing creation now thousands of years old, was deeply symbolic, with meanings that were superimposed, as it were. The traditional garden of the Persians was a sacred space that is said to have joined together within its rectangle four parts representing the four parts of the world, with a space even more sacred than the others which was like the umbilicus, the navel of the world at its center (this was the location of the basin and the fountain); and all the garden's vegetation was supposed to be distributed within that space, within that figurative microcosm. As for carpets, originally they were reproductions of gardens. The garden is a carpet in which the entire world attains its symbolic perfection, and the carpet is a kind of garden that moves through space. The garden is the smallest parcel of the world and the whole world at the same time. Since early antiquity the garden has been a sort of blissful and universalizing heterotopia [...]." ("Different Spaces" 181-182)

This "blissful and universalizing heterotopia" makes its appearance in two short stories by Katherine Mansfield and Elizabeth Bowen and in a poem by Maureen Duffy. In all three instances, the image of the garden is evoked to denote a space of queer possibility, a space in which female same-sex desire can be felt and – sometimes – realized. The garden appears in these texts as a (queer) heterotopia, a place variously metaphoric and real.

In Katherine Mansfield's short story "Leves Amores", written in 1907 and published posthumously as an appendix in Claire Tomalin's *Katherine Mansfield: A Secret Life*, an unnamed first-person narrator relates her stay at the Thistle Hotel and her encounter with another female hotel guest, whom she asks out to dinner and to an opera performance. The female hotel guest invites the narrator to her room before dinner: she cannot lace up her evening bodice on her own, "it was hooks at the back. Very Well" ("Leves Amores" 259). The narrator is given an opportunity to observe the female hotel guest – she is washing "[i]n her petticoat bodice and a full silk petticoat" when the narrator enters her room, "sponging her face and neck" (259). An intimate, suspenseful atmosphere is thus being set up between the narrator and the female hotel guest, which is however undercut by the narrator's description of the somewhat dingy surroundings of the cheap hotel room. The "one filthy window faced the street"; the low bed is "draped with revolting, yellow, vine-patterned curtains"; the wardrobe has "a piece of cracked mirror attached"; and the wallpaper hangs "in tattered strips from the wall. In its less discoloured and faded patches I could trace the pattern of roses – buds and flowers – and the frieze was a conventional design of birds, of what genus the good God alone knows" (259). The hotel guest herself is at the same time alluring and repelling to the narrator, who watches her pull on her thin stockings, "saying 'damn' when she could not find her suspenders"; she feels within her "a certainty that nothing beautiful could ever happen in that room, and for her I felt contempt, a little tolerance, a very little pity" (259). Besides the obvious shabbiness of the room, the narrator attributes the "dull, grey light" which for her "hovered over everything", making even the female hotel guest look "dull and grey and tired", to her own advancing age. Sitting on the bed, she ponders somewhat melodramati-cally, "Come, this Old Age. I have forgotten passion, I have been left behind in the beautiful golden procession of Youth. Now I am seeing life in the dressing-room of the theatre" (259).

And yet, something changes over the course of the evening, over dinner, over attending the opera performance, for the narrator emerges from it transformed. The narrator does not spell out what, exactly, prompts the transformation, sum-marizing the proceedings of the evening in a mere single sentence. One possible way of filling this gap in the narrative as a reader is to assume, following the obser-vations of Terry Castle in *The Apparitional Lesbian*, that the opera performance must have been the agent of change. Castle points to the space of the opera as one space in which female same-sex desire and attraction could be openly acknowl-edged as early as the mid-nineteenth century. Castle refers to female opera stars of the time period such as Jenny Lind and others and their fervent female fan base, from Queen Victoria to the composer Ethel Smyth.

> "Where else but in the plush darkness of Covent Garden, the Met, or the Opéra Comique, say, might a respectable woman of the nineteenth century have spent two or three hours staring raptly at another through binoculars? Before very recent times, the opera house (along with the theater) was one of only a few public spaces in which a woman could openly admire another woman's body, resonate to the penetrating tones of her voice, and even imagine (from a distance) the blood-warmth of her flesh – all in an atmosphere of heightened emotion and powerful sensual arousal." (*The Apparitional Lesbian* 202-203)

A change must indeed have taken place: When the narrative of "Leves Amores" picks up again, it is late, "late and cold" (259). Their walk back to the hotel takes the narrator and her friend down a "white pathway fringed with beautiful golden lilies, up the amethyst shadowed staircase" (260). The mood has quite obviously changed, for the narrator, the story's only focalizer, to be framing her visual observations in term of precious, beautiful metals and gems, making her question her earlier assessment of the time in life for passion to be over. Has the "golden procession of Youth" mentioned earlier returned?

> "*Was* Youth dead? … *Was* Youth dead?
>   She told me as we walked along the corridor to her room that she was glad the night had come. I did not ask why. I was glad, too. It seemed a secret between us." (260)

A passionate encounter is to follow, and this is, accordingly, foreshadowed and phrased in terms of the secret, which as per Eve Kosofky Sedgwick in *Epistemology of the Closet* at least since the turn of the century has always denoted or been linked to sexual knowledge and, most of the time, deviant sexual desires.[3] What secret the night holds must then be framed, accordingly, in terms of darkness: "I went with her into her room to undo those troublesome hooks. She lit a little candle on an enamel bracket. The light filled the room with darkness" (260). Under cover of night, a secretive sexual encounter can take place.

> "Like a sleepy child she slipped out of her frock and then, suddenly, turned to me and flung her arms round my neck. Every bird upon the bulging frieze broke into song. Every rose upon the tattered paper budded and formed into blossom. Yes, even the green vine upon the bed curtains wreathed itself into strange chaplets and garlands, twined round us in a leafy embrace, held us with a thousand clinging tendrils.
>   And Youth was not dead." (260)

What happens between the narrator and her female companion is not spelt out beyond the mention of a passionate embrace. Instead, the narrative conjures up the heterotopic space of the garden as a metaphor for lesbian love and lesbian lovemaking. But the garden in Mansfield's story is both metaphoric and real. The shabby hotel room magically transforms its features into a place that is at the same time cut off from the outside world, like the *hortus conclusus*, and beautiful, like the *locus amoenus*. The birds on the frieze come to life; the flowers on the wallpaper start to blossom; the vine on the bed curtains starts to wind itself around the two lovers in a "leafy embrace". The "Leves Amores" of the title, the leaves of love, denote a space of possibility for forbidden desires, for an extraordinary experience both transcendent and sublime. The actual details of the experience, presumably a sexual and romantic encounter between the two women, remains in the realm of the unsayable. The typographic gap – the long indentation before the story's

---

3   Cf. Sedgwick, *Epistemology* 73-74.

final line – denotes as much, with the narrator affirming in her last sentence that, indeed, Youth, as well as (female same-sex) passion presumably, are not dead.

The story, remarkably written by a nineteen-year-old Mansfield and which Claire Tomalin deems "undisguisedly lesbian" (37) even though the narrator's gender is never openly revealed but has to be inferred, coincides with a time period in Mansfield's life when she was back in New Zealand after attending boarding school in England. Mansfield herself, her diaries reveal, experienced a crush on a female friend at the time, Edith Bendall.[4] A copy of the story has survived among the papers of Vere Bartrick-Baker, a close friend of Katherine Mansfield's from school.[5] Mansfield evidently liked it enough that she decided to share it, together with a few other stories, with one of her closest friends. Whether she considered publishing it, or whether she indeed tried to submit it to the *Native Companion*, which had published some of her other vignettes, is not known.[6] What is known is that Mansfield asked Martha Putnam, her father's secretary, to type up the story for her – Putnam had typed up other stories for her previously which she had considered for publication. Tomalin cites a letter from Mansfield to Martha Putnam from December 1907: "She [Mansfield] apologized for it [the story] in advance, saying, 'I'm afraid you won't like Leves Amores – I can't think how I wrote it – it's partly a sort of dream'" (42).[7] Whether we are to believe Mansfield here or not is unclear, since other letters show that she was also prone to flirting with Miss Putnam. Another letter that Tomalin quotes reads: "Well – I must go to bed – Shall I build a castle with a spare room for you – Yes I will – so please return the compliment" (Mansfield qtd. in Tomalin 42).[8] Her intention – aside from the usefulness of having someone at hand to produce a typescript of the story – may have been as well to either shock Martha or indeed flirt with her through the content of a story on female same-sex passion. In this way, the story – the earliest text of the present archive of this book – can be shown not only to contain elements of female same-sex desire on the level of content, but was also evidently employed and circulated by its author to help maintain connections to female friends and acquaintances with a curious undercurrent of female same-sex attachment and desire. It thus rightfully deserves its place in the lesbian 'canon' and has, accordingly, been

4 Cf. Tomalin 36-37.

5 Cf. Tomalin 37 and 259.

6 Cf. Tomalin 41-43.

7 Tomalin speculates that Martha Putnam may have shared Mansfield's writing with her employer and that the content of "Leves Amores" may have been one of the reasons for her father's decision to rescind his permission for her to return to London to attend college in early 1908 – Mansfield was eventually to return to London to continue her education, so her father's resistance to the idea proved to have been only temporary (cf. Tomalin 42).

8 See Tomalin 42 for more quotes of letters from Mansfield to Martha Putnam.

anthologized in two seminal collections of lesbian writing, Margaret Reynolds'
Penguin Book of Lesbian Short Stories and Terry Castle's *Literature of Lesbianism*.

The garden as queer heterotopic space also makes its appearance in Elizabeth
Bowen's short story "The Jungle", which was first published in 1929 in the short-
story collection *Joining Charles and Other Stories*. In the words of Terry Castle, it
is "the second of a pair of stories – the other is called 'Charity' – involving the
schoolgirl Rachel, whose skittish friendships with other girls are at once bitter-
sweet, abortive, yet full of emotional portent" (*Literature of Lesbianism* 839). Rachel,
who attends boarding school, finds the Jungle at the age of fourteen on "a silent
July evening, an hour before supper" (Bowen, "The Jungle" 251).

> "Towards the end of a summer term Rachel discovered the Jungle. You got over the
> wall at the bottom of the kitchen garden [...] and waded through knee-high sorrel,
> nettles and dock, along the boundary hedge of Mr Morden's property until you
> came to a gap in the roots of the hedge [...] where it was possible to crawl under.
> Then you doubled across his paddock (this was the most exciting part), round the
> pond and climbed a high board gate it was impossible to see through into a deep
> lane. You got out of the lane farther down by a bank with a hedge at the top [...], and
> along the back of this hedge, able to be entered at several points, was the Jungle.
> It was full of secret dog-paths threading between enormous tussocks of bramble,
> underneath the brambles there were hollow places like caves; there were haw-
> thorns one could climb for a survey and, about the middle, a clump of elders gave
> out a stuffy sweetish smell. It was an absolutely neglected and wild place; nobody
> seemed to own it, nobody came there but tramps." ("The Jungle" 251)

Getting to this secret, wild place is, quite obviously, an arduous journey and an
adventure in and of itself, and forms part of the allure of the Jungle for Rachel.
This wild garden, which "nobody seemed to own", enclosed by hedges on all sides,
is presented as a liminal, heterotopic space already in the description of Rachel's
first entering it as well as in her emotional reaction to it. "She had felt a funny
lurch in her imagination as she entered the Jungle, everything in it tumbled
together, then shook apart again, a little altered in their relations to each other, a
little changed" (251). Things, one feels, can exist in the Jungle that cannot exist, or
be imagined or felt, elsewhere. The Jungle is also presented as a space of romantic
female friendship and thus connected to passionate same-sex attachment right
from the story's beginning. Rachel, the narrator reveals, "had no best friend at the
moment, there was an interim" (251); yet the Jungle "gave her a strong feeling that
here might have been the Perfect Person, and yet the Perfect Person would spoil
it. She wanted it to be a thing in itself: she sat quite still and stared at the impene-
trable bramble-humps" (251). Rachel wants the Jungle to be her own private space;
at the same time she longs to have a friend again, the "Perfect Person" with whom

to share everything including, presumably, the Jungle. Elise, the potentially new best friend from one form below, emerges on the train on the way to the summer holidays. "Elise had her hair cut short like a boy's and was supposed to be fearfully good at French but otherwise stupid. She had a definite quick way of doing things and a thoughtful slow way of looking at you when they were done" (252). During the summer holidays, during which she turns fifteen, Rachel has a recurring, disturbing dream about both Elise and the Jungle.

> "It was something to do with a dead body, a girl's arm coming out from under the bushes. She tried to put the Jungle out of her mind; she never thought of it, but a few nights afterwards she was back there again, this time with some shadowy person always a little behind her who turned out to be Elise. When they came to the bush which in the first dream had covered the arm she was trying to tell Elise about it, to make sure it *had* been a dream, then stopped, because she knew she had committed that murder herself. She wanted to run away, but Elise came up beside her and took her arm with a great deal of affection." (252-253)

If the Jungle is for Rachel the liminal space where deep and passionate same-sex attachments are possible and, as was revealed to her there, desirable, then it is also a space that is for her tinged with a notion of abjection, guilt and shame: in the first dream she finds a dead girl's body there; in the second dream it turns out she has committed the murder herself. There is something deeply disturbing to her about the nature of her passionate feelings for her best friend. Still, in the dream Elise does not share in the sensation of homosexual phobia and panic. Elise takes her arm "with a great deal of affection".

The following term sees Elise and Rachel picking apples from a tree in the kitchen-garden, the domesticated garden setting for their next encounter. They discuss the topic of names and Elise, the more athletic of the two, confides that she thinks she really "ought to have been a boy' [...]. She rolled a sleeve back. 'Feel my muscle! Watch it – look!'" The invitation to touch prompts Rachel's inviting Elise to join her in the Jungle.

> "'I say, Elise. I know of a rather queer place. It's near here, I discovered it. I call it the Jungle, just to distinguish it from other places. I don't mean it's a bit exciting or anything [...]. But it is rather what I used to call 'secret'.'" (255-256)

The sharing of a secret space is clearly an attempt at initiating a more intimate friendship with Elise. The place that Rachel describes as being "rather queer", that is strange, is also a space of freedom and possibility. Away from the prying eyes of their school environment, it is also a place outside of school norms and regulations. They decide to go to the Jungle together right away, where Rachel promises there

"may be blackberries" (256). On entering the Jungle, Rachel finds it "an even better place than she had remembered", even though she is reminded of the dreams
she had: "Here was the place where the dead girl's arm, blue-white, had come out
from under the bushes. Here was the place where Elise, in the later dream, had
come up and touched her so queerly" (256). Elise's "queer" touch, which had in the
earlier narration of the dream been described as a touch of great affection, clearly
takes on a meaning other than that of the merely strange here; it describes a touch
that speaks to a desired, though forbidden form of intimacy. Elise, of course, loves
the Jungle, which she deems "an awfully good place [...]. Wish *I'd* found it" (256),
declaring it the perfect place to build camp fires and go to sleep, an idea that Rachel
deems rather extraordinary. The two girls do neither, though, but go on picking
blackberries while making conversation, with the narrator stressing Elise's tom-
boyish nature; Rachel is both drawn to Elise's physicality and finds herself disturbed by it: "just like a compact, thick boy in her black tights she was sprawling
over the great pouffe of brambles, standing on one foot, balancing herself with
the other, reaching out in all directions. But for that way she had of sometimes
looking towards one, blank with an inside thoughtfulness, one couldn't believe
she had a life of her own apart from her arms and legs. Rachel angrily doubted it"
(257). On their return to school they are late for chapel and punished accordingly,
but as the narrator maintains, "[b]eing punished together was intimate; they felt
welded" (257). Soon after, however, their friendship develops a number of strains.
Elise is, in Rachel's eyes, rather bossy, and Rachel does not enjoy being ordered
around, especially from someone from a lower form. Her class-mates make fun
of her friendship with Elise and besides, there is the matter of Elise's other best
friend Joyce, of whom Rachel is quite clearly jealous. They have a falling-out over
supper, and, consequently, take a break on their developing friendship. The narrative skips over the following three months and takes up again on a Sunday in
December, which sees Rachel returning to the Jungle on her own, pondering how
nice it is to come back, but then finding, to her great shock, the first of her dreams
to have come true.

> "Coming out from the brambles, an arm was stretched over the path: 'Not, O God, in
> this lonely place,' said Rachel – 'let there not be a body!'
> [...] The hand lay a yard ahead of her – she could have taken three steps forward
> and stepped on it – the thumb bent, the red, square-tipped fingers curling on to
> the palm." (261-262)

The body turns out to be the sleeping Elise. "Her knees were drawn up, her other
arm flung back under her head which rested, cheek down, on a pile of dead leaves
as on a pillow and was wrapped up in a muffler" (262). Asleep, Elise looks different
to Rachel. "She was Elise, but quenched, wiped-away, different"; Rachel also, for

the first time, really allows herself to observe Elise's face up-close. "Rachel had never looked full at her without having to pass like a guard her direct look; her face now seemed defenceless" (262). Rachel steps on a twig, waking Elise, but it turns out that Elise is not disturbed to find Rachel hovering over her. Elise is also, as it turns out, open to both of them renewing their friendship.

> "'Oh, by the way,' said Rachel, 'congratulations about your colours.'
> Elise, her hands clasped under her head, had been lying looking at the sky. 'Thanks so much,' she said, now looking at Rachel.
> 'Aren't we mad,' said Rachel uneasily, 'doing this in December?'
> 'Why shouldn't we if we're warm enough? Rachel, why shouldn't we? – Answer.'
> 'It'll be dark soon.'
> 'Oh, dark in your eye!' said Elise, 'there's plenty of time ... I say, Rachel, I tell you a thing we might do –'" (263)

It is in this heterotopic space, too, that Elise is the daring one, with Rachel being the one concerned with what constitutes proper and improper behaviour; not in the least because of the way Elise, and Elise's being completely unconcerned about normative behaviour, make her feel and the yearning she experiences in Elise's presence: "She had a funny feeling, a dancing-about of the thoughts; she would do anything, anything" (263). It turns out that Elise wants her to "turn round and round till you're really comfy, then I could turn round and put my head on your knee, then I could go to sleep again ..." (263). Rachel complies with Elise's wishes.

> "The round cropped head like a boy's was resting on Rachel's knees. She felt all constrained and queer; comfort was out of the question. [...]
> The dog had stopped barking, the Jungle, settling down into silence, contracted a little round them, then stretched to a great deep ring of unrealness and loneliness. It was as if they were alone on a ship, drifting out ...
> 'Elise,' whispered Rachel, 'do you think we –'
> But the head on her knees had grown heavy. Elise was asleep." (263)

The close intimacy makes Rachel feel "constrained and queer", though not in an uncomfortable way but rather in a way that feels both exciting and forbidden. The Jungle as queer heterotopic space has enabled an intimate encounter between Rachel and her once-again close friend; but the Jungle has become also, for better or worse, a place of isolation and "unrealness". As is suggested by Rachel's trying to start a conversation while Elise has drifted off to sleep, the possibility remains that Elise's feelings do not run as deep as Rachel's, that Rachel may be alone in her crush on Elise.[9] Complying with Elise's wishes leaves Rachel not quite satisfied. It remains unclear whether Rachel herself knows what kind of intimacy she is truly yearning for, but the one suggested by Elise, while a start, does not seem to be entirely it. The ambivalent ending to the short story is not unusual for Bowen, for whom Castle attests "an undertow of melancholia present in so much of her writing" (*Literature of Lesbianism* 839). Still, the story is remarkable in that it links female same-sex desire and attachment so clearly and unambiguously to the space of a wild, enclosed garden, a place in which forbidden desires can rise to the surface and be acted on, a heterotopic space of lesbian love.

Finally, Maureen Duffy, in her poem "Mulberries" from the poetry cycle *The Garland* published in 1985, also employs the trope of the garden as queer heterotopia, as both a real place and as the symbolic space of a lesbian relationship that proves to be for the speaker a return to a kind of paradisiacal state of happiness. In the poem, the speaker describes herself picking ripe mulberries in her lover's actual garden. It is a scene where fruit is plentiful, where in the speaker's perception the sexual and the sensual constantly mingle. The garden is also a playground of the imagination, a place where children are free to roam, pretending to be pirates, where rules of the outside world do not apply. The speaker's actual reaching up to pick fruit takes on an additional symbolic meaning when she compares her life previous to this point as filled with struggle, a feeling, however, which has now ceased to be true and which has been replaced by a sense of arrival, a sense of homecoming, of happiness, gratitude, of peace and of fulfillment. "It seems all my life has been a reaching up. / Now in this autumn in your garden love / Falls about me prodigal as shook down fruit" (*Collected Poems* 266).[10] Her lover's garden, a private, secluded space, has become a world unto itself, which is at the same time the whole world, filled to the brim with ripeness and abundance, a kind of private Eden. The interpersonal space of the speaker's and her lover's relationship has at the same time become a symbolic Eden, a queer heterotopia.

Interior Landscapes as Safe Space: Robert Duncan's "Often I am Permitted to Return to a Meadow"

There is a long tradition of psychotherapeutic settings seeking to work with a client's resilient aspects of self, or resources, that draw on the powers of the imagination of client – and sometimes also therapist, though the focus will generally

---

9   Though Elise's falling asleep with her head in Rachel's lap could also be read as a sign of ultimate trust on Elise's part.

10 The literary trope of fruit as a conduit for female same-sex desire can be traced back to at least Christina Rossetti's poem *Goblin Market* (cf. Castle, *The Literature of Lesbianism*).

be on enabling the client to make use of the space of the imagination by themselves, rendering the therapist eventually superfluous. Imagination here denotes an exercise of the powers of fantasy that is not restricted to visualization only but draws on all sensory experience, including the aural, visual and the senses of touch and smell as well as bodily sensations (cf. Stein 129). C.G. Jung's depth psychology for instance makes use of the imagination in his methodology of active imagination (cf. Kast). Working with guided imagery has a long tradition in a number of psychotherapeutic schools (cf. Stein); it also has its place in a somewhat simplified version in stress management programmes geared towards the general public. Another methodology, Luise Reddemann's *Psychodynamisch Imaginative Traumatherapie*, makes use of the imagination first and foremost in exercises that are employed primarily as a way of stabilizing clients suffering from post traumatic stress (cf. *Imagination als heilsame Kraft*). Reddemann provides the examples of conjuring up and imaginatively inhabiting a safe space ("der innere Ort der Geborgenheit"; *Imagination als heilsame Kraft* 57-59), which may or may not be the same space as the one conjured up in her exercise "der innere Garten" (66-67), as well as an exercise conjuring up inner helpers ("die inneren hilfreichen Wesen" 60). These exercises, when engaged in repeatedly, can help clients to stabilize themselves whenever they are triggered and experience feelings of anxiety or panic, or when they are overcome by troubling and intrusive images.[11] Employing the imagination as a healing space has been part of the oldest healing traditions on Earth (e.g. shamanism),[12] and has over the course of the past two decades been fruitfully explored by neuroscientists, who point out that the brain activates similar neural networks when confronted with imaginary and with actually perceived sensory input.[13] It stands to reason, then, that experiences taking place in that imaginary inner space can have as much of an impact on how we feel and think

---

11 There is a long tradition for this kind of work. Reddemann quotes Viktor Frankl, who already in the 1940s gave similar recommendations for the treatment of patients: "In diesem Sinne empfehlen wir unseren Patienten beizeiten, sich dem Gefühl der inneren Ruhe und Ausgeglichenheit, eben der seelischen Entspanntheit, ganz hinzugeben ... Hierbei ist es ratsam, zur Vertiefung solcher Erlebnisse Phantasievorstellungen zu Hilfe zu rufen. Als brauchbare Hilfsvorstellung dieser Art hat sich uns erwiesen: die Vorstellung, ein sturmbewegtes Meer zu sehen, dessen aufgepeitschter Wellengang sich allmählich verringert [...]. Aber es empfiehlt sich, dem Kranken in der Wahl seiner Lieblingsvorstellungen freien Spielraum zu lassen, ja sie zu freier Erfindung solcher Vorstellungen zu animieren. Die selbstgewählte Vorstellung ist immer die wirksamste; und je phantastischer sie ist, umso wirksamer pflegt sie zu sein. Besonders bewährt hat sich uns aber eine solche Erfindung einer Patientin – die Vorstellung nämlich, sie liege auf einer blumigen Sommerwiese und blicke zum tiefblauen Himmel hinauf, auf dem die Wolken stetig ihres Weges ziehen" (Frankl in Reddemann, *Imagination als heilsame Kraft* 56).

12 Cf. Reddemann, *Imagination als heilsame Kraft* 53.

13 Cf. Kosslyn et al., "Topographical representations of mental images in primary visual cortex". See also Stein 129; Hüther, *Die Macht der inneren Bilder*; and Kosslyn, Ganis and Thompson, "Neural

about a situation and on actions that we consequently take, as experiences that we make in the actual outside world. I want to propose exercises such as the ones conjuring up inner safe spaces (which may or may not take the form of a garden) as internal heterotopic spaces. I furthermore want to propose that Robert Duncan's poem "Often I am Permitted to Return to a Meadow" conjures up exactly such an internal heterotopic space, a space of well-being that is both a place "made-up by the mind" and "a place of first permission".

The poet Robert Duncan is best known for his work dating from the 1950s and 1960s, most notably the poetry collections *The Opening of the Field* (1960), which opens with the aforementioned "Often I am Permitted to Return to a Meadow", and *Bending the Bow* (1968). Part of the Berkeley Renaissance as well as the San Francisco Renaissance, he is also discussed in the context of the Black Mountain group of poets around Charles Olson, who invited Duncan to teach at Black Mountain College for two terms in the mid 1950s (cf. Jarnot). Raised by theosophist foster parents, Duncan's poetry is steeped in mysticism while also being concerned with the legacy of modernism (he wrote a series of essays which together form a book on the poetry of H.D.) and with emerging postmodernist questionings of poetics and form (cf. Johnson). Duncan became aware of his own homosexuality while studying at the University of California at Berkeley in the 1930s; he was discharged from the U.S. army in 1941 on grounds of his homosexuality, which amounted to a psychiatric discharge at the time (cf. Jarnot). In 1944, Duncan published an essay titled "The Homosexual in Society" in the journal *Politics*, in which he revealed that he himself was gay. In the essay, Duncan places the struggles of homosexuals alongside the struggles of other minoritarian groups such as Jews and African Americans, demanding recognition by the majoritarian culture in terms of a common shared humanity while at the same time attacking separatism in what he refers to as "the homosexual cult"; his vision is one of "a devotion to human freedom" and a disowning of "*all* the special groups (nations, churches, sexes, races)" ("The Homosexual in Society" 11). The essay was reprinted with an introduction and afterword by Duncan himself in 1959, in which he states that the 1944 essay amounted, as far as he knew, to "being the first discussion of homosexuality which included the frank avowal that the author was himself involved" ("The Homosexual in Society" 5). The publication of the essay was not to be without consequences for Duncan. The editor of the *Kenyon Review*, for instance, immediately withdrew a poem by Duncan which had already been accepted for publication (cf. Johnson 3-4). Duncan summarizes the central concerns of the 1944 essay in 1959 as follows:

Foundations of Imagery" for a further exploration of the topic from a neuroscientific point of view.

"[T]he inspiration of the essay was toward something else, a public trust, larger and more demanding than the respect of friends. To be respected as a member of the political community for what one knew in one's heart to be respectable! To insist, not upon tolerance for a divergent sexual practice but, upon concern for the virtues of a homosexual relationship! I was, I think, at the threshold of a critical concept: sexual love wherever it was taught and practiced was a single adventure, that troubadours sang in romance, that poets have kept as a traditional adherence, and that novelists have given scope. Love is dishonoured where sexual love between those of the same sex is despised; and where love is dishonoured there is no public trust. It is my sense that the fulfilment of man's nature lies in the creation of that trust; and where the distrusting imagination sets up an image of 'self' against the desire for unity and mutual sympathy, the state called 'Hell' is created." ("The Homosexual in Society" 12)

If Duncan's vision includes a world in which the heterosexual majority is able to recognize and value same-sex love for what, he says, it actually is, namely love itself regardless of its particular human guise, this is of course a vision that he will find far from realized in the United States of both 1944 and 1959. Duncan himself found enduring love when he met the painter Jess Collins in 1950; the two set up a common household in 1951, and their relationship lasted until Duncan's death in 1982 (cf. Jarnot). Even teaching at Black Mountain College, Duncan and Jess never concealed their relationship: as Lisa Jarnot relates, "the couple's living space became a salon", and for proto-gay students such as Tom Field, "their openly homosexual partnership was a source of wonder" (Jarnot 152).[14] But even living openly in a relationship with his partner and being surrounded by a community

14 Not every poet who earned part of his livelihood by teaching was in the position to be as out as Duncan was able to be at the progressive Black Mountain College as well as later at the liberal New College of California. Duncan records the case of an "eminent poet" whom he had asked in 1945 if he (Duncan) could "attempt an essay on his [the poet's] work in the light of my concept that his language had been diverted to conceal the nature of his sexual life and that because he could never write directly he had failed to come to grips with immediacies of feeling" ("The Homosexual in Society" 14-15). To this daring request, Duncan reports, the unnamed eminent poet (possibly W.H. Auden?) replied:

"... I am very sorry but I must ask you not to publish the essay you propose. I'm sure you will realise that the better the essay you write, the more it will be reviewed and talked about, and the more likelihood there would be of it being brought publicly to my attention in a way where to ignore it would be taken as an admission of guilt.

As you may know, I earn a good part of my livelihood by teaching, and in that profession one is particularly vulnerable. Further, both as a writer and as a human being, the occasion may always arise, particularly in these times, when it becomes one's duty to take a stand on the unpopular side of some issue. Should that ever occur, your essay would be a very convenient red-herring for one's opponents. (Think of what happened to Bertrand Russell in New York).

of artistic peers, some of whom were homosexual themselves, Duncan admits to feelings of daunting and stress when making new acquaintances and friends, of whose acceptance of his homosexuality he could never be certain. In his afterword to "The Homosexual in Society", he reviews what has changed for him by 1959 (as opposed to 1944) and what apprehensions have remained the same:

> "In the fifteen years since the writing of "The Homosexual in Society," my circum-stances have much changed. Life and my work have brought me new friends, where the community of values is more openly defined, and even, in recent years, a companion who shares my concern for a creative life. Distressed where I have been distressed and happy where I have been happy, their sympathy has ren-dered absurd whatever apprehension I had concerning the high moral resolve and radical reformation of character needed before I would secure recognition and understanding. It is a kinship of concern and a sharing of experience that draws us together.
>
> The phantasmic idea of a 'society' that was somehow hostile, the sinister affiliation offered by groups with whom I had no common ground other than the specialized sexuality, the anxiety concerning the good opinion of the community – all this sense of danger remains, for I am not a person of reserved nature; and con-ventional morality, having its roots in Judaic tribal law and not in philosophy, holds homosexual relations to be a crime. Love, art and thought are all social goods for me; and often I must come, where I would begin a friendship, to old moments of trial and doubt when I must deliver account of my sexual nature that there be no mistake in our trust." ("The Homosexual in Society" 11-12)

While the circumstances of his private and home life have indeed changed, clearly the apprehensions surrounding the act of coming out to a new potential friend have not lessened for Duncan (who seems to consider himself an extrovert who enjoys and thrives on making new acquaintances) in those fifteen years, nor have the feelings of distress changed that he experiences around the fact that he finds himself still living in a "somewhat hostile" society which regards "homosexual relations" as criminal acts. I propose that the creation and existence of an inner safe space, such as the one provided by the vista opened up by Duncan's poem "Often I am Permitted to Return to a Meadow", has the propensity to work as a counterbalance to these feelings of distress for Duncan, and can work as a coun-terbalance to similar feelings of distress as well for the reader encountering Dun-can's work.

I hope you will believe me when I say that for myself personally I wish I could let you publish it, and that anyway I hope that other essays will be as good as you would like them to be." ("The Homosexual in Society" 15)

The speaker of Duncan's poem "Often I am Permitted to Return to a Meadow" invents and makes use of an inner space which takes the form of a meadow, an "eternal pasture" (l. 4), and later the form of a hall, an interior space of subject-hood, "Wherefrom fall all architectures I am" (l. 8). It is an imaginary space, a space that is "a property of the mind" (l. 20), and a place that "certain bounds hold against chaos" (l. 21) – thus it is a nurturing space, a counterbalancing space to the chaos wreaked by the outside world, which I take to mean the psychic threat experienced by the subject who does not fit into the order imposed on him by this outside world. It is also "a place of first permission" (l. 22), an important notion for any poet because the place of permission is the place where creativity is allowed to unfold, and it is an important notion for the queer poet, because it is a place where the subjectivity of a queer sexual self is allowed to unfold. It is also an "everlasting omen of what is" (l. 23), which I take to mean a revelation of a greater mysterious order beyond or below the ordinary meaning of things.

"Often I am Permitted to Return to a Meadow

as if it were a scene made-up by the mind,
that is not mine, but is a made place,

that is mine, it is so near to the heart,
an eternal pasture folded in all thought
so that there is a hall therein

that is a made place, created by light
wherefrom the shadows that are forms fall.

Wherefrom fall all architectures I am
I say are likenesses of the First Beloved
whose flowers are flames lit to the Lady.

She it is Queen Under The Hill
whose hosts are a disturbance of words within words
that is a field folded.

It is only a dream of the grass blowing
east against the source of the sun
in an hour before the sun's going down

whose secret we see in a children's game
of ring a round of roses told.

Often I am permitted to return to a meadow
as if it were a given property of the mind
that certain bounds hold against chaos,

that is a place of first permission,
everlasting omen of what is."

The imaginary space of the meadow is for Duncan's speaker both "mine" (l. 3) and "not mine" (l. 2), a space originating from an elsewhere and yet a place that feels like it is his to inhabit.[15] He is "permitted to return" to it, as the poem's title states: It appears to him as if he had found this place, not made it up himself, as if it were coming from an elsewhere, possibly what C.G. Jung would call the Collective Unconscious; it feels to him somehow pre-cognitive, revealed to him not from the conscious but his unconscious mind, as if found in a hypnotic state of trance. Both the meadow and the hall share these traits of being imaginary, yet somehow archetypal, "made" places (l. 2 and 6), and both provide the speaker with a safe inner space, an internal heterotopia.

A number of characters make their appearance in this imaginary scene, some of them reminiscent of Reddemann's inner helpers: the "First Beloved" (l. 9), the "Lady" (l. 10), the "Queen Under The Hill" (l. 11) and finally, children playing a game "of ring a round of roses" (l. 18). Duncan works with archetypal figures, in fact mere sketches of figures, and leaves it up to the reader to imaginatively fill these sketches.[16] In a lecture given at the Poetry Center in San Francisco in 1959, Duncan explains that for him, the poem works as a kind of tapestry, a weaving of

---

15 As line 2 indicates, the speaker is allowed to return to this meadow "*as if* it were a scene made-up by the mind" (italics by S.J.). The simile indicates, I think, that this place feels more real to the speaker than a mere invention of the mind, and yet it clearly is a scene conjured up by the mind (of the poet). What is more, lines between dream and reality blur for the speaker; the meadow is "only a dream of the grass blowing" (l. 14), a nod to Whitman's *Leaves of Grass* and also a citation of a much earlier image for the transient. It is worth mentioning that Duncan is drawing on some of his own childhood dream material in this poem. As Mark Andrew Johnson relates, Duncan "had a recurring 'Atlantis dream' as a child: the dream's motifs – of a hill, a field that seemed alive, a circle of children dancing in the field, an underground cavern, a stone chair, a flood – recur in much of Duncan's poetry, most notably in *The Opening of the Field*" (2). Elsewhere Duncan stresses the importance he places on his own earliest memories: "I have consciously proposed that I would keep alive and at work as primaries earliest experiences and structures. I would not reprove the child in me in my also being adolescent, in my also being gown-up. Hence I seek out and fortify even embarrassing sentiments – sentimentalities they can be seen to be by those critics who have put away childish things" (qtd. in Johnson 10).

16 In fact, as Duncan relates, as soon as the line is written, he himself becomes a reader of the work, joining us in filling in the sketches conjured up by the words (Cf. Duncan, "Reading").

sorts, where one thread rises to the surface, followed by another, then another.[17] For different readers, different threads rise to the surface at different points in Duncan's poem. Virtually all critics read the hall "that is a made place, created by light / wherefrom the shadows that are forms fall" (l. 6-7) as an allusion to Plato's Allegory of the Cave from the *Republic*, which argues that the "shadows" are only a surface reality perceived by us; but hidden underneath this surface reality lies a realm of ideas or forms that is not accessible to us, governed by a mysterious, hidden order (the soul of the world) that we do not have access to but that lies underneath everything. From this hall, the poem goes on, "fall all architectures I am" – the speaker's subjectivity – which are "likenesses of the First Beloved" (l. 9). Here different readers see different personages in Duncan's archetypal figure. For me, the "First Beloved" signifies one's mother, foundation of one's subjectivity in psychoanalytic terms; this is also Donald K. Gutierrez' reading of this scene (cf. Gutierrez). Yet Jeanne Heuving, for whom the Platonic thread has not yet ended, reads the First Beloved as "the beloved in Diotima's speech in Plato's *Symposium*" (Heuving 128); and Duncan himself, reading his own poem, sees another thread already emerging, this time a biblical thread: for him, the First Beloved is Adam, the first human in Genesis (cf. "Reading"). The following line with its image of "flames lit to the Lady" follows up on this thread, conjuring up the image of a scene of prayer before the figure of the "Lady" who is read by Gutierrez (and Duncan himself) as the Virgin Mary, a reading with which I concur. The "Lady" morphs in line 11 into the archetype of the "Queen Under The Hill", which to me brings up another thread, the one of fairy tales and folklore.[18] I read the Queen Under The Hill as the fairy queen, as does Duncan himself (cf. "Reading"), whereas Gutierrez perceives in the Queen Under The Hill "a primeval Earth Mother or pre-Christian Mediterranean matriarch as well as a dead female personage" (cf. Gutierrez), and Heuving sees in her Kore and Persephone, queen of the Greek underworld, and the emerging field here as related to "Eleusinian mysteries" (cf. Heuving 129). Line 17 and 18 see children playing a game of "ring a round of roses". Mark Andrew Johnson convincingly reads the allusion to the nursery rhyme, "the medieval chant to ward off the plague inverted to a game", as a central metaphor for Duncan: "blossoming is followed by decay, destruction inevitably follows upon realization and

---

17 This is a different way of describing the effect created by what Duncan terms elsewhere his idea of his poetry as collage art. As Johnson notes, "Duncan has spoken of his poetry as a collage in which a number of new elements enter the poem to create new complexes of meaning" (16). And Jeanne Heuving estimates that with *The Opening of the Field*, Duncan "creates a poetry of process and collage – a writing that allows for an increment of association, both temporally and spatially" (111). Duncan's partner Jess preferred to work with collage as well in his visual art. With his poetics of the poem as collage art, Duncan is also heir to modernists such as Ezra Pound.

18 Duncan himself values the cultural archive of fairy tales, regarding them as "the immortal residue of the spirit that seeks to find its place in the hearts of each generation" (qtd. in Johnson 11).

is superseded in its turn by renewal. Dust returns to dust inevitably, but this is a fertilizing decay from which new life, phoenixlike, arises" (65). This is the secret revealed in the children's game – death as part of a life-affirming circle of destruction and (creative) renewal. The poem itself seems to operate in mythic time, somehow outside of real time and space, just like the meadow, an "eternal pasture folded in all thought" (l. 4), seems to exist outside of time itself. Indeed, it is the poem itself that is "a field folded" (l. 13). As the central stanza of the poem (literally the symmetrical centre of the poem) reveals, this is the field created by words, and by the hidden meaning behind words and behind the associations evoked by the combination of words that make up poetry itself (the "disturbance of words within words" as line 12 has it). The archetypal Queen Under The Hill functions then as a source of creativity itself, helper of the poet; it is her hosts which are "a disturbance of words within words / that is a field folded" (l. 12-13).

In his creative writing workshops at Black Mountain College, Duncan had his students experiment with the various building blocks that make up a poem, revealing some of his notions about his own poetics. These building blocks consisted of vowels, consonants and rhyme (which he discusses in his notebooks in terms of the "tone" of a poem), as well as syllable, word, phrase, line, paragraph and sentence (which he discusses in terms of "movement"); together they contribute to the larger "form" a poem may take; they also relate to the artist's concerns addressed in the poem (cf. Jarnot 155). Together these building blocks, or objects as Charles Olson would call them, make up the field of the poem. Duncan addresses his idea of composition by field in the introduction to *Bending the Bow*: "The artist, after Dante's poetics, works with all parts of the poem as *polysemous*, taking each thing of the composition as generative of meaning, a response to and a contribution to the building form" (ix). As Michael Davidson explains, this poetics "– what Charles Olson called 'open field' or 'projective' verse – is indebted to modernists like Pound and Williams and was forged among conversations with Duncan's contemporaries: Olson, Robert Creeley, Denise Levertov, Robin Blaser, and Jack Spicer" (xv). Importantly, it employs a kinaesthetic aesthetics, stressing the role of the body in the creation and reception of poetry. As Davidson says, "'Open form' casts poetry as a participant in, not a container for, realms of value that lie obscured from view. Where Pound hoped to erect a dynastic edifice against social decay or Eliot sought an objective correlative against solipsism, Duncan's peers emphasized the role of the body, perception, and cognition in reengaging art with the human and natural world" (xv). Duncan especially develops his ideas on rhyme further. As he describes in an interview, "[r]ime, or meter, which is the same word in English, is simply a sense of measure being present. And while measure may be like a ruler – 12 marks, and all of them equal – a measure actually means you're feeling something did happen before or did not happen before. Any sense of resemblance or any sense of disresemblance indicates the presence of rime" (qtd.

in Johnson 67). Johnson takes this to mean that for Duncan, rhyme "is not only a matter of sound, but also of image, emotion, and thought" (67), that is of any pattern that reoccurs in the poem. In my opinion, these recurring patterns – of alliteration, of internal rhyme, of the repetition of words, phrases and images, of a semi-regular meter and linebreaks that are modelled organically (as Charles Olson proposed) on the length of the human breath – add to the hypnotic, tranceinducing quality of "Often I Am Permitted to Return to a Meadow": patterns create rhythms, and rhythms form the basic structuring units of human experience in time.[19] There is a mysterious meaning and order beneath everything in the world, the poem seems to imply, reassuringly, I find. Whether we regard this mysterious order as being orchestrated by a Platonic world soul, by God the Creator of the Old Testament or by the archetypal figures of Jung's Collective Unconscious is a matter of preference or personal belief. All names ultimately try to describe the numinous, Mystery itself, which holds everything together. Duncan himself reflects on his relationship to the numinous in one of his essays on the poet H.D.: "My eyes have seen the veil, the double or triple moving depths of bead curtain, that in my work may still be my fascination with the movement of meaning beyond or behind meaning, of shifting vowels and consonants – beads of sound, of separate strands that convey the feeling of one weave ... There is something about looking behind things. There is the fact that I am not an occultist or a mystic but a poet, a maker-up of things" (qtd. in Johnson 1). Duncan the poet is not just the one who sees the veil and sees behind things, and then becomes the maker-up of things. He is also the one who finds things. Like this space of the meadow, the field, the pasture or the garden that he finds – an internal heterotopia – in the space of his own (subconscious) mind.

Creating Queer Spaces and a Space to Belong: San Francisco, the Emergence of the Castro as a Queer Space and Harvey Milk's Legacy of Hope

The following subchapter traces the creation and development of queer urban space in the city of San Francisco from the beginning of the twentieth century to the 1970s, focussing on the emergence of the Castro as a (mostly) gay neighbourhood in the 1970s and the figure of the "unofficial mayor of Castro Street", Harvey Milk, the first openly gay official elected to public office in the U.S., as a figure who was instrumental in shaping the Castro into the queer urban space it would eventually become (Shilts 87). Prior to his assassination, Milk had become an important leader in the emerging gay rights movement. As this chapter is going to argue,

---

19 For an audio sample, cf. Duncan's rendition of this poem in his reading at the Poetry Center.

someone like Harvey Milk could only achieve what he did achieve by being part of and operating from an emerging queer space like the Castro; at the same time he was an instrumental figure in the shaping of the Castro as a queer space. Milk's vision, which is laid out in his archive of speeches, includes a society where discrimination against LGBTQ people has ended. At the same time, an ethical concern, the trope of hope emerges as a central concept in his speeches, a structure of feeling essential for resilience which I am going to analyse in terms of José Esteban Muñoz' utilization of Ernst Bloch's concept of educated hope in *Cruising Utopia*.

San Francisco, and the Castro and its adjacent neighbourhoods, have served for the last forty years as 'home' spaces – as safe spaces and as a space to belong – for its queer residents and visitors. For Cecile Sandten and Kathy-Ann Tan, the "notion of home [...] commonly entails four dimensions: 1. a spatial dimension – with reference to real places, landscapes, towns, cities, regions, countries or nations; 2. a temporal dimension – since often a particular time period or a period of time decides whether a person will feel at home after having been relocated; 3. a social dimension – home is where the family is and where friends are"; and finally, "4. a cultural dimension – home is where familiar traditions and customs are maintained, where 'local' delicacies are eaten and local dialects spoken" (3). To these I would add the following three affective dimensions: 1. a sense of belonging – to a place and to a community of others living in the same space with whom one shares past and present experiences and thus a sense of community and a sense of connection; 2. a sense of attachment to a place, 'topophilia' – the love of a place; 3. a sense of safety, that is on the one hand a sense of physical safety connected to a space where one feels one is (relatively) free from attack, violation and discrimination, but also a sense of safety connected to a space where one feels at ease, comfortable and comforted, secure and held. John D'Emilio delineates the significance San Francisco and the Bay Area held for LGBTQ people already in 1981:

> "For gay men and for lesbians, San Francisco has become akin to what Rome is for Catholics: A lot of us live there and many more have made the pilgrimage. The gay male subculture in San Francisco is more visible and more complex than in any other city; lesbians in the Bay Area also sustain more institutions than their sisters elsewhere. San Francisco is one of the very few places where lesbians are residentially concentrated enough to be visible. For gay men and for lesbians, San Francisco is a special place." ("Gay Politics and Community" 456)

The feeling conveyed by D'Emilio of San Francisco as a gay and lesbian (and by now also bisexual, transgender and queer) "mecca" or home still holds true even thirty-five years later (Stryker and Van Buskirk 4).[20] The Castro may have become more gentrified and the geography of some of the predominantly queer neigh-bourhoods may have shifted a couple of blocks since its heyday in the late 1970s and early 1980s; but the significance of the city and its queer neighbourhoods for the LGBTQ imaginary has not changed. There is still a giant rainbow flag flying over the corner of Castro and Market Streets (now Harvey Milk Plaza), a symbol invented by Gilbert Baker for the 1978 San Francisco Gay Freedom Day Parade (cf. Wright 173). I regard the creation of queer urban spaces such as the Castro and its adjoining neighbourhoods (and the participation of its queer inhabitants and visitors in marches such as the annual Pride Parade which momentarily extends the boundaries of openly queer space), the moving to a queer urban space and the visiting of a queer urban space as spatial resilience strategies for queer sub-jects that can help foster feelings of safety, connection and a sense of belonging. Equally, I argue, even forty years after Milk's death, hope still emanates from these queer urban spaces and propels forward the communities who constantly remake them.[21]

Since the 1970s, the Castro has become known as *the* example of queer urban space in San Francisco *par excellence*, but pockets of queer space already existed earlier dispersed among the city as well. The early 1900s saw the Barbary Coast, a waterfront neighbourhood of this old port city and "old San Francisco's infamous saloon and brothel district" (Stryker and Van Buskirk 18) in what was to become later North Beach, as a male-male sociosexual meeting space. As Les Wright relates, "the Dash, a dance hall and saloon which featured female impersonation, became San Francisco's first identifiably 'gay' bar, opening and closing its doors in 1908" (168). Various cruising sites existed for men along the Embarcardero and the new public transit system along Market Street; public bath houses such as the now defunct Sutro Baths near Ocean Beach and later the Third Street Baths and public toilets also served as potential sites for male-male sexual encounters (cf. Wright 169-170). Finnochio's, a popular gay bar during the 1930s and 1940s, opened during the age of Prohibition as a speakeasy in 1929, featuring female impersonators (Wright 171). As Susan Stryker and Jim Van Buskirk point out, the countercultural

---

20 Susan Stryker and Jim Van Buskirk rightly point out that "[t]here has never been one monolithic queer community in the Bay Area. Rather, there is a bewildering variety of intersecting subcul-tural scenes, separatist enclaves, political factions, ethnicities, genders, and classes"; still, they suggest, "living in the same geographical location creates a set of overlapping experiences with-in local queer cultures" (*Gay by the Bay* 5).

21 In a similar vein, John D'Emilio, writing about "Gay Politics and Community in San Francisco since World War II", concludes that by the early 1980s, "[w]hat was once a secret, despised identity had become the basis for an urban community, sharing many of the characteristics of more tradi-tional ethnic groupings. And the community had, in turn, spawned a vigorous politics that gave it unusual national influence and served as a beacon of hope for others" (473).

space of the speakeasies allowed many "middle-class white people [to] first [mix] socially with people from different economic and ethnic backgrounds", prefiguring the notion of queer culture as part of a larger countercultural social movement (26). Other popular meeting places in North Beach included Mona's, "the city's first lesbian establishment", as well as the Black Cat Café, "which would become an icon of San Francisco bohemian culture in the postwar years" (Stryker and Van Buskirk 23). Different bars catered to different kinds of audiences. Furthermore, private spaces existed where LGBTQ people could meet and socialize. Stryker and Van Buskirk point for example to the circle of friends around poet Elsa Gidlow, who came to San Francisco in 1926 and moved to a cabin in nearby Marin County in 1940 (21-23). They also point out that due to the "racial segregation of many public places", bar culture was "more important for white lesbians and gays than it [was] for African Americans and other people of color. The first black-owned and oriented gay bar in the city, the Big Glass on Fillmore, did not open until 1964" (24).

The Second World War proved to have a great impact on the gay and lesbian population of San Francisco. The war uprooted millions of young men, who suddenly found themselves away from their families in homosocial environments. At the same time, millions of women took up previously male labour, often also in homosocial environments. This opened up the possibilities of same-sex sexual and romantic encounters for many who felt themselves drawn to members of their own sex. As John D'Emilio summarizes his own research and the research of Allan Bérubé, who has worked on the experience of lesbian and gay GIs in World War II, "[f]or some it simply confirmed a way of living and loving they had already chosen. For others, it gave meaning to little-understood desires, introduced them to men and women with similar feelings [...]. For still others, the sexual underside of the war years provided experiences they otherwise would not have had and that they left behind when the war ended" ("Gay Politics" 459). San Francisco served as a major point of departure for the Pacific theatre of war; the city was also a point of return for members of the U.S. military who had been dishonourably discharged on account of their homosexuality, and many gay and lesbian service members, regardless of whether they had been discharged honourably or dishonourably, were reluctant to return to their places of origin and chose instead to remain in the Bay Area after the end of the war (cf. Wright 173). The postwar period, then, saw American culture and politics turn increasingly conservative. Police raids on gay bars intensified, and a rescripted California Penal Code redefined its notion of what constituted sodomy, proscribing all male-male sexual acts (cf. Stryker and Van Buskirk 33; and Wright 173). D'Emilio convincingly argues that this renewed conservatism helped forge a group consciousness among those persecuted in postwar America as 'sexual deviants': "If the war years allowed large numbers of lesbians and gay men to discover their sexuality and each other, repression in the postwar decade heightened consciousness of belonging to a group. [...] The tightening web of oppression in McCarthy's America helped to create the minority it was meant to isolate" ("Gay Politics" 459).

One reaction on the part of homosexual men and women to this renewed conservatism was the formation of homophile groups, i.e. groups that sought to influence public opinion and the opinion of members of the establishment such as doctors, psychologists and lawyers on the subject of homosexuality (cf. D'Emilio, *Sexual Politics*). They also provided meeting spaces for homosexual men and women and published magazines which were distributed nationwide. The most prominent of the homophile organizations, the Mattachine Society, was founded in 1950 by Harry Hay and others in Los Angeles; Hay had been a member of the Communist party who had grown impatient with the homophobia he perceived in the Communist movement (cf. D'Emilio, *Sexual Politics*). However, the Mattachine Society soon split from its more radical founders and dedicated itself to a slow-paced, less radical intervention in American society. The headquarters of the society, which had chapters all over the U.S., moved to San Francisco in 1957 (cf. Stryker and Van Buskirk 41). Also in San Francisco in 1955, Phyllis Lyon and Del Martin and others founded the Daughters of Bilitis, a lesbian political organization which published its own magazine, *The Ladder*, likewise extending its sphere of influence beyond San Francisco alone (cf. Stryker and van Buskirk 41). The early 1960s saw the foundation of the Society for Individual Rights, another homophile organization keen on working towards providing social space for gays and lesbians, opening in 1966 the first gay community centre in the U.S. (Cf. D'Emilio, *Sexual Politics* 190-191). D'Emilio emphasizes the lasting legacy of the Mattachine Society and other homophile groups who laid the ground for what would follow in terms of gay liberation in the 1970s: "Mass movements for social change do not spring into existence fully grown, nor do institutional arrangements and cultural beliefs generally alter as suddenly as those that pertained to homoeroticism in the 1970s"; he contends that "the relative ease with which gay liberationists accumulated victories can only be explained by the persistent, plodding work of the activists who preceded them" (*Sexual Politics* 240).

The 1950s also saw the development of a literary and countercultural bohemia in San Francisco's North Beach. The poets of the San Francisco Renaissance, whose three most prominent authors, Robert Duncan, Jack Spicer and Robin Blaser, were all gay, gathered in North Beach cafés and houses, often with a coterie of younger writers. D'Emilio quotes a conversation he had with poet Stan Persky, who describes his experiences as a young poet and the community provided for him by Duncan, Spicer and Blaser in the 1950s:

> "[They] not only kept alive a public homosexual presence in their own work, but kept alive a tradition, teaching us about Rimbaud, Crane, and Lorca. ... They *carried* into the contemporary culture the tradition of homosexual art and were sen-

sitive to the work of European homosexual contemporaries. There was a conscious searching out, in fraternity, of homosexual writers. Thus, in my 'training' as a poet, homoerotic novels would be recommended to me. ... This was at a time when the English departments of the country told us that Walt Whitman *wasn't* gay." (qtd. in *Sexual Politics* 180)

The North Beach artistic community also temporarily included queer beat poets such as Allen Ginsberg, whose famous Six Gallery reading of *Howl* in 1955 marked the starting point of a much more public presence of openly queer work. Ginsberg's *Howl* was the subject of an obscenity trial for its publisher Lawrence Ferlinghetti, the owner of City Lights bookstore (located also in North Beach), and as such gained more public attention and sold more copies than it might otherwise have done. This is remarkable from a queer point of view as, as D'Emilio points out, *Howl* did not shy away from openly acknowledging male homosexuality: "In describing gay male sex as joyous, delightful, and even holy, Ginsberg [turned] American values inside out" ("Gay Politics" 462).

Police raids on gay bars in San Francisco continued during the 1950s and 1960s; the largest bar raid saw police arrest 81 men and 14 women in 1961 (Stryker and van Buskirk 43). Also in 1961 it came to light that police officers were regularly taking bribes from gay bar owners to prevent their bars from being raided. This scandal led to the formation of the Tavern Guild, a business association of owners of gay bars who sought to defend their clients' rights to frequent the bars without police harassment (cf. Stryker and Van Buskirk 44). In San Francisco, as opposed to other cities of the U.S., from the bar culture itself, political activism was thus emerging. Another instance of political consciousness raising and cultural critique was to be found in the weekly operatic revues put on by José Sarria, a waiter and drag performer at the Black Cat Café. Sarria's disidentificatory performances were testament to what José Esteban Muñoz in his book *Disidentifications* describes as the worldmaking power of queer performance art.[22] D'Emilio describes one such performance:

> "Sarria's act departed dramatically from the female impersonation found in some gay male circles. Donning an outlandish hat to sing *Carmen*, for example, he reworked the script for his audience and its milieu. The heroine would be in Union Square, a gay cruising area in downtown San Francisco, scurrying through the bushes in an attempt to avoid capture by the vice squad. An overflow crowd of 200 or more cheered Carmen's escape." (*Sexual Politics* 187)

---

22 For a further elaboration of Muñoz' concept of disidentification cf. the narrative strategies chapter.

In celebrating Sarria's escape, as Carmen, from the vice squad, audience members were undoubtedly celebrating their own imaginary triumph over persecution and harassment. Sarria also used the Black Cat's communal space as a space to evoke an atmosphere of hope, the kind of hope Harvey Milk would later try to evoke in his queer audience by means of his political speeches. D'Emilio quotes George Mendenhall, an audience member and pre-Stonewall activist, who describes the kind of effect Sarria's usual, non-satirical ending of his show had on its audience:

> "[A]t the end … of every concert, he would have everybody in the room stand, and we would put our arms around each other and sing, 'God Save Us Nelly Queens.' It sounds silly, but if you lived at that time and had the oppression coming down from the police department and from society, … to be able to put your arms around other gay men and sing 'God Save Us Nelly Queens' … We were not really saying 'God Save Us Nelly Queens.' We were saying 'We have our rights too.'" ("Gay Politics" 463)

Presumably, this was exactly the kind of effect Sarria, the artist/activist, was hoping for, as, foreshadowing once more Harvey Milk, Sarria decided to run as city supervisor in a 1961 election – not in an effort to win (he collected a respectable 5,600 votes), but as he himself put it, in an effort to try to "prove to my gay audience [...] that I had the right, being as notorious and gay as I was, to run for public office, because people in those days didn't believe you had rights" (qtd. in D'Emilio, "Gay Politics" 464). A broader allegiance between activists from the homophile movements and members of various liberal Protestant churches was finally to take place in 1964 with the foundation of the Council on Religion and the Homosexual, an organization working towards eliminating homophobia from mainstream churches (cf. Stryker and Van Buskirk 41). Its fundraiser, a New Year's Day Mardi Gras Ball which was once again raided by police, exposed the attending liberal heterosexual ministers for the first time to the kind of harassment prevalent at gay venues, helping raise consciousness for the social legitimacy of anti-homophobic activism also for allies of the homophile movement.

To sum up, apart from the private homes of its LGBTQ residents, queer spaces existed in San Francisco prior to the 1970s for the most part in a number of bars, as well as in the meeting spaces of a number of homophile groups. A number of neighbourhoods, such as for instance North Beach, featured several gay or gay-friendly venues. However, no one neighbourhood existed that could be understood to appear as predominantly gay or queer as was to be the case with the Castro from the 1970s onwards. Queer space, prior to the 1970s, was always precarious space, and its visitors open to attacks from the police, arsonists and murderers; still, for the people frequenting these spaces, they provided a place to encounter likeminded folks, be that in a bar or in known cruising grounds, and later also a space to seek to engage in politics and community building – mostly at first as a result of trying to curb the ongoing harassment by police and in an effort to make these spaces safe for LGBTQ people.

With the advent of the 1970s, the geography of queer San Francisco significantly changed. City neighbourhoods like the formerly working-class Castro were emptying out due to its residents' moving to the suburbs. The countercultural Beat movement had been replaced by the late 1960s by the hippie movement, centred around Haight-Ashbury, and gay hippies were being drawn to the neighbouring Castro due to both the cheap living spaces as well as the existence of a number of gay bars in the vicinity; the summer of 1971 then saw an additional four gay bars opening in the Castro itself (cf. Stryker and Van Buskirk 64). Wright describes the Castro as "a roughly 34-block neighborhood in the geographic center of San Francisco. Originally known as Eureka Valley and formally demarcated by the Most Holy Redeemer Church parish boundaries of Sixteenth, Dolores, Twenty-Second and Douglass Streets, the Castro took its name from the movie palace which anchored the commercial corridor of Castro and upper Market Streets" (181). A number of gay newspapers began publishing in the early 1970s, such as *Gay Sunshine*, the *Bay Area Reporter* and *The San Francisco Sentinel*, contributing to the creation also of an imagined community of LGBTQ San Franciscans; further gay businesses were opening, such as baths, clubs, bookstores, gyms and coffee houses (cf. Stryker and Van Buskirk 71). San Francisco was touted as a gay capital by mainstream U.S. magazines, thus drawing a growing number of gays and lesbians from all over the U.S. to the Bay Area (D'Emilio, "Gay Politics" 467). The Castro also saw the emergence of a new type of fashion and grooming style, what became later known as the Castro clone. The fashion style of blue jeans combined with tight-fitting tee shirts or flannel shirts and hooded sweatshirts was born, as Randy Shilts describes, "out of the J.C. Funky secondhand clothing store"; the fashion was both affordable and "proved functional for the city's Mediterranean climate", and it also "matched a new gay attitude. The clothing spoke of strength and working-class machismo, not the gentle bourgoise effetism of generations past" (86). However, 1970s Castro was also not without its problems: both racism and sexism remained a troublesome issue. Wright relates how in bars, "[p]ractices such as subjecting black patrons to the three-photo ID policy while ignoring it for white patrons or point blank refusing entrance to women and mixed groups of gay men and women (lesbian or straight), were prevalent" (183). If the Castro was a space that was predominantly male, lesbian space was primarily aligned in 1970s San Francisco with women's separatist spaces in, for instance, the Mission. Also, homophobic crime was still happening in San Francisco. By 1976, gay murders "accounted for 10 percent of the city's homicide rate" while, throughout the 1970s, "[g]ay businesses were frequent targets of bombings and arson" (Stryker and Van Buskirk 77). Still, a new phenomenon existed from the 1970s onwards: the development of gay residential neighbourhoods as home spaces and a space to belong for queer individuals. An early article appearing in the *SF Free Press* in January 1970, Carl Wittmann's "Refugees from Amerika: A Gay Manifesto", already hails San Francisco as "a refugee camp" for homosexuals (qtd. in Wright 179). The metaphor of the refugee camp expresses the feelings attached to a prior experience of space elsewhere: the non-existence of queer space; the demarcation of heteronormative space, which is established by acts of ostracism and violence, creating feelings of non-belonging in queer individuals and of being under attack, or creating the pressure of having to hide one's sexuality; this is in opposition to the feelings expressed around queer space in San Francisco: feelings of safety, and the expression of hoping to find or create a queer home space. D'Emilio astutetely summarizes the changes taking place in 1970s San Francisco as pertains to queer space:

> "By the mid-1970s San Francisco had become, in comparison to the rest of the country, a liberated zone for lesbians and gay men. It had the largest number and widest variety of organizations and institutions. An enormous in-migration had created a new social phenomenon, residential areas that were visibly gay in composition: Duboce Triangle, Noe Valley, and the Upper Mission for lesbians; the Haight, Folsom, and above all the Castro for gay men. Geographic concentration offered the opportunity for local political power that invisibility precluded." ("Gay Politics" 468)

And local political power for San Francisco's gay community was connected in the mid to late 1970s first and foremost with the name of Harvey Milk.

Milk had been one of the gay hippies moving to San Francisco in the early 1970s, leaving behind the mundane existence of a Wall Street financial analyst in New York City. He moved to the Castro in 1972, opening up a camera store at 575 Castro Street with his boyfriend Scott Smith (Shilts 65). He had lived in San Francisco briefly two years earlier and had now, in his early forties, decided to move there permanently. Randy Shilts describes Castro Camera in his biography of Harvey Milk, *The Mayor of Castro Street*:

> "When Harvey was in, Castro Camera became less a business establishment than a vest-pocket City Hall from which Harvey held court. [...] Harvey could often be found on his frumpy couch when new Castro residents came to find where to look for apartments, what to do with a lover who had an alcohol problem, or how to find that first job. Local merchants discovered that Harvey was the man to go to if police took too long to answer a suspected burglary or if the sewer overflowed; Harvey always knew whom to call at City Hall, or the reporter to buzz with the proper story of moral indignation if nothing was done. The store's large picture windows displayed announcements of upcoming demonstrations, environmen-

tal protests, commission hearings on Castro issues, or neighborhood meetings."
(Shilts 87-88)

Not only the person to go to with any neighbourhood problems, Milk also actively
networked to connect with other neighbourhood businesses. He sought contact
not only with other gay business owners but also with the established old-time,
mostly Irish Castro businessmen, becoming an "ex-officio liaison" between the
two groups (Shilts 87). With other gay merchants, he resurrected the Castro Village Association (CVA) and "was dutifully elected president [...], if for no other reason than nobody else wanted the job" (Shilts 89-90). In 1974, he got the other CVA
members to organize an annual Castro Street Fair, which over 5,000 attended. By
1976, the number of visitors had grown to 100,000 (Morris and Black 18). He was
thus already emerging as a neighbourhood leader, working towards creating in
the Castro a space to belong for its LGBTQ residents. As Shilts estimates, "[a]fter
years of searching and drifting, Castro Street had become Harvey's hometown,
and he had worked to make it a hometown for tens of thousands of homosexuals
from around the world" (xii).

It is perhaps not surprising that Milk proceeded to get interested in running
for the position of city supervisor, thus trying to extend his sphere of influence
beyond the neighbourhood of the Castro alone, as well as in an effort to better
serve the interests of the Castro and the gay community at large; he was passionate about all the San Francisco neighbourhoods and concerned with the developments he saw happening with inner city space all over San Francisco, the influence of major corporations on neighbourhood development and the demolition of
living space for parking garages and freeways. His vision was one where people
who worked in the city also lived in the city, and one of "a city that breathes, one
that is alive and where the people are more important than the highways" (Milk
qtd. in Morris and Black 16). He ran unsuccessfully for supervisor in 1973 and 1975
(discarding for his second attempt the hippie hair and clothing style for a more
conventional haircut and a suit in order to gain greater credibility among the voting public), as well as – once again unsuccessfully – for the state assembly. His
efforts were finally successful in 1977, when he was elected to the Board of Supervisors as a representative of District 5, which comprised the Castro and adjacent
neighbourhoods (Stryker and Van Buskirk 64). Milk was adamant about a number
of things: that more gay San Franciscans should actually vote; that an openly gay
person elected to city hall would do more for the gay community than a straight
ally, who might promise to address concerns of the gay community in order to get
elected but then change his mind when under pressure once elected (cf. Robinson xx). He was in favour of a coalition with other groups such as the unions (for
instance supporting them in the Coors Boycott), or other minority groups, reasoning that the fight against discrimination would be more effective if the different

groups helped each other (cf. Morris and Black 18-19). He understood the discrimination against gays to be a civil rights issue, arguing in the *Sentinel* in 1974 that "the only important issue for homosexuals is Freedom. All else is meaningless. ... Many people think that they are FREE because they have a lot of money and live in 'good' neighborhoods. But the homosexual is not free until there are NO laws on ANY books suppressing him and not until he, if he so wishes, can join the police force or any government agency as an open homosexual. It is as simple as that" (Milk qtd. in Morris and Black 17). Milk's first official act as a supervisor then, once elected, was the introduction of an "anti-discrimination ordinance assuring gay rights in all employment, housing, and public accommodations in San Francisco" (Morris and Black 32). In his victory statement in the *Bay Area Reporter*, he stated: "I understand the significance of electing the first Gay person to public office and what his responsibility is not only to the people of San Francisco but to Gay people all over. It's a responsibility that I do not take lightly. Whoever shoulders that responsibility must be willing to fight. It won't be an easy task" (Milk qtd. in Morris and Black 31-32).

Two occurrences helped raise the scope of Milk's activism beyond his immediate concerns with the city of San Francisco to a state and national level. In Florida, a gay rights ordinance was repealed in 1977 in Dade County following a campaign by Anita Bryant, a former beauty queen utilizing a Religious Right discourse of painting homosexuals as sexual deviants and a danger to society and especially children. A California State Senator, John Briggs, jumped on the same bandwagon shortly after, introducing an initiative that would ban LGBTQ teachers from teaching in California public schools. This initiative, Proposition 6, would be on the ballot for California citizens in 1978 (cf. Stryker and Van Buskirk 78). Protest marches and rallies ensued in all major cities in the U.S. in reaction to Bryant's victory, with Milk emerging as a speaker and leader in the San Francisco rallies, giving voice to the anger and frustration felt by the crowd and at the same time deescalating a potential riot (cf. Shilts 159). Milk then took on Briggs in a series of public debates, countering Briggs' defamations of lesbians and gays with actual factual numbers concerning the abuse of and violence against children (perpetrated in the vast majority of cases by heterosexuals) as well as in an effort to educate the general public about and dispel prevalent myths around the topic of homosexuality. Charles E. Morris and Jason Edward Black estimate that Milk's efforts cast a decisive edge in the final voting result and the defeat of Proposition 6 by a fifty-eight percent majority in the fall of 1978 (cf. Morris and Black 36). Milk acutely felt the need to react to Bryant and Briggs and the emerging Religious Right which he considered dangerous. In his Gay Freedom Day Speech, reprinted in the *Bay Area Reporter* in June 1978, he memorably called on gays to stop the infighting and to come out in an effort to dispel myths and lies about homosexuals. He called on the powers that be to end discrimination and harassment against gays, whether this concerned local or state politicians, moderate religious leaders or Jimmy Carter, the president of the United States:

> "My name is Harvey Milk — and I want to recruit you for the fight to preserve your democracy from the John Briggs' and the Anita Bryants who are trying to constitutionalize bigotry. [...] We will not win our rights by staying quietly in our closets. [...] For I am tired of the conspiracy of silence. [...]
>
> Gay brothers and sisters, what are you going to do about it? You must come out. [...] Come out only to the people you know and who know you. Not to anyone else. But once and for all, [...] destroy the lies and distortions for your own sake, for their sake, for the sake of the youngsters who are being terrified by the votes coming from Dade County to Eugene. [...]
>
> And finally, most of all, I'm tired of the silence from the White House. [...]
>
> Jimmy Carter, listen to us today. Or you will have to listen to all of us from all over the nation as we gather in Washington next year. For we WILL gather there and we will tell you about America and what it really stands for. [...] On the Statue of Liberty it says, 'Give me your tired, your poor, your huddled masses yearning to be free...' In the Declaration of Independence it is written, 'All men are created equal and they are endowed with certain inalienable rights...' [...] No matter how hard you try, you cannot erase those words from the Declaration of Independence. [...]"
> ("Gay Freedom Day Speech" 215 – 220)

Cleverly referencing in his opening line Bryant and Briggs, who had accused gays and lesbians of 'recruiting' minors, Milk drew on a rhetoric that linked gay rights with other civil rights discourses and with American liberation, quoting the Declaration of Independence and the inscription on the Statue of Liberty, as well as aligning his vision with that of Martin Luther King Jr. and his dream of an America free from discrimination against minorities, calling on a march on Washington which was to take place in 1979.[23] Operating from a visibly queer space, San Francisco's Castro, and the temporarily queer space of the Gay Freedom Day rally, Milk as the first openly gay elected official called on other gays and lesbians to come out of the closet, hoping that enhanced queer visibility, being aware of the fact that people in their immediate surroundings whom they already knew were actually lesbian or gay, would help change the consciousness of the heterosexual majority. Enhanced queer visibility would also, he argued, engender hope in queer people living elsewhere in the U.S., "the youngsters who are being terrified by the votes coming from Dade County to Eugene". Throughout all of his speeches

---

23 And indeed, Harvey Milk has been described by Harry Britt, one of his aides, as "the Martin Luther King of this nation's gay-liberation movement" (qtd. in Morris and Black 8).

and writings, this was Milk's other major concern, apart from the issue of gay civil rights: to give young queer people hope.

The trope of hope emerges in Harvey Milk's writings as early as 1964 in a letter written to his former boyfriend Joe Campbell, who had attempted to commit suicide: "people in worse situations than you have come back strong – have been against worse odds and won – only because they felt that somewhere there was some reason for living – they are not sure, but they had hope" (qtd. in Shilts 37). Hope is thus, for Milk, a prerequisite for survival, a similar understanding, perhaps, to Sören Kierkegaard's conception of hope as the opposite of despair: for Kierkegaard, hope is what can balance out despair in the end.[24] In his inauguration speech as well, Milk stressed the importance of hope: "A true function of politics is not just to pass laws, but to give hope" (Milk qtd. in Shilts 190). Indeed, hope had already been one of the central themes in his speech at the San Francisco Gay Community Center in June 1977, when he had announced his candidacy: "We must give people outside our community the chance to judge us by our Gay legislators and leaders. A gay person in office can set a tone, can command respect not only from that larger community but from young people in our own community who need both examples and ... hope" ("You've Got to Have Hope" 153). Indeed, Milk said, he had been running "so persistently for public office" because "I'll never forget what it was like coming out" (154).

> "And I'm running for public office because I think it's time we've had a legislator who was gay and proud of that fact and one who will not walk away from the responsibilities that face such a legislator. [...] I walked among the angry and sad gay sisters and brothers last night at City Hall and late last night as they lit candles and stood in silence on Castro Street reaching out for some symbolic thing that would give them hope.
>
> These were strong people. [...] They were strong and even they needed hope ... and those young gays in Des Moines who are 'coming out' and hear the Anita Bryant story – to them the only thing that they have to look forward to is hope. And YOU have to give them hope.
>
> Hope for a better world.
> Hope for a better tomorrow.
> Hope for a place to go to if the pressures at home are too great.
> Hope that all will be alright.
>
> Without *hope* not only the gays but the blacks, the seniors, the poor, the handicapped [...] give up ... if you help me get elected, that election. No, it is not my election, it is yours – will mean that a green light is lit. A green light that says to all who feel lost and disenfranchised that you now can go forward – it means *hope* and

---

24 Cf. Lutz, *Der Hoffende Mensch* 337-339.

we – no you and you and you and, yes, you got to give them hope." ("You've Got to
have Hope" 155)

Utilizing the theme of hope as a campaign strategy may appear to be also a strategic decision on Milk's part. But there can be no doubt that he was also sincere
in his conception of hope as the ethical groundwork for a queer futurity. In his
political will, recorded a year before his actual assassination by fellow supervisor
Dan White in late November 1978, Milk stressed: "I have never considered myself
a candidate. I have always considered myself part of a movement, part of a candidacy. I've considered the movement the candidate", and he expressed his wish
that his successor would be someone who regarded him- or herself as part of the
movement and about the movement as well ("Political Will" 246). Milk's political
will, too, closes on the theme of hope:

> "And that's all I ask. That's all. I ask for the movement to continue, for the movement
> to grow because last week, I got a phone call from Altoona, Pennsylvania, and my
> election gave somebody else, one more person, hope. And after all it's what this is
> all about. It's not about personal gain, not about ego, not about power – it's about
> giving those young people out there in the Altoona, Pennsylvania's hope. You gotta
> give them hope." ("Political Will" 249)[25]

Wendy O'Brien, drawing on Hannah Arendt's concept of natality or beginning,
conceives of hope as an action, a doing, it is the first step of beginning anew:
imagining otherwise. "To hope is to begin anew. [...] To begin necessitates [...] an
understanding of the circumstances framing the present. It is to recognize that

---

25 Milk's political will is also utilized as a framing device in Gus Van Sant's biopic from 2009. The
movie *Milk* weaves archival material from a 1984 documentary, Rob Epstein's *The Times of Harvey Milk*, into the fictional narrative portraying both Harvey Milk and the gay community and
queer space in San Francisco in the 1970s. *Milk* thus performs important memory work for an
LGBTQ community which, too often, fails to remember its not too recent histories (cf. Morris
and Black 37-38). The movie also features parts of Milk's Gay Freedom Day Speech and the public
debates with Senator Briggs. Screenwriter Dustin Lance Black made use of his Academy Award
acceptance speech to take up Milk's message of hope and carry it into the present moment by
addressing, himself, the queer youth of 2009:
"When I was 13 years old ... I heard the story of Harvey Milk. And it gave me hope. It gave me
the hope to live my life, it gave me the hope to one day live my life openly as who I am and that
maybe even I could fall in love and one day get married ... If Harvey had not been taken from us
30 years ago, I think he'd want me to say to all of the gay and lesbian kids out there tonight who
have been told that they are less than by their churches or by the government or by their families
that you are beautiful, wonderful creatures of value and that no matter what anyone tells you,
God does love you and that very soon, I promise you, you will have equal rights, federally, across
this great nation of ours." (qtd. in Morris and Black 41-42)

there are things that are not as they should be. [...] Those who hope live [...] as if the world was as it should be, as it could be. It is an act of defiance, one that exhibits freedom" (33-34). Those who hope do not only "believe that things can be different, they make the stronger, normative claim that things should be different" (34). Not to be confused with optimism, hope is, as Václav Havel points out, "not the conviction that something will turn out well, but the certainty that something makes sense, regardless of how it turns out" (qtd. in O'Brien 30). Thus, O'Brien argues, "the purpose of hope lies not in changing the world so much as it resides in changing the person. It is through hope that individuals take up their role as agents and citizens, that is, it is through these acts of freedom that they exhibit their humanity" (34-35). And it is herein that lies, for O'Brien, the resilience of hope. To further elaborate on what hope can do for the individual: Following Wendy O'Brien, I argue that hope is a prerequisite for agency. Hope enables someone to take action. It is not to be conflated with optimism. Hope does not expect a certain result or outcome. It is, as O'Brien states, not a matter of vision but of sight (cf. O'Brien). Hope builds on the possibility of a future alternative outcome but does not necessarily expect that this outcome will come true exactly as envisioned. (That is what optimism does; pessimism presumes to know that the outcome will not be achievable and achieved at all. It is as sure as optimism is as to predicting the future.) I regard hope as open-ended. Hope knows that things will be okay in the future, whether a certain outcome has been achieved or not. An open-ended vision of the future propels the individual who hopes forward, who may then take action, where pessimism would keep the individual locked in immobility or cause him or her to retreat. Optimism presumes to know the future. Hope does not do that. Nevertheless hope endows an individual with the ability to see that things could be different in the future. It thus enables future-directed action. It is a future-directed and thus a utopian structure of feeling, pointing, in the here and now, towards a future then and there. To the remarks of his fellow supervisor Dianne Feinstein that hope was fine, "but you can't live on hope" (Shilts 191), Milk was quick to reply that the "important thing is not that we cannot live on hope alone, but that life is not worth living without it" ("A City of Neighborhoods" 172). If Milk wanted to engender, with his election, in others (and especially in other gays and lesbians) hope "for a better world", "for a better tomorrow", "for a place to go to if the pressures at home are too great" and finally, hope "that all will be alright", his vision was undoubtedly one of both changing the world *and* empowering (young) LGBTQ people. Thus, Milk relates in an interview after his election victory:

"When the mayor asked me a year ago what my motivation [for running for the position of city supervisor, S.J.] was, I told him that I remember what it was like to be 14 and Gay. I know that somewhere today there is a 14 year old child who discovers that he or she is Gay and learns that the family may throw that child out of the house. The police will harass that child. The state will say that the child is a criminal and that the intelligence of the Anita Bryants will be screaming at that child. Maybe that child read in the newspaper, "Homosexual Elected in San Francisco," and that child has two options: move to San Francisco or stay in San Antonio or Des Moines and fight. The child has hope." ("Harvey Speaks Out" 161)

The potentiality of hope lies for Milk in the vision of a queer futurity that includes and at the same time extends beyond even what he and others were already trying to build in the Castro: a community and a place to belong and a space free from harassment and discrimination for LGBTQ people. Milk's concept of hope comes close to the kind of hope advocated by queer theorist José Esteban Muñoz, who takes up philosopher Ernst Bloch's notion of educated hope in both "Hope and hopelessness" and in his book *Cruising Utopia*. Educated hope, says Muñoz, is not "a mode of hope that simply keeps one in place within an emotional situation predicated on control" but is instead a "practice of hope that helps escape from a script in which human existence is reduced. Utopia has often been described as the education of desire. To want something else, to want beside and beyond the matrix of social controls that is our life in late Capitalism, is to participate in this other form of desiring" (Duggan and Muñoz, "Hope and hopelessness" 278). Muñoz comes to a similar conclusion about the potentiality of hope as does Wendy O'Brien: Hope is about seeing that things could be different, which is the first step in moving towards the realization of a utopian impulse.

> "Practicing educated hope is the enactment of a critique function. It is not about anouncing the way things *ought* to be, but, instead, imagining what things *could* be. It is thinking beyond the narrative of what stands for the world today by seeing it as not enough. Concrete Utopianism is rooted in a kind of objective possibility. [...] Concrete Utopia is [...] the goal of enacting a world, the actual creation of that goal and the actual movement towards that goal. The concept of *docta spes* (educated hope) is the intellectual and material force that potentially produces concrete utopian thought. We need hope to counter a climate of hopelessness that immobilizes us both on the level of thought and transformative behaviors. [...] [I]f the point is to change the world we must risk hope." ("Hope and hopelessness" 278-279)

Muñoz links this utopian impulse explicitly to the notion of queer. For him, queerness with its gesture of indeterminate openness entails the notion of futurity. It is in this sense that queerness "is not yet here"; and it is in this sense that the "future is queerness's domain. Queerness is a structuring and educated mode of desiring that allows us to see and feel beyond the quagmire of the present"; it is now for Muñoz queerness that "is that thing that lets us feel that this world is not enough, that indeed something is missing" (*Cruising Utopia* 1). What Muñoz has taken away from Bloch and his notion of educated hope is the utopian impulse Bloch detects in hope and in the act of hoping, an impulse the project of queer shares with Bloch's notion of hope. "Queerness", says Muñoz, "is essentially about the rejection of a here and now and an insistence on potentiality or concrete possibility for another world" (1). Educated hope as a structure of feeling underlies, I have endeavoured to show, already Harvey Milk's thinking about the concrete queer utopia he was trying to build in the Castro. It is this framework of hope that he and others were hoping to inspire in and provide for others in need of it, living in San Francisco or elsewhere. Utopia emerges here not as a place or space that is no place, but as a space that is not yet here; as a space that can be accessed conceptually in the here and now to create a then and there. Notably, many of the textual examples in *Cruising Utopia* in which Muñoz finds traces of a queer utopian impulse and educated hope also date from the late 1960s and early 1970s, the immediate pre- and post-Stonewall years (cf. *Cruising Utopia* 3). Hope is for Muñoz also a "modality of emotional recognition that structures belonging" (97). Sharing in this structure of feeling creates relationality and sociality and thus community.

Milk's vision of the future of San Francisco, which he expressed in an interview with activist Jack Davis shortly before his death, was finally one where gays and heterosexuals were living side by side. "I could never have imagined five years ago that it would become like today", he furthermore states, as Shilts relates (259). Harvey Milk's experiences and feelings around the Castro were surely shared by many:

> "I came out at fourteen. Even though I lived at home for several more years, it was never 'home' again, for in that home, I was closeted. In fact, I never had a home again and especially no hometown. Then came Castro Street. Castro Street became my hometown. For the first time in my life, there was a place to live, to shop, to play, to be where I felt at home. To many, Castro Street became their hometown. Even if for only a short time. It has become a symbol to many gay people – a symbol of being. You can go home again." (Milk qtd. in Shilts 259)

By the late 1970s, the Castro as an openly queer space had thus become a home space and a place to belong for its queer residents and visitors. It had additionally become a symbol for a whole community from which sprang a political movement that promised action towards attaining equal rights for lesbian and gay U.S. citizens. And it embodied the utopian longing of a queer futurity, the spirit of hope for a better tomorrow and a better elsewhere for LGBTQ people everywhere.

Bodily Strategies

In this chapter I will take a closer look at strategies of queer resilience that make use of or relate in some form or other to the body, to its representations in literature and film, to bodily experiences and to the cultural meanings attached to them. The strategies I present range from what I term the 'art of postpornography', a way of looking at, and visually representing the myriad possibilities of sexual desire beyond the confines of heteronormativity, which I will elucidate with a close-reading of John Cameron Mitchell's movie *Shortbus* and Mark Wunderlich's poem "The Trick", to an epistemology privileging bodily sensations and feelings as well as the sense of touch, which I will trace through the poetry of May Swenson, Thom Gunn, Pat Parker and Carol Ann Duffy. I link these poems to neuroscientific research and therapeutic schools working with and through the body in an effort to further an individual's resilience. The body and bodily experiences emerge in a number of different ways in all of these literary and cultural texts as potential resources for queer subjects.

The Art of Postpornography: John Cameron Mitchell's *Shortbus* and Mark Wunderlich's "The Trick"

In her introduction to *The Invention of Pornography*, historian Lynn Hunt argues that our understanding of the pornographic in art as well as in mass media productions can be traced back to the late seventeenth and early eighteenth century, the beginning of modernity. Hunt and others have pointed out that the invention of 'pornography' itself and the creation of a binary of pornographic vs. non-pornographic art forms has more often than not been instrumentalized for a policing of boundaries: From the late eighteenth century onward, it has been used mainly as a tool for inscribing a new sex/gender system and a proto-heteronormative social order. Our current sex/gender system and the heterosexual hegemony governing twentieth and early twenty-first century gender relations, as they have been theorized by Gayle Rubin, Judith Butler, Eve Kosofksy Sedgwick and others, can be directly related to these past and still ongoing acts of policing, to the ongoing debates around 'pornography'.[1]

Feminist and queer inquiries into pornography to date have focused mainly on two issues: An earlier strand of criticism devoted itself to a feminist critique of sexism in mainstream pornography (cf. Dworkin; Schwarzer), whereas a younger generation of scholars, following the work of Linda Williams and others, is providing increasingly more sophisticated analyses of both mainstream straight and gay male pornography, of the newly developing market of feminist erotica and porn, of pornographic performance art, and more recently also of independently produced lesbian and queer porn (cf. Williams, *Hard Core* and Williams, *Porn Studies*).

This subchapter is going to explore the work of artists who have been influenced by these latest developments in mass-market pornography and pornographic art. However, I am going to focus on what I term 'postpornographic' art, that is to say on works, communities and artists that purposely disregard the ideological boundaries we have inherited and whose origins can be traced to the eighteenth century: pornographic vs. non-pornographic art forms, or sometimes more simply art/porn or decent/indecent modes of artistic expression. Postpornographic art as I understand it undoes the pornographic vs. non-pornographic binary by simply disregarding its interpellating call. Among other things, as I am going to argue, it thus performs the cultural work of rendering visible the ideological investments underlying this binary and their mechanisms of inscription. The term 'postpornography' has been put to a number of different usages already by both critics and artists. Georg Seeßlen employs it to describe a mode of depicting sexuality in postmodern film that aims at distancing the viewer: "Im post-pornografischen Blick ist die Sexualität zerfallen. Die Naheinstellung fetischisiert nicht mehr, sondern dokumentiert die Fremdheit. Der post-pornografische Blick ist vor allem ein gespaltener, einer, der sich vor lauter Verzweiflung darüber, dass sich das Objekt der Begierde umsomehr entzieht, je genauer man es ansieht, in seine analytische Strafe verkehrt" (qtd. in Rall 318). Performance artist Annie Sprinkle puts a different spin on 'post porn' in shows such as *Post Porn Modernism*, in which the material body becomes a stage and the sex worker as artist turns her gaze back on the viewer (cf. Schneider, *The Explicit Body in Performance* 52-65).

In the following I will look at an example of postpornographic art that employs the medium of contemporary film to explore these issues, John Cameron Mitchell's independent movie *Shortbus* from 2006. First and foremost, I wish to enquire what this particular artist's concern is regarding the creation of his work of art. What does Mitchell achieve by employing the pornographic as just another (equally valid) mode of artistic expression? Analyzing the story arc of the charac-

---

1 A shorter version of this subchapter has already been published as part of Susanne Jung, "Prisms of Desire".

ter of James in particular, I will also explore how, as *Shortbus* posits, bodily experiences can be employed to work through queer stress and trauma individually and collectively. Mark Wunderlich's poem "The Trick" will serve as a second example for what I term the art of postpornography. For Cameron's movie and Wunderlich's poem, I argue, similar issues are at stake.

Shortbus, which was collaboratively created and independently produced, revolves around the lives of a number of characters living in a post 9/11 New York City. 'Shortbus' is the name of a fictional bohemian salon run by real life queer performance artist Justin Bond, who plays a version of himself in this movie. Other queer subcultural stars make an appearance, lending the salon an air of authenticity as a mixture of queer art/performance space that includes its very own play area, the aptly titled Sex-Not-Bombs room. Justin Bond describes 'Shortbus' as "a salon for the gifted and challenged", referring to the U.S. system of short yellow school buses for 'gifted and challenged' students. He characterizes the salon's atmosphere as being "like the Sixties, only with less hope" (cf. *Shortbus*). The movie's protagonists include Sofia, a sex therapist who has never had an orgasm, and her husband Rob. Sofia is counselling James and Jamie, a gay couple who are considering opening up their relationship to include other men, one potential candidate being Ceth, an ex-model and singer-songwriter they meet at Justin Bond's 'Shortbus'. Then there is Severin, a female sex worker who frequents 'Shortbus', who may or may not be able to help Sofia out with her problem. And finally, unnoticed by most of the characters throughout the first half of the movie (but far from unnoticed by the viewer), there is Caleb, a character in his mid-twenties who lives in an apartment just across from James and Jamie and who has a habit of observing his neighbours through the tele lens of his camera. Caleb has lately taken to stalking the two Jamies, seemingly with the intention of 'saving' their relationship, though his actual function remains unclear for the first two-thirds of the movie.

John Cameron Mitchell explains his motivation for making *Shortbus* as wanting to make a movie that uses "real sex, unsimulated sex, in the context of an emotional narrative", a narrative that is, as he describes it, "non-pornographic" but that is connected to other aspects of our lives, aspects like "emotion, ideas, humor". Mitchell sets his vision also apart from recent European films: "I'd seen a lot of films in the late 90s coming out of Europe that were using unsimulated sex, and they were interesting – some of them were very good – but all of them were very bleak, and that seemed to be just as negative a view of sex as, say, Jerry Falwell's [U.S. televangelist, S. J.] view" (cf. Mitchell). Despite Mitchell's protestations, it could be argued that *Shortbus* does employ the typical tropes of pornography, albeit mostly in a manner that is tongue-in-cheek. It alludes to, and at the same time sends up, pornographic genre conventions as they have been theorized by Linda Williams in *Hard Core*: there is an explicit depiction of genitals and sexual acts as well as a number of 'money shots' (depictions of male ejaculation as proof

of the achievement of pleasure); these climaxes are worked into a variety of narratives and a variety of sexual numbers in the manner of musical numbers in a
musical feature film. Says Williams, "hard-core feature film is a kind of musical,
with sexual number taking the place of musical number" (*Hard Core* 124). These
numbers usually vary according to sexual acts, sexual positions and the number
of people involved. In Williams' view, feature-length pornography does not lack
a narrative. The narratives may be mostly clichéd and any real character development mostly lacking, but in order to achieve its effect on the viewer, episodic narrative and sexual numbers still inform each other (cf. *Hard Core* 128-151). Interestingly, Mitchell uses the same comparison as Williams, describing that he wanted
to use sex in *Shortbus* the way he used music in his earlier film *Hedwig and the Angry
Inch*, a musical feature (cf. *Gifted and Challenged*). However, the pleasures evoked
for the viewer in the case of *Shortbus* are not first and foremost scopophilic but are
largely influenced by the viewer's emotional investment in the narrative and the
characters, with the plot ranging from comedy to drama, and by the dominating
aesthetic: a lighthearted atmosphere of *joie de vivre* and a carnivalesque humour
that also embraces the kitsch, the camp, and the sentimental and that is achieved
primarily by an intermingling of mimetic realism with animated sequences of a
fairy-talesque cityscape and elements of magical realism.[2]

The sex scenes themselves are in turn funny, boring, playful, quotidian or
adventurous, and often strategically placed at moments of emotional conflict for
the characters. The desires and sexual acts depicted involve various ethnicities,
and run the gamut from gay to bisexual to straight to polyamorous, including references to cross-generational desires and the depiction of sadomasochistic sexual
practices. By presenting 'deviant' sexual practices alongside 'normal' ones (speaking in terms of a heteronormative ideology of sex and gender), *Shortbus* undermines heteronormative hierarchies, graphically illustrating the manifold forms
human sexual desire can take, without rendering abject queer sexual desires and
practices. It thus works against the erasure of queer possibilities that is intrinsic
to the majority of mainstream cultural productions. It presents a fictional (and
in some cases only semi-fictional) world of queer subcultural urban communities and spaces and as such forms part of the living archive of a culture of radical
sex and kinship. Already Michel Foucault proposed that what scares straight culture the most are not the 'deviant' sexual acts queer people might indulge in but
the new forms of kinship, new ways of living and being in the world they might

---

2 As a side note however, scopophilia, the sexual pleasure derived from watching and observing
   other people, is acknowledged in the movie as a non-deviant form of desire both for the movie's
   characters and for its audience, forming part of a legitimate transaction in the economy of desire. After all, as one of the sextras in the Sex-Not-Bombs room explains to Sofia, "voyeurism *is*
   participation".

invent (cf. Foucault, "Friendship as a Way of Life"). Foucault argues that these new forms of kinship might pose a greater threat or challenge to the existing social order. From the vantage point of queer activism, of course, they provide a promising potential for larger cultural processes of social transformation and change. Queer archives function here in several ways: For one, archives that document the activities of queer subcultures work against the erasure of queer possibilities from the cultural imaginary and help conserve LGBTQ history for future generations (cf. Halberstam, *In a Queer Time and Place* 169-170); as archives of feelings, they also function as sites of collective memory and mourning, and provide space for a collective and individual working through of queer trauma (cf. Cvetkovich, *An Archive of Feelings* 268-270).

However, in *Shortbus* sex itself is also presented as a potentially cathartic experience, a healing art. James' plot arc may serve as one example for how the sex scenes tie into a larger narrative, and into questions of character development and social context. James' story, I propose, is an investigation into the affective life of queer male stress and trauma. Recent work by e.g. Ann Cvetkovich has focused on the long-term traumatic effects on the individual psyche of social structures of oppression as they relate to queer subjects and communities (cf. Cvetkovich). For a queer subject traumatic effects can be produced by a whole range of acts of homophobic violence, from everyday experiences of discrimination to singular traumatic events such as rape or physical assault. Stress and trauma may also add up over the course of a lifetime. It is part of the intrinsic psychic structure of trauma that the actual traumatic event(s) may not be fully accessible cognitively for the traumatized subject, what Cathy Caruth has come to refer to as "unclaimed experience" (cf. Caruth). The typical effects of trauma an individual may experience and by which it is therefore mostly known, include dissociation and flashbacks, emotional states of numbness or hyperarousal, and the compulsion to repeat (cf. Cvetkovich 17-19; van der Kolk, "Posttraumatic stress disorder" and *The Body Keeps the Score*). For the damaged psyche to heal, the trauma has to be recovered individually and collectively. Since in the case of queer trauma, the trauma is tied to entire social systems, specifically to being a minoritarian queer subject in a heteronormative social order, two more strategies become necessary: one, the individual subject has to develop strategies to cope with the shaming interpellation by which the heteronormative social order inscribes itself into its queer subjects, rendering them abject (cf. Hotz-Davies); and two, on a communal level, a politics of social transformation becomes necessary to ultimately alleviate and counter the structural basis of such trauma. Both of these, I would argue, fall within the realm of what I term strategies of queer resilience, one on the level of the individual, the other on the level of the communal or social.

To illustrate: In *Shortbus* the character of James is portrayed from the outset as disconnected from his own self and from the people around him, including his partner Jamie. Diagnosed with clinical depression, the symptoms he exhibits can be better understood, I suggest, as the psychic and physical effects of sustained insidious stress or trauma relating to his subject position as a gay man; or phrased differently, the contemporary heteronormative sex/gender system serves here as a vulnerability factor for this queer subject. Throughout the movie he is shown to be working on a performance tape, a documentary of his life with Jamie in which the idyllic routine of a gay male couple is interspersed with a montage of shots illustrating James' tormented interior life: In one shot, James as a young boy violently beats up an adult-sized papier mâché dummy, in another, the naked adult James looks back at the viewer from the surface of a mirror, his body and face covered in band aids. Whereas young James rebelled against the pressures put on him by a malign social order by acting out, adult James has turned the violence against himself. The image of his mute, battered body serves as an externalization of his psychic pain and injury. The tape can be understood to consist of the affective archive of James' trauma. Performance art – an obvious influence for James' film project is Jonathan Caouette's *Tarnation* – is here employed as a form of testimony and a working through the effects of trauma. Both Cvetkovich and José Esteban Muñoz in *Disidentifications* point to a tradition in queer culture of using performance art as a vehicle for containing and working through negative affect individually and collectively (cf. Cvetkovich; Muñoz, *Disidentifications*). The viewer learns that James' past included growing up gay in a small town; for lack of a better role model he turned to movies in an effort to cope with his emerging sexuality; however, unable to appropriately disidentify with his fictional heroes (that is to perform the cultural work of identifying only with those aspects of his chosen cultural role models that are beneficial to the development of a viable gay identity), he followed too closely in the footsteps of the young male hustlers in Gus Van Sant's *My Own Private Idaho*, turning to hustling himself in an attempt to connect meaningfully with other gay men. This attempt mostly fails, and by the time he meets Jamie, James has successfully internalized the abject position of the gay subject in a heteronormative social order. Ultimately, sustained stress and trauma can erode the sense of a coherent self, and James' real impetus for opening up his and Jamie's relationship is, as we later learn, so that Jamie will not be left alone by James' attempted suicide. The suicide attempt fails because Caleb finds James in time, and released from hospital, James returns not to his own apartment but to Caleb's, where he learns that Caleb has been obsessively observing and following him for quite some time. In the sexual encounter that follows, Caleb penetrates James, a sex act that he had until then not allowed anyone to perform on his body. Only as a consequence of this transformational encounter is James able to return to his partner and take up his old life with Jamie, their friends and the queer community around 'Shortbus'.

In an early twentieth century model of the psychic mechanisms of trauma, Sigmund Freud uses the image of a living organism for a human consciousness that is protected against outside stimuli by a protective shield (cf. "Jenseits des Lustprinzips" 25-27). He describes as 'traumatic' any outside stimuli that are strong enough to break through the protective shield. In reaction to these traumatic penetrations of the shield, the organism develops a defensive crust through the death of its outer layers. Freud's metaphor illustrates how traumatic response can take both the form of numbness and hyperarousal. – Freud's metapsychological model works mostly only as metaphor but he is not quite wrong in his choice of a specifically *bodily* metaphor here: The Cartesian mind/body divide has come under attack in recent years also due to neuroscientific findings, some of them in the field of trauma studies. The body *does* keep the score, as Bessel van der Kolk and others have shown. Physiologically, trauma manifests in neurotransmitter and hormonal changes; also, traumatic memories are mainly processed by subcortical areas of the brain (which process somatic and affective experiences), and only to a lesser extent by the left hemisphere and prefrontal cortex (which process rational thought and verbal communication). Traumatic memories are thus less accessible to cognitive processing, which has caused leading clinicians in the field to call for a further integration of body-oriented therapies in current trauma treatment regimes (cf. van der Kolk, "Posttraumatic stress disorder"). For James, emotional numbness induced by trauma is linked to his refusal to be penetrated.[3] With regard to his partner, James describes to Caleb how he can see Jamie's love all around him, "but it stops at my skin. I can't let it inside". The actual physical act of penetration becomes therefore for him a form of body therapy: The repetition of trauma with a difference, in a safe context and under controlled circumstances, cuts through all of his defences. Penetrative sex goes beyond metaphor here in that the boundaries of external/internal, physical/psychic, body/mind collapse. But the body is also, as Cvetkovich aptly remarks, an "imaginary locus of meaning" and a "vehicle for the materialization of symbolic meanings" (70). For James to achieve a state of vulnerability by an active process of reception means that he is also finally coming to terms with a cultural imaginary that renders gay male subjectivity and the penetrable male body abject (cf. e.g. Bersani).

Drawing on the work of Judith Butler and Eve Kosofsky Sedgwick, Ingrid Hotz-Davies has demonstrated how ideologies inscribe themselves into their subjects via the affect of shame: "[Die Scham] ist im Zentrum der Prozesse angesiedelt, mit denen Kulturen ihre ideologischen Inhalte in die Subjekte einschreiben" (196). Judith Butler has theorized that becoming a subject entails an act of sub-

---

3 Anne Cvetkovich finds the same in lesbian butch-femme culture, where sexual and emotional styles can (though they do not automatically have to) also inform each other, especially regarding the tropes of butch untouchability and femme receptivity (cf. Cvetkovich 49-82).

jection to power; according to Louis Althusser, it is the ideological state apparatuses (school, church, the family) that interpellate (hail) us, and "[i]ndem ich mich
umdrehe, erkenne ich die Macht dieser Institution an, mich zu konstituieren. Im
Gegenzug werde ich zum Subjekt und zum Unterworfenen dieser Institution"
(183). Hotz-Davies suggests that the affect of shame is what makes us obey this
interpellating call. It is next to impossible for an individual to resist being interpellated into e.g. a subject position in their contemporary sex/gender system if the
individual does not want to lose their identity as a human being, and this is true
even if the subject position in question is an abject one as in the case of queer subjects. Individual differences do exist as regards the strength of one's shame theory
(i.e. how susceptible one is to the affect of shame) and as regards the coping strategies one develops for dealing with the affect of shame (cf. Hotz-Davies 187-196).[4]
Shame, following Silvan Tomkins, is directly related to an economy of the gaze.
"The innate activator of shame", he writes, "is the incomplete reduction of interest
or joy. Hence any barrier to further exploration which partially reduces interest
[...] will activate the lowering of the head and eyes in shame and reduce further
exploration or self-exposure. [...] Such a barrier might be because one is suddenly
looked at by one who is strange, or because one wishes to look at or commune with
another person but suddenly cannot because he is strange, or one expected him to
be familiar but he suddenly appears unfamiliar, or one started to smile but found
one was smiling at a stranger" (qtd. in Sedgwick, *Touching Feeling* 97). It is pertinent here that Caleb, the voyeur character, the one who sees but does not judge, be
the one to penetrate James. Caleb acts as both witness to James' trauma and as the
one providing a benign gaze to counter the toxic effect of James' shame. It is only
through him that James can weather the shaming interpellation of a heteronormative social order and let himself be vulnerable and work through both trauma
and shame to reclaim his own self and a viable gay identity for himself.

James' arc is not the only plot arc that explores issues of trauma but it is the
one that most clearly elucidates notions of queer trauma and bodily strategies of
queer resilience. On the level of the collective, *Shortbus* celebrates queer subcultural urban space as a space conducive to creativity and a variety of performances;
performative and therefore transformative, it is home to a living, breathing culture that can absorb and work through a myriad of affects and thereby form the
basis of an activist politics of social transformation and change. *Shortbus* depicts
such a space, and at the same time it is created from such a space. With its investigation into the trauma culture surrounding oppressive social systems, and as

---

4 Silvan Tomkins' theory of high and low shame theories corresponds to recent neurological findings that different people may have different sensitivities, i.e. they perceive and process different amounts of stimuli from the same environment (cf. Aron, *The Highly Sensitive Person*; Aron and
   Aron, "Sensory Processing Sensitivity").

a post 9/11 film, it also points to alternative ways of dealing with trauma to the dominant U.S. cultural reaction to the national trauma of 9/11. 9/11 is referenced directly in *Shortbus* when the camera pans across Ground Zero, pulling back to the location of a nearby hotel room. "You're taking a picture of yourself at Ground Zero. Do you smile?" Jesse, Severin's client, asks her. The question remains unanswered, and maybe unanswerable for both Severin and the equally interpellated viewer. Severin understands it to be not an interrogatory speech act but a provocation that demands punishment (and that was probably uttered by Jesse just with this consequence in mind). As such it stands as a forbidden speech act proposing an improper reaction to the "unclaimed experience" (Caruth) of national trauma. *Shortbus* suggests that there is a more beneficial reaction to the haunting of the phantom trauma produces than a hyperbolic demonizing of the Other: In the words, or rather song lyrics, of Justin Bond, we may all "bear the scars"; yet "as your last breath begins", you may "find your demon's your best friend, and we all get it in the end" (cf. *Shortbus*).

Similar to the story of James in *Shortbus*, the speaker of Mark Wunderlich's poem "The Trick" from his poetry collection *The Anchorage* (1999) describes the experience of growing up in a homophobic environment and delineates his adolescent struggle to deal with his gay male sexuality; the poem lays out the ways the speaker has found to rework this challenging experience as a queer adult. It describes the speaker's coming to terms with and giving voice to a set of desires rendered unthinkable in his adolescence:

"The Trick

I made love with a man—hugely muscled, lean—the body
I always wished for myself. He kept pulling my arms
up over my head, pinning them there, pressing me down

with his entire weight, grinding into me roughly,
but then asked, begged, in a whisper of such sweetness,
Please kiss me. Earlier that evening, he told me

he'd watched a program about lions, admired
how they took their prey—menacing the herds at the water hole
before choosing the misfit, the broken one.

What surprised him was the wildebeests' calm
after the calf had been downed, how they returned to their grazing
with a dumb switching of tails. Nearby the lions looked up

from their meal, eyed the hopping storks and vultures,
before burying their faces, again, in the bloody ribs.
As a teenager, I wished to be consumed,

to be pressed into oblivion by a big forceful man.
It never happened. Instead I denied myself nourishment—
each un-filled plate staring back satisfied me, deprivation

reduced to a kind of bliss I could lie down in
where I remained unmoved, untouched.
Early on I was taught that the body was a cage,

that illness was a battle fought with chaos,
the viruses themselves unnatural; that sex lived
in some pastel chamber that gave way to infants,

first cousins, the handing down of names.
No one ever mentioned being taken in the dark,
or wanting to be broken open, pushed beyond words,

tongue thickening in another human mouth,
or how a person could be humiliated and like it.
To my surprise, I found myself struggling under this man,

pushing me chest up against his chest, arms straining
against the bed, until some younger, hungrier
version of myself lay back on top of me and took it—

the heaving back, the beard, the teeth at the throat."

The first stanza establishes a scene of erotic domination and submission in which the speaker is depicted voluntarily submitting to a powerful male other. The second stanza reveals the encounter as consensual and even tender, with the powerful male other asking the speaker "in a whisper of such sweetness" to kiss him. The poem then takes several detours before returning to the sexual scene at hand. First, an extended image of another violent scene is evoked: a television programme featuring a scene of lions capturing and devouring their prey; then the speaker links his current and past desires to a theme of violence: he expresses both a desire to be violated and at the same time narrates the violation visited upon his subjectivity by the interpellation of a heteronormative sex/gender system in his youth that rendered queer sexualities and desires abject. The poem addresses, I argue, the notion that hegemonic power structures, such as heteronormativity, can have a traumatizing (in the sense of wounding; trauma in its original sense translated from the Ancient Greek means wound) effect on an individual's interior experience. The allusion to the documentary on lions and other predatory animals serves in this poem as a metaphoric field of resonance for the violence the speaker feels he had to submit to as a queer teen – in fact as a field of resonance for both the voluntary and non-voluntary states of vulnerability and submission to a powerful Other, the ones he feels were forced upon him then and the ones he voluntarily seeks out now. The speaker's conscious use of S&M sex in the present serves here as a means of actively and consciously reworking the wound produced by the heteronormative interpellations of his upbringing, the notion that "sex lived / in some pastel chamber that gave way to infants", where "[e]arly on [he] was taught that the body was a cage" and where the gay male body was constructed as riddled with disease. The speaker successfully reworks past experiences of a compromised sexual subjectivity by submitting to this other male in the present and thus finds ways of actively coping with the legacy of his queer adolescent self. As Jessica Benjamin has argued in *The Bonds of Love*, "[t]the fantasy of erotic domination embodies both the desire for independence and the desire for recognition" (52). As Benjamin sees it, "especially in voluntary submission to erotic domination", a paradox occurs "in which the individual tries to achieve freedom through slavery, release through submission to control" (52). How can this be achieved? Benjamin argues that "the desire for submission represents a peculiar transposition of the desire for recognition", where submission is revealed as "a search for recognition through an other who is powerful enough to bestow this recognition. This other has the power for which the self longs, and through [the other's] recognition [the submissive] gains it, though vicariously" (56). I would argue that Benjamin's ideas around erotic submission can be fruitfully employed for a reading of the present poem. Indeed, the potential vicariousness of the experience taking place is hinted at in "The Trick" in the very first stanza, when the speaker reveals that his sexual partner has "the body / I always wished for myself". "The Trick" thus presents erotic submission as a bodily experience that can be used to alleviate queer trauma and shame. The experience enables an act of recognition by a powerful other and a vicarious experience of power and control.[5] The speaker of "The Trick" experiences

---

5   It is worth mentioning at this point that I regard countering the bodily archive of queer trauma with an act of erotic surrender as *one* possible way of dealing with a potential heritage of queer stress and trauma. It is not *the* way. Still I want to present a voluntary act of surrender as an act of resilience that consciously makes use of a bodily experience to counter shame and gain recognition. Also, this is of course not all there remains to be said on the subject of erotic submission. Working through abject feelings and gaining recognition is *one* of the things such an experience can do for the one choosing to undergo the experience. There are more things potentially gained from a masochistic or submissive experience that is set up in a safe, consensual way.

in the poem's present both agency and the giving up of control in a setting of his own design. This sense of agency is already expressed in the poem's first line (and indeed already in the first word of the poem, namely "I"), which stresses that it is he, the speaker, that "makes love" with this other man. Similarly, the experience of an act of surrender is the subject of the very last line, which lacks a personal pronoun; the experience has obliterated the "I" of the poem's beginning; all that is left are bodily sensations: "the teeth at the throat".

At the same time the poem opens up another way of reading BDSM experiences, pointing to the notion that, more generally speaking, BDSM may also be understood as merely a personal sexual preference, one that "[n]o one ever mentioned" to the speaker as a queer teen but that, as he discovers as an adult, one may just happen to "like". The poem can thus also be read to be presenting scenes of consensual domination and submission as a non-deviant form of sexual desire that has been rendered abject by the heteronormative sex/gender system (cf. Rubin), but that the speaker, as a queer adult, can now claim for himself free from any connotations of deviancy.

Postpornographic works of art like *Shortbus* and "The Trick", I propose, privilege pleasure (*jouissance*) and bodily and somatic forms of knowledge, using the body and bodily expressions and experiences as an epistemological tool. They privilege affect over cognition and render visible the ideological nature of our current sex/gender system and its mechanisms of inscription. At their best they manage to point beyond the Cartesian mind/body divide and its concurrent ideological implications of sex, gender and kinship. Like optical prisms refracting the light to reveal a myriad of spectral colours to the naked eye, these works of art render visible and viable what has culturally been abjected or cloaked by past and present regimes of reglementation policing the boundaries of the decent and the indecent: the myriad forms human desire can and does take.

The Body as Resource: An Epistemology of Sensing/Feeling in the Poetry of May Swenson, Thom Gunn, Pat Parker and Carol Ann Duffy

This subchapter is concerned with the following set of questions: How can queer subjects employ the body as a resource to further their resilience? And how is this portrayed in literary and cultural texts? In recent neuroscience as well as bodily oriented therapies and pedagogies, attention to what goes on inside the body, one part of what might be termed subconscious mind/body processes, has been proposed as an avenue into furthering an individual's resilience as well as a way to undo the traces of trauma and ongoing stress in both body and mind.[6] This chapter is concerned with what I term an epistemology of sensing/feeling. I focus on the processing of bodily feelings and sensations, that is I discuss internal processes that have been subsumed in recent neuroscientific and somatic research under the heading of 'interoception'.[7] I also consider, when discussing processes of sensing/feeling, sensory experiences involving the sense of touch, which often, in the texts analysed in this chapter, include an interpersonal dimension. If 'epistemology' tries to trace the question of how we come to know what we know about ourselves and the world, it seems to me that it would be wrong to limit the focus of our attention to what can be grasped by processes of cognition and/or perception only. In the wake of the work of Antonio Damasio and others, bodily oriented therapists such as Peter Levine have suggested to amend Descartes' famous dictum *Cogito ergo sum* to include the dimension of sensing/feeling in a bottom-up processing of consciousness. 'I think therefore I am' then becomes: "I sense, I act, I feel, I perceive, I reflect, I think and I reason; therefore I know I am" (Levine 282). Recent queer affect theory has helped foreground theories of affect in theorizations of queer subjectivities and lives, studying the relation between subjects, texts and emotions or the function of emotions in texts from a cultural studies perspective, but it has been less inclined to study bodily feelings and sensations alongside affects or emotions.[8] Notable exceptions include Eveline Kilian's discussion of bodily experiences and how they relate to gender, transgender and transsexual identities, which include a dimension of "leiblich-affektive Wahrnehmung" (213) of bodily experiences (cf. Kilian 202-220). In this chapter I will present readings of several poems that illustrate, I argue, what epistemologies of sensing/feeling, what employing the body as a resource and consciously experiencing bodily feel-

---

6 Cf. the work of neuroscientists such as Antonio Damasio, trauma and somatic therapists such as Bessel van der Kolk, Peter Levine and Robert Schleip, as well as the pedagogies developed by Moshe Feldenkrais, F. M. Alexander and Ida Rolf. A genealogy of bodily oriented therapies to which Peter Levine and others are indebted would include concepts developed by e.g. Wilhelm Reich, Alexander Lowen, Fritz Perls and Eugene Gendlin (cf. Levine).

7 I use the terms 'bodily feelings' and 'sensations' interchangeably throughout this chapter.

8 Note that I also use the terms 'affects' and 'emotions' interchangeably. I am following Ann Cvetkovich in this regard (cf. Cvetkovich in Ahmed 205-206). I am aware that a different usage of these terms can found in the work of some cultural theorists. A critical discussion, with which I would concur, of the so-called affective turn and of a conceptual differentiation between 'affect' and 'emotion' can be found in the second edition of Sara Ahmed's *The Cultural Politics of Emotion* (cf. 205-211). In the discipline of psychology, Silvan Tomkins differentiates between these terms, employing the term affects only to a limited number of emotions which are similar to the emotions described already by Charles Darwin as primary emotions and studied extensively by Paul Ekman and others. Emotions in this stricter definition of the term would then apply to an unlimited number of emotional states that one can make out to describe various shades of emotional experience (cf. Tomkins; Levine).

ings can do for queer subjects. The poems discussed range from the 1950s to the 1980s and include work by May Swenson, Thom Gunn, Pat Parker and Carol Ann Duffy.

To begin, and to illustrate what I mean by bodily feelings, here is a simple exercise: If you experience shame or joy, disgust or fear (just call up a memory of a time when you last experienced one of the aforementioned emotions), where in your body do you experience this feeling, that is to say, which bodily feeling or sensation goes along with this affect or emotion, what Antonio Damasio would refer to as the 'somatic marker' of that particular experience (cf. Damasio, *Descartes' Error*)? And if you focus your attention on the bodily feeling or sensation in a mindful way (that is stay with it in the present moment, which at the same time means: with an open mind to what happens next, as the present knows no future), what happens then? Does it shift, change? Does a tension or a holding pattern that you noticed start to soften? And what happens then? Since you are now already 'inside' (both Bessel van der Kolk and Peter Levine refer to this focused mindful attention on bodily feelings and states, this engaging of what Eugene Gendlin refers to as the 'felt sense', as 'going inside'; cf. van der Kolk, *The Body Keeps the Score*; Levine), can you locate areas of your body that feel good from the inside, maybe warm, maybe comfortable? What you are doing right now is engaging in what somatic researchers such as Robert Schleip refer to as 'interoception'.[9] This is usually not

---

9 A.D. Craig provides the first extensive neuroscientific description of this feature of internal body awareness and demonstrates how it differs neurophysiologically from proprioception, that is the internal awareness of the orientation of the body in space (cf. Schleip and Jäger). According to Robert Schleip and Heike Jäger, current "concepts describe interoception as a sense of the physiological condition of the body" that includes, for example, internal sensations of warmth, coolness, muscular activity, pain, tickle, itch, hunger, thirst, air hunger, sexual arousal, wine tasting (in sommeliers), heartbeat, vasomotor activity, distension of bladder, distension of stomach, rectum or esophagus as well as sensual touch. "These sensations are triggered by stimulation of unmyelinated sensory nerve endings (free nerve endings) [located in fascia of the skin, visceral connective tissue of internal bodily organs and muscular tissues, S.J.] that project to the insular cortex [in the human brain, S.J.] rather than to the primary somatosensory cortex which is usually considered as the main target of proprioceptive sensations. Feelings from these sensations not only have a sensory, but also an affective, motivational aspect and are always related to the homeostatic needs of the body. They are associated with behavioural motivations that are essential for the maintenance of physiological body integrity" (89). Schleip and Jäger describe the sense of "sensual or pleasant touch" as a "recent and surprising addition to the [...] list of interoceptive sensations". Human skin, it has been discovered, "contains interoceptive C-fiber endings which trigger a general sense of well-being". According to Schleip and Jäger, "[i]t is concluded that human skin contains particular touch receptors which form a system for social touch that may underlie emotional, hormonal (for example oxytocin), and affiliative responses to caress-like, skin-to-skin contact between individuals. The profound importance of such a system for human health and well-being has long been indicated" in previous research; it has now been given a neurophysiological basis (89-90). Schleip, who is a manual therapist as well as a somatic researcher also de-

at the forefront of your consciousness but a background process, and yet it is the basis, as Damasio and others have argued, for an experience of a core sense of self (cf. Damasio, *The Feeling of What Happens*).[10] So, if you take a moment to go back inside, do you notice a chronic tension in your body somewhere, a chronic holding pattern, or an area of your body that feels numb? Chances are, this is a residue of stress, or possibly trauma, that is either ongoing (in the case of stress) or that your body was not able to completely shake off on its own when returning to homeostasis after a stressful or overwhelming event. What happens when you start 'pendulating' with your attention between the area that feels tense or numb and the area that feels comfortable or good? Does the area that feels tense start to soften up a little bit? If it does, this is the beginning of your body returning to a state of homeostasis. 'Pendulation' is one of the principles employed by Peter Levine and Bessel van der Kolk when working with traumatized patients (cf. van der Kolk, *The Body Keeps the Score*; Levine). The body/mind that shut down in response to an overwhelming event can be brought to a state of homeostasis again by activating bodily feelings of overwhelm or numbness and pendulating between uncomfortable and comfortable sensations. This titration process (that is the overwhelming

---

scribes interoceptive sensations that can be released by manual therapists applying myofascial tissue manipulation, which can effect changes in the autonomic nervous system. These sensations include "[s]ubjective sensations of warmth, lightness/heaviness, spaciousness, density/ fluidity, nausea, streaming, pulsation, spontaneous affection, or a general sense of well-being". He concludes that "[m]yofascial as well as visceral therapists should [...] not be surprised when encountering psycho-emotional responses which may include changes in internal body perception, in self awareness, or affiliative emotions", as these may be "triggered by their stimulation of interoceptive free nerve endings in the skin, in visceral connective tissues as well as in muscular tissues" (Schleip and Jäger 93).

10 Bessel van der Kolk explains how our sense of who we are relates to two senses of self: a core sense of self and an autobiographical self. "[W]e possess two distinct forms of self-awareness: one that keeps track of the self across time and one that registers the self in the present moment. The first, our autobiographical self, creates connections among experiences and assembles them into a coherent story. This system is rooted in language. Our narratives change with the telling, as our perspective changes and as we incorporate new input. The other system, moment-to-moment self-awareness, is based primarily in physical sensations, but if we feel safe [and] are not rushed, we can find words to communicate that experience as well. These two ways of knowing are localized in different parts of the brain that are largely disconnected from each other. Only the [latter] system devoted to self-awareness, which is based in the medial prefrontal cortex [which is directly adjacent to and closely affiliated with the insula where interoceptive sensations are processed, S.].], can change the emotional brain" (*The Body Keeps the Score* 236). Drawing on the research of Joseph LeDoux and others, van der Kolk comes to the conclusion that engaging in interoceptive processes is the only way that we can consciously access and influence the amygdala (that is our emotional brain). "Neuroscience research shows that the only way we can change the way we feel is by becoming aware of our *inner* experience and learning to befriend what is going [on] inside ourselves" (*The Body Keeps the Score* 206).

feelings are activated gradually and only to the extent that the body does not go into shutdown) will allow for the traces of trauma to be fully integrated in the body/mind.[11]

The human body is excellently equipped and can deal and withstand stressful and potentially traumatizing events by activating several pathways of the autonomous nervous system (that is parts of the nervous system beyond conscious control). These pathways are fast and efficient, activating action patterns and sequences that will ensure that response to perceived danger is swift and effective. All human beings and all mammalian animals share them.[12] Wild animals, Peter Levine noted when studying the work of ethologists, shake off their trauma by trembling, reintegrating frozen or activated energy and returning to a state of homeostasis. This observation led Levine to try to find ways the human body, too, can be helped to restore its natural equilibrium, resulting in the development of a

---

11 Sometimes, the completion of aborted movements the body, directed by the autonomous nervous system, made in order to protect itself, is also necessary to fully integrate a traumatic event, such as an accident or an attack. A skilled therapist will notice pre-movements the body wants to make and can call these to the attention of the patient who then can consciously complete the action and movement pattern so the aborted movement is no longer held as a tension pattern in the body (cf. Levine). Levine's therapeutic system of Somatic Experiencing employs a bottom-up processing of trauma, which takes bodily sensations as its starting point but also includes processing images and emotions; once these are dealt with and any implicit memories related to the traumatic events have been integrated into autobiographical episodic memory and have lost their emotional charge, the autonomous nervous system has been able to discharge its activated energy (which caused hyperarousal) and vagal tonus has been restored (which may have caused freeze, dissociation and collapse), new cognitions will spontaneously arise, that is the client will automatically come to reevaluate the traumatic event as well as its effect on his or her own perception of him- or herself (e.g. as someone helpless to prevent what happened) and arrive at new meanings without any attempts by the therapist to reframe thoughts or beliefs connected to the trauma (cf. Levine; Payne, Levine and Crane-Godreau).

12 These quick, life-saving responses comprise the fight/flight response (activated via the sympathetic nervous system) as well as the response to collapse or freeze (activated via the parasympathetic nervous system). Stephen Porges has been able to expand this schematics of the autonomous nervous system in recent years. As Peter Payne, Peter Levine and Mardi Crane-Godreau note, Porges "postulates that the [autonomic nervous system] has three, not two, divisions. While the sympathetic is associated with mobilization in response to threat, the parasympathetic serves to support survival through its two different evolutionary branches, the dorsal and ventral vagal complexes. The evolutionarily older system, the dorsal vagal, promotes shut-down and immobility, while a more recent branch, the ventral vagal, governs social engagement. This includes the supra-diaphragmatic vagus as well as the cranial nerves which serve eye contact, speech, hearing and feeding behaviour. Porges suggests that the ventral vagal serves as a complex and nuanced way of inhibiting excess sympathetic activation ('stress') through engaging socially with others" (8). To seek to socially engage with others is thus regarded as an additional instinctual response to threat to the ones mentioned earlier and known for much longer (fight/flight or freeze/collapse).

therapeutic intervention he has termed Somatic Experiencing (cf. Levine; Payne, Levine and Crane-Godreau). Its goal is to help the patient enhance interoception and facilitate the self-regulation of their nervous system. Someone who is trained in noticing bodily sensations and used to using their body as an anchor for their consciousness, who can pendulate between comfortable and uncomfortable sensations will be able to withstand uncomfortable and distressing emotions better and will know how to return themselves to homeostasis after stressful experiences. Someone who is good at this process, at shaking off stress and integrating trauma (and with the integration of trauma will come a renewed sense of agency) will naturally be better at bouncing back and will thus further their resilience, with the help of the resource of their own body.

The marvel of the wonder of the human body, which is so much like the body of other mammalian animals, and the marvel of the wonder of an existence in and with the human body, is at the root of the following poem by lesbian poet May Swenson from her poetry collection *Another Animal* (1954):

"*Question*

Body my house
my horse my hound
what will I do
when you are fallen

Where will I sleep
How will I ride
What will I hunt

Where can I go
without my mount
all eager and quick
How will I know
in thicket ahead
is danger or treasure
when Body my good
bright dog is dead

how will it be
to lie in the sky
without roof or door
and wind for an eye

With cloud for shift
how will I hide?"

The speaker of this poem employs various animal metaphors for talking about her body, the "house" for her subjectivity: the body is likened to a "horse" (or "mount") as well as to a "dog" (or "hound"), invoking both the horse's speed and strength as well as the dog's trustworthiness: the body will be strong and quick, the body will not let you down. Without the trusted body, how will "I know / in thicket ahead / is danger or treasure", the speaker asks in the third stanza. This is, as we now know, a very astute and intuitive observation on the part of poet and speaker and also, as it turns out, neurophysiologically correct. For it is our 'gut feelings', our enteric brain, that alerts us to danger (cf. Levine 125-127). Similarly, when we are on to a 'treasure', once more it is your 'gut feelings', your somatic markers, that will let you know. If so much of our sense of self is directly tied up with bodily experiences, what indeed, will happen to the subjectivity of the speaker when the body ceases to exist? The question the poem poses remains, for now, unanswerable. To take joy in consciously experiencing this living, breathing animal body, is maybe what the poem invites the reader to do. The metaphysical question then cedes to the background of the reading experience as well as to our experience of life generally. "Animals aren't human beings, but human beings are animals", the author May Swenson observed in an interview, adding that "[p]eople should not lose their animal nature" (qtd. in Crumbley 138).

An invitation to 'go inside' the physical body and into bodily feelings can also be found in Swenson's poem "The Process" from her collection *A Cage of Spines* (1958). When consciousness is grounded in the body at ease, the poem invites us to consider, the creative mind will fly.

"The Process

Lie down upon your side
and fold your knees
 Bend your hands at the wrist
 against your chest
  as a cat or dog does in repose

 Close your eyes and feel
  your brow smooth out like a small
  cloth in the wind
   or a brook slipping
    to gentle waterfall

Now wait for what will happen
Something will

Beneath this hill of breathing hair
a steep mine
Within this ear
oracles of echoes seep
Wide and clear the eyelid's dome
a galaxy where suns collide
and planets spin and moons begin
Words are birds perceived
in a secret forest
Fed by nerve and vein they hop
from twig to twig and up
an ivory ladder to the top
where it is light and they remain
and are believed"

The speaker describes the creation of textual art as a bottom-up process grounded in the mindful attention to bodily experience. The poem is an exercise in using the body as an anchor for one's consciousness in the creation of a work of art. The poem is phrased as an invitation for the reader to join the speaker in a guided exercise that begins with a pose of mindful resting, one the speaker has observed cats and dogs take. In this poem, too, the human speaker takes points from the study of animal behaviour. Rest is helped along by the positioning of arms and wrists and knees; the closing of the eyes allows for the conscious mind to focus inside. "Feel" the reader is instructed at the end of line 6. The line break affords the word a special emphasis; the ensuing slight pause is where the reader's attention can follow the speaker's direction. The smoothing out of the brow is invited along not only by a direct instruction but it is helped along by images invoked by the speaker meant to help evoke the sensation of ease: a piece of cloth fluttering in the wind; water cascading straight down a waterfall. Indeed the typographic printing of the poem on the page emulates this image of the cascade: Follow one step of this process and the others will inevitably follow. Get your conscious mind, your train of thoughts, out of the way for now and let happen what wants to happen, let unfold what wants to unfold. Like in the body-oriented therapies of Levine and van der Kolk, waiting with an open mind for what happens next when consciousness is grounded in the body at ease is maybe the crucial step in the process of the poem's title, for "[s]omething will" happen, as the speaker assures us in line 12. The interior universe that unfolds behind the closed eyes of speaker and addressee is of a creative richness in image and sensory experience. Auditory and visual experiences are the first that arise, followed only at the very top of this bottom-up process by language, by words. The poetic language lets the reader share in the richness and exuberance of this experience, the creation of a whole cosmos. Internal rhyme elevates this experience where "planets spin and moons begin" (l. 19). The words that rise from the subconscious realm to the realm of consciousness, that "hop / from twig to twig and up / an ivory ladder to the top" (l. 22-24), the twitter of birds that finally registers in the prefrontal cortex as language "where it is light and they remain / and are believed" (l. 25-26) is the final result of all the faculties of body/mind working together to create text, speech, language, art, this poem.

Swenson's poem "Standing Torso", written in 1950 but published only posthumously in 1994, widens the scope of bodily feelings and sensations evoked to include the sensory experience of desire.

"Standing Torso

My eyes
flicker over you
like flames
to lick you up

are cooled
by your beauty

blue loops
ripple you
like tongue-tips

furling with
the serpents
of your thighs

into the whorl
of your haunches
and the slender trap
of your waist

gliding the
gulled column
of your back

your neck and head
its ornament

over your
belly's plateau
flat and palpitant

to your breasts
which are
perched birds
plump and alert
their little beaks
sharply lifted

You stand in Egyptian
stillness
accomplished
calm as bronze

and the fuses
of my veins
fill with quickfire"

The speaker's gaze becomes touch in this poem which abounds with extended fire metaphors. The speaker's eyes, which "flicker" over the figure of the beloved "like flames" (l. 3), "licking" her up, or rippling her "like tongue-tips" (l. 9), trace the outline of the naked body of the beloved. The reader follows the speaker's gaze along the contours of this "standing torso" – the title of the poem evokes the aesthetic of classical sculpture, with the speaker finding additional metaphors for each body part traced and discovered along the way: the thighs are serpents, the back is a column, the belly a plateau, the breasts "perched birds / plump and alert" (l. 27-28), the neck and head mere ornaments of this magnificent torso which seems to contain for the speaker a whole universe. The short lines and frequent line-breaks add an element of slowness to the movement of the speaker's gaze and a dimension of the slowing down of time to the poem, contributing to an effect of the reader being drawn into sharing the focussed attention the speaker brings to observing the body of the beloved. The gender of the beloved is only revealed to be female in line 27. The gender of the first-person speaker is never revealed. I still read the poem as lesbian and the speaker as female (inferred from the gender of the author), but there is undoubtedly a deliberate vagueness in the use of first-person speaker and second-person addressee, which leaves the matter of both the speaker's and the beloved's gender identity in a realm of either ambiguity or non-importance. Paul Swenson, May's brother, situates the poem among a number of love poems Swenson wrote "in the first bloom of her liaison" with one of her long-time companions, Pearl Schwartz, while living in New York's Greenwich Village (33). In his estimate, the "universality and pliant malleability of most of May Swenson's love poems, applicable in their metaphorical dexterity to both heterosexual and homosexual love, was undoubtedly a deliberate artistic conceit that also served to protect the poet's private life" (29). Fellow queer poet Mark Doty, writing in 1999, regards Swenson's treatment of same-sex desire in her poetry as a "thrilling dance of reticence and self-disclosure" (qtd. in Juhasz 187). As the penultimate stanza reveals, the power dynamics between observer and observed are balanced out: the speaker's gaze is caress, discovery and worship while the beloved, who stands "in Egyptian / stillness / accomplished / calm as bronze", is not a passive object submitting to being looked at but possesses instead the poise and self-contained presence of an Ancient Egyptian statue, of a Greek bronze sculpture. The last stanza brings the speaker's and reader's attention to the effect this activity of observing the body of the beloved has on the speaker. What follows is a metaphorically rich description of an experience of interoception on the part of the speaker, drawing again on fire imagery: the bodily feeling of desire the observation evokes is described as an experience of "quickfire" filling the "fuses / of [her] veins". Touch and interoception – both sensory experiences – serve in this poem as cornerstones for the way the speaker gains an understanding of herself and the world and thus as epistemological tools. These sensory processes, I argue, can be used as bodily resources and strategies of resilience not just by the speaker of this poem but by pretty much everyone. Where there is so much focussed attention on the experience of bodily feelings of goodness, of enjoyment and discovery or interest, there is no room for feelings of shame for experiencing (and indulging in) what others in 1950, the year the poem was written, would consider 'deviant' sexual desires, as literally, you cannot engage in both the affects of interest/enjoyment and shame – and the bodily feelings going along with them – at the same time. It is neurophysiologically impossible (cf. Tomkins, Levine).[13]

Swenson's poem "Neither wanting more", published in 1991, covers some of the same territory. If the previous poem explored the sensory experience of desire, this poem explores the sensory experience of love and companionship.

---

13 This may also be why queer physician-poet Rafael Campo offers his patients a 'prescription' of the following in his poem "What I Would Give": a sense of wonder and surprise rooted in sensory experiences as well as the joy and comfort found in a sense of connection to a beloved person and a home space, to balance out feelings of anxiety around a medical diagnosis or chronic illness (cf. Campo).

"Neither wanting more

To lie with you
in a field of grass
to lie there forever
and let time pass

Touching lightly
shoulder and thigh
Neither wanting more
Neither asking why

To have your whole
cool body's length
along my own
to know the strength
of a secret tide
of longing seep
into our veins
go deep ... deep

Dissolving flesh
and melting bone
Oh to lie with you
alone

To feel your breast
rise with my sigh
To hold you mirrored
in my eye

Neither wanting more
Neither asking why"

The experience of sensing, touch, leads to an experience of being in the present moment and a being at peace, feeling safe and comforted in the presence and companionship of the beloved, an experience from which the dimension of time seems to have vanished. The togetherness in the space of the relationship between speaker and beloved is explored via the senses: speaker and beloved lie in this "field" of grass, "[t]ouching lightly / shoulder and thigh" (l. 5-6), with the address-ee's "whole / cool body's length" (l. 10) alongside the speaker's own body. Again, this poem makes use of a first-person speaker and a second-person addressee, rendering the experience described subjective but also elevating it to the level of the universal. This is what it feels like, on a visceral level, to experience a moment of intimate connectedness with a beloved human being, regardless of the genders of the people involved; and this level of connectedness, experienced through the senses, is the foundation for the feeling of contentment and absolute presence expressed in the recurring chorus of arriving at a state of "Neither wanting more / Neither asking why" (l. 7-8, 25-26). The sensory experience of desire, "a secret tide / of longing", which seeps "into our veins / go deep ... deep" is part of this intimate relationship, but it neither raises concern for the speaker nor does it need to be explained, the adjective "secret" the only code word hinting at the fact that the relationship described is probably a same-sex relationship. The sensory experience of connection opens up to include the sense of sight almost as an afterthought to the sense of touch in the penultimate stanza: "To feel your breast / rise with my sigh" describes a moment of visceral attunement between speaker and addressee that is rendered again through an experience of interoception ("feeling") before the sense of sight becomes involved; but even the speaker's gaze, which holds the beloved "mirrored / in my eye" makes use – with the verb 'to hold' – of a metaphor of touch. Again, it is by grounding her experience in her senses, most prominently the sense of touch and the experience of interoception, that the speaker of this poem arrives at a state of feeling comforted and good, at ease with both her own subjectivity and her (presumably same-sex) relationship.

May Swenson is not the only LGBTQ poet exploring the physicality of touching, sensing and using sensory experiences as the starting point of an epistemology that privileges the sense of touch. In Thom Gunn's poem "The Hug" from his collection *The Man with Night Sweats* (1992), the gestalt of a decades-long relationship is revealed to the speaker in the symbolic and experiential form of a hug.[14] Both typographical arrangement of the lines and the rhyme pattern used mirror the content of the poem and its central image of an embrace between long-time companions. The occasion for the hug, as outlined in the first stanza, is the addressee's birthday dinner which finds the speaker in the aftermath falling asleep but rousing when his partner joins him in bed. The second stanza describes the speaker's experiencing the hug, which comes upon him all of a sudden, from behind, as does the epiphanic insight he gains into the meaning and significance of their relationship to him by means of his bodily experience of this hug. The sensation of two bodies touching is described, "the full lengths of our bodies pressed: / Your instep to my heel, / My shoulder-blades against your chest", the focus of attention of speaker (and reader) directed to significant points of contact, to where the

---

14 The entire poem can be read at the website of the Poetry Foundation, www.poetryfoundation. org.

speaker can exactly feel the two bodies lining up. Bodily feeling leads to knowing in this poem: the speaker can feel the strength of his partner's body "locking me to you". The strength, brace and lock of the hug is also at the same time the strength and holding container of a loving relationship which has lasted since both were twenty-two. The sensory experience of the present embrace blurs with the sense memory of a past embrace; a long-time relationship is hinted at but now all intervening time seems to vanish and time itself is suspended in the experiencing of the present moment; this moment in which the speaker knows – a knowledge gained via sensory experiencing – nothing but this: "The stay of your secure firm dry embrace", a feeling/knowing – which in this bottom-up process is also a noticing and a realizing – of being held secure, of finding an anchor for both consciousness and experience in both hug and relationship. An autobiographical reading of the poem would regard Gunn as the speaker of the poem and his long-time partner Mike Kitay as the poem's addressee. The two met while studying at Cambridge university and Gunn left the U.K. to follow Kitay, who is American, to the U.S. in 1954. They settled in San Francisco, where they lived in a domestic arrangement that included a communal household shared with friends, and remained committed in an open relationship that lasted until Gunn's death in 2004 (cf. Sleigh).

The sense of touch and the knowledge that sensing/feeling may lead to is also explored in Thom Gunn's poem "Touch" from the collection of the same name, published twenty-five years earlier and written this time in free verse. Here, it is the addressee, once again presumably Kitay who is Jewish, who is already asleep when the speaker joins him in bed. The speaker describes leaving behind his ordinary, day self when joining his lover in bed, his skin slightly "numb with the restraint / of habits", a habitual self covered, even, in a "black frost / of outsideness", which can refer to both the coldness of having been literally outside but also, metaphorically, to a status of outsiderness (as a British expat living in America or as a queer man living in a heteronormative society). The speaker's numbness and cold recede in this bed (which they share with the cat), by being under the covers and by drawing on the warmth of the addressee's body. Feeling can return to a body that had to temporarily harden to brace itself for dealing with the demands of the outside world.[15] The fourth stanza offers, with the indentation, a pause for speaker and reader. The 'turn' of the poem arrives with the addressee's turning in bed to hold the speaker tightly. This holding is presented as a universal human gesture of comfort and connection, visceral body connecting with visceral body. It is the place where attunement is first learned in the relationship between mother

---

15 Note that Gunn's usage of the word 'resilient' (to describe hard(i)ness) in this poem differs slightly from the concept of resilience discussed in this book. Where Gunn sees hardness and hardiness, I see elasticity and the ability to bounce back when making use of the word and the concept of resilience.

and infant, one nervous system learning from another; it is the comfort provided in an intimate partnership as here between the speaker and the addressee, and it is the survival strategy of the persecuted finding themselves in the direst of circumstances, one human nervous system leaning on another and finding a temporary bodily anchor amidst chaos and danger.[16] The speaker's musings as to who he is or stands for in this specific moment in the perception of his sleeping lover, cover the whole range of benign human interpersonal experience. The speaker himself describes in the final stanza his own relaxation into the state created by touch – as he is about to fall asleep – as a sinking into an old "big place, it is / there already, for / you are already" there, as is the cat. It is a place that is "not found but seeps / from our touch in / continuous creation". Cocoon-like, it is a dark "wide realm where we / walk with everyone". It is the metaphoric space of connection between all human beings as well as the animals, the space of the living. But for the speaker of the poem, this space, created by touch, seems to be more than a merely metaphoric space. It is a holding container; connectedness itself. It is a space that emanates from touch, that connects living surfaces. It is also a space that, conceptually, derives from the sameness of humans as well as animals. We are made of the same basic building blocks, the poem seems to suggest, and we all dream and we are joined in sleep and deep rest in a state of quasi-mystical connection.[17]

The speaker of African-American lesbian feminist poet Pat Parker's "My lover is a woman" from her poetry collection *Pit Stop* (1973) uses bodily connection, touch and sensory experiences to counter toxic feelings of shame around her queer sexuality and interracial desire and the hurt and anger at her surroundings' reaction to her as a Black lesbian who is in a relationship with a white woman. In this poem, Parker employs a process which is similar to Peter Levine's concept of dealing with bad sensations/feelings: the pendulation between good and bad bodily feelings. Having access to the good feelings makes the bad feelings bearable. Having access to the good ones means the bad ones can be felt and experienced without getting stuck in them. Once they have been felt without the nervous system being overwhelmed and either dissociating from them or tensing up against them, the body does not need to hold on to them. They will not be archived in a body that oth-

---

16 This corresponds to Stephen Porges' hypothesis of the seeking out to socially engage with others as an instinctual response to threat (cf. Payne, Levine and Crane-Godreau 8).

17 Bessel van der Kolk finds a similar concept of connectedness to Gunn's "realm where we / walk with everyone" in the South African principle of Ubuntu, relating: "My most profound experience with healing from collective trauma was witnessing the work of the South African Truth and Reconciliation Commission, which was based on the central guiding principle of *Ubuntu*, a Xhosa word that denotes sharing what you have, as in 'My humanity is inextricably bound up in yours.' Ubuntu recognizes that true healing is impossible without recognition of our common humanity and our common destiny" (*The Body Keeps the Score* 349).

erwise eventually carries the heavy burden of prolonged stress and trauma. The human body will not never experience them again – and in the case of anger that is not held onto, they can also serve as the starting point for embodied, empowered action – but fully experienced, they will also soon go away again. They will pass like the weather.

"My lover is a woman

I.
my lover is a woman
& when i hold her
feel her warmth
  i feel good
  feel safe

then – i never think of
my family's voices
never hear my sisters say
bulldaggers, queers, funny
  come see us, but don't
  bring your friends
    it's ok with us,
    but don't tell mama
    it'd break her heart
never feel my father
turn in his grave
never hear my mother cry
Lord, what kind of child is this?

II.
my lover's hair is blonde
& when it rubs across my face
it feels soft
  feels like a thousand fingers
  touch my skin & hold me
    and i feel good

then – i never think of the little boy
who spat & called me nigger
never think of the policemen
who kicked my body & said crawl

never think of Black bodies
hanging in trees or filled
with bullet holes
never hear my sisters say
white folks hair stinks
don't trust any of them
never feel my father
turn in his grave
never hear my mother talk
of her backache after scrubbing floors
never hear her cry
Lord, what kind of child is this?

III.
my lover's eyes are blue
& when she looks at me
i float in a warm lake
  feel my muscles go weak with want
    feel good
    feel safe

then – i never think of the blue
eyes that have glared at me
moved three stools away from me
in a bar
never hear my sisters rage
of syphilitic Black men as
guinea pigs
  rage of sterilized children
    watch them just stop in an
    intersection to scare the *old*
    white bitch
never feel my father turn
in his grave
never remember my mother
teaching me the yes sirs & ma'ams
to keep me alive
never hear my mother cry
Lord, what kind of child is this?

IV.
& when we go to a gay bar
& my people shun me because i crossed
the line
& her people look to see what's
wrong with her
  what defect
  drove her to me

& when we walk the streets
of this city
  forget and touch
  or hold hands
    & the people
    stare, glare, frown, & taunt
      at those queers

i remember
  every word taught me
  every word said to me
  every deed done to me
    & then i hate
i look at my lover
& for an instant
  doubt

then – i hold her hand tighter
  & i can hear my mother cry.
  Lord, what kind of child is this?"

The speaker's diction carries the emotional intensity often found in spoken verse poetry and is powerfully embodied by the poet who performs her own work, as Parker, who was involved as an activist in the Black Panther Party as well as the Black Women's Revolutionary Council and in gay and lesbian organizations, was wont to do (cf. Garber).[18] In aesthetic and form, Parker draws on the black oral

---

18 Apart from various printed poetry collections, Parker published a record of her spoken poetry alongside Judy Grahn in 1976. Together with Grahn, whom she met in 1969, she held poetry readings, performing her poetry in public venues in the San Francisco Bay Area and elsewhere. As Linda Garber states, Parker is "considered by many" to be "the first African American lesbian and one of the first lesbian poets to acknowledge her sexual identity in public poetry readings" (63).

tradition. Linda Garber notes that her "work is often autobiographical and always complex, if seemingly simple because of Parker's diction" (82), and to do her poetry justice, "[n]early all commentators on Parker agree that her poetry needs to be heard, not just read" (75). Structurally, the poem makes use of repetitions of words and phrases and oscillates in each section between the description of a sensory experience between the speaker and her lover and an experience where she was ostracized, beaten, insulted or made to feel bad in an other way about her lesbianism and her interracial relationship. In the first section, the description of good bodily feelings and sensations includes the speaker holding her lover, which makes her "feel good / feel safe". The second section has sensory experiences of the lover's hair touching the speaker's face, feeling to her "like a thousand fingers" touching her skin and holding her, making her once again "feel good". The third section has the speaker looking into her lover's eyes, which makes her feel both suspended "in a warm lake" as well as bodily experience sexual desire in the form of her muscles going weak; this encounter makes her once again – this is her mantra – "feel good / feel safe". These descriptions of experiencing her relationship, viscerally, as a space of safety and goodness is followed in each section by a depiction of instances where the speaker experiences homophobic or racist discrimination and violence, making her feel bad. She is, among other things, put down by her sisters, assaulted by the police, frowned upon when walking down the street holding her lover's hand and ostracized even in the lesbian community by both groups of Black lesbians and white lesbians. Her father and mother are both scandalized by her same-sex desire. The structural format of two parts – one outlining the good experiences within the relationship followed by a description of the challenging ones outside of it – is only reversed in the final stanza, where descriptions of situations that make her feel bad are then followed by a stanza that has the speaker once again make use of the bodily resource of making bodily contact with her lover in the form of holding "her hand tighter", which grounds her, which makes her feel good, which enables her to withstand the shame incurred by an imagined (and presumably previously experienced and thus experienced now as a cognitive intrusion) outcry by her mother who is scandalized by her daughter's lesbianism: "Lord, what kind of child is this?" – the other, darker chorus of

---

Garber describes her as a "revolutionary activist whose poetry overlaps the categories of African American, lesbian, and feminist literary traditions"; as a black, lesbian, working-class poet and activist, she "expressed a multifaceted, politically situated identity that calls into question the orthodoxies of every movement in which she participated" (63). What is more, in her "insistence on multiple, shifting identities", Garber contends, "Parker was a poet whose grassroots vernacular theorizing prefigured some of the most important insights of queer theory" (96). In her book *Identity Poetics*, Garber convincingly argues for a reassessment of the work of lesbian feminist poets, like Parker, as foundational for concepts around gender, sexuality, class and race which would emerge in the 1990s as queer theory.

this poem, counterpart to the feelings of goodness and safety. The poem is thus both: it is as much a poetry of witness – of homophobic and racist discrimination and violence – and can thus be performed as a rousing call to working towards social transformation and change; but it is also a demonstration of the art of survival and even thriving – by engaging in bodily contact and by consciously and viscerally experiencing bodily feelings of goodness as well as fully experiencing challenging feelings without either becoming overwhelmed or shutting down,[19] but instead moving through them and then balancing them out with feelings of goodness and safety. As the poem demonstrates, the speaker's feelings make themselves felt equally within the relationship and in the speaker's consciousness in the form of intruding memories, images and cognitions; these can however be borne by going 'inside' and fully experiencing them and focussing then on bodily feelings of goodness: her lover's touch, and interoceptive experiences of feeling held, loved and desired.

Finally, Carol Ann Duffy's poem "Warming Her Pearls" from her collection *Selling Manhattan* (1987) describes an instance of cross-class desire between a maid and her mistress in terms of an epistemology of sensing/feeling. The poem is set in an unspecified past before the advent of the automobile and centres around the practice of a servant wearing her mistress' pearl necklace during the day to imbue it with the warmth of her skin. Duffy was alerted to this historical practice by Judith Radstone, to whom the poem is dedicated (cf. O'Day).[20] In Duffy's poem, the speaker, who is the maid, does not experience the wearing of the pearls as a chore but rather submits to this practice willingly. The poem reveals that the maid desires the mistress, and the pearl necklace represents for her an object that symbolizes or stands in for a relationship and a person, her love object. The pearl necklace becomes thus imbued with meaning; it becomes a material presence of a part of the beloved other in the case of absence of the other, when maid and mistress go about their separate daily activities. The pearls touching the speaker's skin come to stand in for a yearned-for experience of her own body touching her mistress' body. A connection between lover and beloved is established via the sense of touch, and sensing/feeling the object connects lover and beloved and evokes the presence of the beloved mistress. The necklace, which the speaker describes as a rope, connects her to her mistress in voluntary bondage and servitude. What separates lover and beloved in this poem is, on the one hand, the class barrier between maid and mistress. The poem does furthermore not reveal whether the

---

19 This would constitute, variously, trauma and dissociation.

20 The entire poem can be read at the website of the Poetry Foundation, www.poetryfoundation.org.

maid's desire is actually reciprocated by the mistress.[21] The speaker finds herself unable to voice her desire: When brushing her mistress' hair, she watches in the mirror her own lips merely parting as though wanting to speak. Instead, she fulfils her duties and dreams about her mistress, lying in her attic bed, and imagines her mistress wearing the pearl necklace to a social event she cannot be a part of. Her desire becomes evident to the reader at the latest when, in the fifth stanza, she assures the reader that she sees, in the evening, "her every movement in my head ... Undressing, / taking off her jewels, [...] slipping naked into bed". This could refer to either an elaborate fantasy on the part of the speaker or to the speaker sharing with the reader a previous event that has indeed happened. In this case, the speaker has actually previously seen her mistress undress and slipping into bed naked. The ellipses then hint at what the speaker once again cannot, or does not want to share: what she either wants to happen, or what has already happened, between the mistress and herself, an intimate, presumably sexual encounter. As the final stanza reveals, on this night at least, mistress and maid do not share a room and a bed. Instead, the speaker lies still awake, "knowing the pearls are cooling even now" in her mistress' room. "All night / I feel their absence and I burn". The speaker experiences a sense of lack and absence around the familiar feeling of the necklace around her throat, and because of this lack – she burns. The lack is experienced as a yearning, a desiring which the speaker experiences viscerally and metaphorically as a sense of burning. This desire, this burning can be fulfilled by only two things, one presumes: her mistress' touch or the touch of the necklace around her throat. With this dramatic monologue, Duffy has imaginatively given voice and agency to a subject usually absent from the texts of the historical archive: the lower-class, female, same-sex desiring servant. By vividly rendering her feelings and sensations, the reader is drawn to share an unusual point of view and witness the embodied life of this historical subject on the margins.[22]

In this subchapter, I have shown what being attuned to bodily feelings and sensations in the present moment can do for (queer) subjects, how the body can

---

21 Since the maid is the only focalizer in this narrative poem, the reader does not get any more insight into what goes on inside the mistress' mind.

22 Another instance where the touch of an object can evoke the presence of a beloved absent other can be found in Daphne Gottlieb's poem "pilot light" from her collection *Kissing Dead Girls* (2008). Here the speaker, who is in love with pilot Amelia Earhart, nuzzles "the fuzz on the inside of her leather cap's earflaps" and fingers "the soft folds of her tan aviator's jacket". Amelia Earhart, in this poem, is only in love with the sky, and yet the speaker reports, "When she nonchalantly breezes through the room, slings her jacket over her shoulder, matador-like, I thrill to the fact that my fingerprints, the tiniest morsels of my skin, travel with her". In contrast to Duffy's poem, the distance between lover and love object adds, in this poem, to Earhart's allure. As the speaker concludes in the poem's last stanza, "She's never more beautiful than when she's completely gone".

be employed as a resource and as an anchor for consciousness, and how body awareness and being in tune with your interoceptive sensations can be used as a roadmap to a resilient self as well as provide a wellspring for comfort, joy and well-being. It can also give you a sense of your own body's boundaries and thus by extension a sense of your boundaries of self. Furthermore, interpersonal touch as well as touching an object that stands in for a beloved person, with the attendant bodily feelings that arise, can also be employed by queer subjects to further their resilience, as the examples of Thom Gunn's, Pat Parker's and Carol Ann Duffy's poems have shown. May Swenson and Thom Gunn have emerged in this chapter as poets who have grasped and written about what fully experiencing and being attuned to bodily feelings and sensations in the present moment can do for all of us half a century before neuroscientists have been able to provide explanatory models for how these processes work on a neurophysiological level. An epistemology of sensing/feeling emerges thus in this chapter as a bodily resilience strategy for queer subjects.

Conclusion

This book has argued that, while heteronormativity as a power structure may indeed pose an affective challenge to queer peoples' lives, queer subjects have had and continue to have strategies of resilience at their disposal to help them weather this challenge and continue to not only survive but also thrive. This book is the first extensive study investigating queer resilience from a literary and cultural studies perspective. I have identified a number of narrative, performative, spatial and bodily strategies that can help promote the resilience of LGBTQ subjects, and I have provided in this book an archive of literary and cultural texts that may serve as exemplary cases of how individuals (LGBTQ artists and fictional characters developed by LGBTQ artists) have put these strategies into practice over the last 110 years.

Many of the strategies discussed in the previous chapters work towards fostering an individual's (self-)recognition and/or sense of connection. This corroborates the findings of social scientists and psychologists who have found both to be particularly salient for queer resilience in a number of studies (cf. Brown and Colbourne; Sadowski; Nodin et al.; Zeeman et al.; Singh). As I have shown in the first chapter, the search for a viable narrative sexual identity (which can be arrived at via processes of identification, disidentification and deconstruction) can foster an individual's self-recognition and their understanding of themselves and the world they live in. The act of writing itself can aid this search; the act of *re*writing one's story can help heal the wounds of a past self, promoting the resilience of the one who writes, as the example of Jeanette Winterson's life writing showed. Engaging in queer intertextual writing practices (both novel writing and history writing) can further the extension of a queer textual archive, and it can further a sense of connection to past and present queer subjects for both writers and readers of this body of work. In this chapter I also outlined resilient and reparative reading practices. These include acts of reading that promote a reader's resilience as well as texts derived from these acts of reading. They can also include creative reader responses to cultural narratives in instances where the cultural archive may not be offering readers and spectators the desired queer subject positions. These lacunae in hegemonic texts can then be filled by an audience, as the example of queer fan fiction has shown; here consumer creativity unfolds unhindered and queer subjectivity ceases to be marginal, becoming the centre of a whole new set of textual worlds produced by a community of writers who connect over their reading practices and their creative work.

In the second chapter I explored a resilient mode of doing subjectivity in another way that I term the art of emptiness. Some queer subjects, I argue, manage to disregard the interpellating hail of Althusser's imaginary policeman into a 'bad' subject position in our contemporary sex/gender-system by performing a 'simple' vanishing act. These subjects let go of the need to be recognized by the social order, thus eluding being interpellated into a subject position of abjection. The poetry of Mary Oliver and the novels of Sylvia Townsend Warner exemplify in the present study one such strand of practicing queer emptiness. Foucault's notion of an 'other' subjectivity that makes use of what he terms technologies of the self, that is a different kind of hermeneutics of the self which he borrows from authors of late antiquity, may serve as a second example of doing subjectivity in another way. Foucault posits a privileging of the care of the self and puts forth an administrative view of the subject that is more concerned with the subject's past, present and future actions than with the finding of personal truths. This comprises an alternative to current ways of 'doing' the self and can also serve to promote a queer subject's resilience.

In the third chapter I traced performative resilience strategies, which included the strategic use of patterns of disclosure and non-disclosure of one's queer sexuality that I outlined with the example of actors Ian McKellen and Zachary Quinto, as well as with George, the protagonist of Christopher Isherwood's novel A Single Man; furthermore the making use of periperformativity, that is the using of utterances around the performative, thus evading the interpellation of the performative; and the engaging in acts of creative sexual citizenship such as the performance of a song as evinced by musician Melissa Etheridge. The strategic non-disclosure of one's queer sexuality can be understood to be an instance where self-recognition becomes paramount for the subject. Being misrecognized by others, a state of affairs the subject has deliberately chosen in order to protect itself, does then not result in a misrecognition of self; but it can result in an experience of disconnection with one's surroundings. This sense of disconnection becomes manageable, however, if the subject is still able to connect with one other person in their daily life around whom they do not need to hide their queer sexuality; this is the case, for instance, for George as regards his friend Charlotte in A Single Man. The forging of connections, the experiencing of belonging and an integration of disavowed and abjected self parts are finally important aspects of ritual, a performative resilience strategy which I outlined with the example of DeObia Oparei's Crazyblackmuthafuckin'self.

In the fourth chapter I delineated spatial strategies of queer resilience. I looked at how, throughout the twentieth century, queer subjects have sought out, made use of, and created spaces that helped promote their resilience. I drew on Foucault's notion of heterotopic space to describe pockets of space, actual or imaginary locations in which same-sex desires could be imagined, felt and at times, realized, and a same-sex desiring self could be acknowledged and recognized. In the short stories I analysed by Katherine Mansfield and Elizabeth Bowen, the garden turned out to be one such space; similarly, for poet Robert Duncan, the internal space of the meadow provided one such imaginary space, a place of first permission. A short historical overview of the development of queer urban space in the city of San Francisco concluded the chapter. I argued that the creation of queer urban space, the relocation to such a space or the visiting of such an openly queer space in San Francisco or elsewhere can be regarded as a spatial resilience strategy for queer subjects, able to provide LGBTQ individuals with a sense of safety, connection and a sense of belonging – to a community and to a 'home' space. Hope furthermore emerged as a central concept in the speeches of Harvey Milk, the 'unofficial mayor of Castro Street' of 1970s San Francisco, a structure of feeling which can promote queer resilience that I analysed with José Esteban Muñoz' conceptualizations around educated hope in *Cruising Utopia*.

In the final chapter I traced a number of resilience strategies that make use of bodily experiences (and of bodily sexual acts or the representation thereof) in literature and culture. I analysed two examples of what I term the art of postpornography, that is art which employs the pornographic as just another, equally valid mode of artistic expression, thus rendering visible the actual diversity of human sexuality which usually gets cloaked by acts of censorship that try to uphold current heteronormative regimes of the 'normal' vs. the 'abject'. I then traced interoceptive processes as a form of experiencing which privileges bodily feelings and sensations and which can be employed in the processing of stress and trauma in the human body/mind. It can also be employed to further the resilience of any subject. Self-recognition takes here the form of a different kind of self-awareness: that of an awareness of internal sensations in the human body, the moment-by-moment experience of a core self. Engaging in the 'felt sense', the tracking of these sensations, allows one to pendulate between comfortable and distressing feeling states; it also allows one to tolerate distressing feeling states for a limited amount of time. I found descriptions that pay attention to bodily feelings and sensations, to internal states of awareness as well as to the sensory experience of interpersonal touch in the poetry of a number of twentieth-century lesbian and gay poets. The chapter outlined a number of ways in which subjects can draw on the body and bodily experiences as resources: on the one hand by employing the art of postpornography; and on the other hand by using sensory experiences such as interpersonal touch and the mindful attention to bodily feelings and sensations as an anchor for their consciousness, thus interoceptively experiencing a sense of connection and a core sense of self, thus promoting their resilience.

Resilience is then more than merely a form of reacting to the challenges posed to a subject by living in an unjust society. It is a highly interactive mode of being in the world which can set free a large amount of creative energy and which in turn can draw inspiration and energy from artistic work. In this book I have explored queer resilience in twentieth and twenty-first century English literature and culture. Further studies could extend the present archive of texts and strategies found; one might include, for instance, texts of the nineteenth century as well as literary works from outside the U.K. and North America and also the visual arts and music in further studies on queer resilience.

The year 2017 saw the introduction of same-sex marriage in Germany as well as, finally, the rehabilitation of those prosecuted under §175 StGB for committing homosexual acts from 1945 until 1994. It also saw the publication of a national report that diagnosed, still, a heightened vulnerability for LGBTQ youth and young adults (cf. Krell and Oldemeier); reports on the situation of young LGBTQ people from the U.K., the U.S. and Canada come to similar conclusions (cf. introduction). Study authors regularly call on policy makers to introduce measures to make schools, youth groups, universities and work places, as well as society as a whole more LGBTQ-friendly; this seems to be a long-term project, indeed. However, vulnerability factors, such as they still can be found to exist, can – for the time being – also be balanced out by resilience factors, as resilience researchers have argued over the last two decades. Studies on the resilience of present and past queer subjects, such as this book, and investigations into how to further the resilience of LGBTQ people now are both timely and relevant.

Credits

Works Cited

Ahmed, Sara. *The Cultural Politics of Emotion*. 2nd ed. Edinburgh: Edinburgh UP, 2014.

Althusser, Louis. "Ideology and Ideological State Apparatuses." *Lenin and Philosophy and Other Essays*. Transl. Ben Brewster. New York: Monthly Review P, 1971.

Amaechi, John. Interview by David Ornstein. "John Amaechi: Football 'toxic' for gay people and minorities." *BBC*. BBC, 8 Jan. 2014. Web. 20 Oct. 2017. <http://www.bbc.com/ sport/football/25660495>.

Andermahr, Sonya. *Jeanette Winterson*. Basingstoke: Palgrave Macmillan, 2009.

Anderson, Benedict. *Imagined Communities: Reflections on the Origin and Spread of Natonalism*. Rev. ed. London: Verso, 1991.

Anderson, Carol S. "anitya." *Encyclopedia of Buddhism. Vol. 1*. Ed. Robert E. Buswell. New York: Macmillan Reference, 2004. 23-24.

Antonovsky, Aaron. *Unraveling the Mystery of Health: How People Manage Stress and Stay Well*. San Francisco: Jossey-Bass, 1987.

Aranda, Kay, Laetitia Zeeman, Julie Scholes, and Arantxa Santa-Maria Morales. "The resilient subject: Exploring subjectivity, identity and the body in narratives of resilience." *Health* 16 (2012): 548-563.

Aron, Elaine N. *The Highly Sensitive Person*. New York: Broadway Books, 1997.

---, and Arthur Aron. "Sensory Processing Sensitivity and Its Relation to Introversion and Emotionality." *Journal of Personality and Social Psychology* 73 (1997): 345-368.

Assmann, Aleida. *Erinnerungsräume: Formen und Wandlungen des kulturellen Gedächtnisses*. München: Beck, 1999.

Assmann, Jan. *Das kulturelle Gedächtnis: Schrift, Erinnerung und politische Identität in frühen Hochkulturen*. München: Beck, 1992.

Atwood, Margaret. *Negotiating with the Dead: A Writer on Writing*. New York: Anchor Books, 2002.

Austin, J.L. *How to Do Things With Words*. Cambridge: Harvard UP, 1962.

Bachmann-Medick, Doris. *Cultural Turns. Neuorientierung in den Kulturwissenschaften*. 5th ed. Reinbek: Rowohlt, 2014.

Balsam, Kimberly F. "Trauma, Stress, and Resilience Among Sexual Minority Women: Rising Like the Phoenix." *Trauma, Stress, and Resilience Among Sexual*

Minority Women: Rising Like the Phoenix. Ed. Kimberly F. Balsam. Binghamton: Harrington Park P, 2003. 1-8.

Barrett, Eileen. "Unmasking Lesbian Passion: The Inverted World of *Mrs. Dalloway.*" *Virginia Woolf: Lesbian Readings.* Ed. Eileen Barrett and Patricia Cramer. New York: New York UP, 1997. 146-164.

Barthes, Roland. "The Death of the Author." *Image Music Text.* Trans. Stephen Heath. London: Fontana P, 1977. 142-148.

---. *The Pleasure of the Text.* Trans. Richard Miller. New York: Hill and Wang, 1997.

Bechtold, Adrian. "Ein Mann, den es eigentlich nicht gibt." *Fluter.* Fluter, 11 Sept. 2012. Web. 20 Oct. 2017. <http://www.fluter.de/ein-mann-den-es-eigentlich-nicht-gibt>.

Benjamin, Jessica. *The Bonds of Love: Psychoanalysis, Feminism, and the Problem of Domination.* London: Virago, 1988.

---. *Like Subjects, Love Objects: Essays on Recognition and Sexual Difference.* New Haven: Yale UP, 1995.

---. *Shadow of the Other: Intersubjectivity and Gender in Psychoanalysis.* New York: Routledge, 1997.

Berg, James J., and Chris Freeman. "Introduction: An American Outsider." *The American Isherwood.* Ed. James J. Berg and Chris Freeman. Minneapolis: U of Minnesota P, 2015. xvii-xxii.

---. "Introduction: The Isherwood Century." *The Isherwood Century: Essays on the Life and Work of Christopher Isherwood.* Ed. James J. Berg and Chris Freeman. Madison: U of Wisconsin P, 2000. 3-8.

---. "A Real Diamond: The Multicultural World of *A Single Man.*" *The American Isherwood.* Ed. James J. Berg and Chris Freeman. Minneapolis: U of Minnesota P, 2015. 95-101.

Bergman, David. "Introduction." *Camp Grounds: Homosexuality and Style.* Ed. David Bergman. Amherst: U of Massachusetts P, 1993. 3-16.

---. "Isherwood and the Violet Quill." *The Isherwood Century: Essays on the Life and Work of Christopher Isherwood.* Ed. James J. Berg and Chris Freeman. Madison: U of Wisconsin P, 2000. 203-215.

Bergmann, Franziska. *Die Möglichkeit, dass alles auch ganz anders sein könnte: Geschlechterverfremdung in zeitgenössischen Theatertexten.* Würzburg: Königshausen & Neumann, 2015.

Berndt, Christina. *Resilienz: Das Geheimnis der psychischen Widerstandskraft.* München: dtv, 2013.

Bersani, Leo. "Is the Rectum a Grave?" *Is the Rectum a Grave? And Other Essays.* Chicago: U of Chicago P, 2009. 3-30.

Berthoud, Ella, and Susan Elderkin. *The Novel Cure: An A-Z of Literary Remedies.* Edinburgh: Canongate, 2013.

Blair, Rhonda. "Reconsidering Stanislavsky: feeling, feminism and the actor." *The Performance Studies Reader*. Ed. Henry Bial. London: Routledge, 2007. 249-261.

Bollinger, Laurel. "Models of Female Loyalty: the Biblical Ruth in Jeanette Winterson's *Oranges Are Not the Only Fruit*." *Tulsa Studies in Women's Literature* 13 (1994): 363-380.

Bosold, Birgit, Dorothée Brill and Detlef Weitz. "Wildes Wissen." *Homosexualität_en*. Dresden: Sandstein, 2015. 190-193.

Bowen, Elizabeth. "The Jungle." *The Collected Stories of Elizabeth Bowen*. London: Vintage, 1999. 251- 263.

Bowleg, Lisa, Jennifer Huang, Kelly Brooks, Amy Black, and Gary Burkholder. "Triple Jeopardy and Beyond: Multiple Minority Stress and Resilience Among Black Lesbians." *Trauma, Stress, and Resilience Among Sexual Minority Women: Rising Like the Phoenix*. Ed. Kimberly F. Balsam. Binghamton: Harrington Park P, 2003. 87-108.

Brannigan, John. *New Historicism and Cultural Materialism*. Basingstoke: Macmillan, 1998.

Bray, Alan. *The Friend*. Chicago: U of Chicago P, 2003.

Breedlove, Lynnee. *One Freak Show*. San Francisco: Manic D Press, 2009.

Brighid. "The Bitten Peach." *Archive of Our Own*. Web. 20 Jan. 2017. <http://archiveofourown.org/works/5657290>.

---. "That Dead Men Rise Up (Never)." *Archive of Our Own*. Web. 20 Jan. 2017. <http://archiveofourown.org/works/944682>.

Bristow, Joseph. "Introduction." *Oscar Wilde and Modern Culture*. Ed. Joseph Bristow. Athens: Ohio P, 2008. 1-45.

Brothers, Barbara. "Flying the Nets at Forty: *Lolly Willowes* as Female Bildungsroman." *Radical Spinsters: Unmarried Women in the Twentieth-Century Novel*. Ed. Laura L. Doan. Urbana: U of Illinois P, 1991. 195-212.

Brown, Marion, and Marc Colbourne. "Bent But Not Broken: Exploring Queer Youth Resilience." *Handbook for Working With Children and Youth: Pathways to Resilience Across Cultures and Contexts*. Ed. Michael Ungar. Thousand Oaks: Sage, 2005. 263-277.

Busse, Kristina, and Karen Hellekson. "Introduction: Work in Progress." *Fan Fiction and Fan Communities in the Age of the Internet: New Essays*. Ed. Karen Hellekson and Kristina Busse. Jefferson: McFarland, 2006. 5-32.

Butler, Judith. *Bodies That Matter: On the Discursive Limits of "Sex"*. New York: Routledge, 1993.

---. *Gender Trouble: Feminism and the Subversion of Identity*. New York: Routledge, 1990.

---. *Undoing Gender*. New York: Routledge, 2004.

Campo, Rafael. "What I Would Give." *Landscape with Human Figure*. Durham: Duke UP, 2002. 16.

Carnicke, Sharon M. *Stanislavsky in Focus.* Amsterdam: Harwood Academic Publishers, 1998.

Caruth, Cathy. *Unclaimed Experience: Trauma, Narrative, and History.* Baltimore: Johns Hopkins UP, 1996.

Castle, Terry. *The Apparitional Lesbian: Female Homosexuality and Modern Culture.* New York: Columbia UP, 1993.

---, ed. *The Literature of Lesbianism: A Historical Anthology From Ariosto To Stonewall.* New York: Columbia UP, 2003.

---. "The Will to Whimsy." *Boss Ladies, Watch Out!: Essays on Women, Sex, and Writing.* New York, Routledge, 2002. 237-243.

Chisholm, Dianne. *Queer Constellations: Subcultural Space in the Wake of the City.* Minneapolis: U of Minnesota P, 2005.

Christensen, Laird. "The Pragmatic Mysticism of Mary Oliver." *Ecopoetry: A Critical Introduction.* Ed. J. Scott Bryson. Salt Lake City: U of Utah P, 2002. 135-152.

Cixous, Hélène. *Three Steps on the Ladder of Writing.* Trans. Sarah Cornell and Susan Sellers. New York: Columbia UP, 1993.

Cleto, Fabio. "Introduction: Queering the Camp." *Camp: Queer Aesthetics and the Performing Subject. A Reader.* Ed. Fabio Cleto. Edinburgh: Edinburgh UP, 1999. 1-42.

Collins, Billy. "Preface." *The Poem I Turn To: Actors & Directors Present Poetry That Inspires Them.* Naporville: Sourcebooks, 2008. xv-xvi.

Conard, Nicholas J. "A female figurine from the basal Aurignacian of Hohle Fels Cave in southwestern Germany." *Nature* 459 (2009): 248-252.

Conard, Nicholas J., Maria Malina, and Susanne C. Münzel. "New flutes document the earliest musical tradition in southwestern Germany." *Nature* 460 (2009): 737-740.

Conradi, Peter J. *Going Buddhist: Panic and Emptiness, the Buddha and Me.* London: Short Books, 2004.

Coppa, Francesca. "Writing Bodies in Space: Media Fan Fiction as Theatrical Performance." *Fan Fiction and Fan Communities in the Age of the Internet: New Essays.* Ed. Karen Hellekson and Kristina Busse. Jefferson: McFarland, 2006. 225-244.

Coupe, Laurence. *Myth.* London: Routledge, 1997.

Cramer, Patricia. "Introduction." *Virginia Woolf: Lesbian Readings.* Ed. Eileen Barrett and Patricia Cramer. New York: New York UP, 1997. 117-127.

Crumbley, Paul. "May Swenson and Other Animals: Her Poetics of Natural Selection." *Body My House: May Swenson's Work and Life.* Ed. Paul Crumbley and Patricia M. Gantt. Logan: Utah State UP, 2006. 138-156.

Cunningham, Michael. *The Hours.* London: Fourth Estate, 1999.

---. Interview by Tony Peregrin. "Michael Cunningham after Hours." *The Gay & Lesbian Review Worldwide* Mar.-Apr. 2003: 30-31.

---. Interview by Michael Coffey. "Michael Cunningham: New Family Outings." *Publishers Weekly* 2 Nov. 1998: 53-55.

Cvetcovich, Ann. *An Archive of Feelings: Trauma, Sexuality, and Lesbian Public Cultures*. Durham: Duke UP, 2003.

Damasio, Antonio R. *Descartes' Error: Emotion, Reason, and the Human Brain*. New York: Putnam, 1994.

---. *The Feeling of What Happens: Body and Emotion in the Making of Consciousness*. New York: Harcourt Brace, 1999.

Davidson, Michael. Foreword. *Robert Duncan: The Ambassador From Venus. A Biography*. By Lisa Jarnot. Berkeley: U of California P, 2012. xiii-xx.

D'Emilio, John. "Gay Politics and Community in San Francisco Since World War II." *Hidden From History: Reclaiming the Gay and Lesbian Past*. Ed. Martin Bauml Duberman, Martha Vicinus and George Chauncey, Jr. London: Penguin, 1989. 456-473.

---. *Sexual Politics, Sexual Communities: The Making of a Homosexual Minority in the United States 1940-1970*. Chicago: U of Chicago P, 1983.

Derecho, Abigail. "Archontic Literature: A Definition, A History, and Several Theories of Fan Fiction." *Fan Fiction and Fan Communities in the Age of the Internet: New Essays*. Ed. Karen Hellekson and Kristina Busse. Jefferson: McFarland, 2006. 61-78.

Derrida, Jacques. *A Derrida Reader: Between the Blinds*. Ed. Peggy Kamuf. New York: Columbia UP, 1991.

DeSalvo, Louise. *Writing as a Way of Healing: How Telling Our Stories Transforms Our Lives*. Boston: Beacon P, 2000.

Dinshaw, Carolyn. *Getting Medieval: Sexualities and Communities, Pre- and Postmodern*. Durham: Duke UP, 1999.

Doan, Laura. "Jeanette Winterson's Sexing the Postmodern." *The Lesbian Postmodern*. Ed. Laura Doan. New York: Columbia UP, 1994. 137-155.

Dollimore, Jonathan. *Sex, Literature and Censorship*. Cambridge: Polity Press, 2001.

Duffy, Carol Anne. "Warming Her Pearls." *Selected Poems*. London: Penguin, 1994. 60-61.

Duffy, Maureen. *Collected Poems*. London: Hamish Hamilton, 1985.

Duggan, Lisa, and José Esteban Muñoz. "Hope and hopelessness: A dialogue." *Women & Performance* 19 (2009): 275-283.

Duncan, Robert. *Bending The Bow*. New York: New Directions, 1968.

---. "The Homosexual in Society." *Collected Essays and Other Prose*. Ed. James Maynard. Berkeley: U of California P, 2014. 5-18.

---. "Often I am Permitted to Return to a Meadow." *The Collected Later Poems and Plays*. Ed. Peter Quatermain. Berkeley: U of California P, 2014. 3.

---. "Reading and Discussion of 'Often I Am Permitted to Return to a Meadow'." Poetry Center, San Francisco. 18 May 1959. Reading. http://writing.upenn.edu/pennsound/x/Duncan.php.

Dworkin, Andrea. *Pornography: Men Possessing Women*. New York: Putnam's, 1981.

Erll, Astrid. *Kollektives Gedächtnis und Erinnerungskulturen: Eine Einführung*. 2nd ed. Stuttgart: Metzler, 2011.

Erskine, Willie. "Aboriginal Epistemology." *First Nations Education in Canada: The Circle Unfolds*. Ed. Marie Battiste and Jean Barmah. Vancouver: UBC P, 1995.

Etheridge, Melissa. "Miss California." *Fearless Love*. Universal, 2010. CD.

Fetzer, Margret. "Reading as Creative Intercourse Michael Cunningham's and Stephen Daldry's *The Hours*." *Anglistik* 19 (2008): 65-83.

Firefly. Prod. Joss Whedon. Twentieth Century Fox Television, 2002-2003.

Flores, Ralph. *Buddhist Scriptures as Literature: Sacred Rhetoric and the Uses of Theory*. Albany: SUNY P, 2008.

Foucault, Michel. "Different Spaces." *Aesthetics: Method, and Epistemology*. Ed. James Faubion. Trans. Robert Hurley and others. *Essential Works of Foucault Vol. Two*. London: Penguin, 1994. 175-185.

---. "The Ethics of the Concern of the Self as a Practice of Freedom." *Ethics: Subjectivity and Truth*. Ed. Paul Rabinow. Trans. Robert Hurley and others. *Essential Works of Foucault Vol. One*. London: Penguin, 1994. 281-301.

---. "Friendship as a Way of Life." *Foucault Live: Collected Interviews, 1961-1984*. Ed. Sylvère Lotringer. Trans. John Johnston. New York: Semiotext(e), 1996. 204-212.

---. *The History of Sexuality Vol. 1. The Will to Knowledge*. Trans. Robert Hurley. London: Penguin, 1976.

---. "Technologies of the Self." *Ethics: Subjectivity and Truth*. Ed. Paul Rabinow. Trans. Robert Hurley and others. *Essential Works of Foucault Vol. One*. London: Penguin, 1994. 223-251.

Fox, Amy. *Heights*. *Thicker Than Water: One-act plays by the members of Youngblood*. Ensemble Studio Theatre. New York: Dramatists Play Service, 2005. 9-28.

---. "*Heights*: A Merchant Ivory Film." *Amy Fox Personal Homepage*. Web. 20 Jan. 2017. <http://heights.amyfox.net>.

Frankl, Viktor E. *Man's Search for Meaning: An Introduction to Logotherapy*. London: Hodder & Stoughton, 1974.

---. *The Unheard Cry for Meaning: Psychotherapy and Humanism*. New York: Simon & Schuster, 1978.

Freeman, Elizabeth. "Time Binds, or, Erotohistoriography." *Social Text* 23 (2005): 57-68.

Fremantle, Francesca. *Luminous Emptiness: Understanding the Tibetan Book of the Dead*. Boston: Shambala, 2003.

Freud, Sigmund. "Der Dichter und das Phantasieren." *Gesammelte Werke* Vol. 7. Ed. Anna Freud. Frankfurt: Fischer, 1966. 213-223.

---. "Jenseits des Lustprinzips." *Gesammelte Werke* Vol. 13. Ed. Anna Freud. London: Imago Publishing, 1955. 1-69.

Frey, Rodney, ed. *Stories That Make the World: Oral Literature of the Indian Peoples of the Inland Northwest. As told by Lawrence Aripa, Tom Yellowtail, and Other Elders.* Norman: U of Oklahoma P, 1995.

Frijling, Jessie L. et al. "Promoting Resilience After Trauma: Clinical Stimulation of the Oxytocin System." *The Resilience Handbook: Approaches to Stress and Trauma.* Ed. Martha Kent, Mary C. Davis and John W. Reich. New York: Routledge, 2014. 299-308.

Fröhlich-Gildhoff, Klaus, and Maike Rönnau-Böse. *Resilienz.* 4th ed. München: Ernst Reinhardt, 2015.

Gamallo, Isabel C. Anievas. "Subversive Storytelling: The Construction of Lesbian Girlhood through Fantasy and Fairy Tale in Jeanette Winterson's *Oranges Are Not the Only Fruit.*" *The Girl: Construction of the Girl in Contemporary Fiction by Women.* Ed. Ruth O. Saxton. New York: St. Martin's, 1998. 119-134.

Garbarino, James. "Foreword." *Handbook for Working With Children and Youth: Pathways to Resilience Across Cultures and Contexts.* Ed. Michael Ungar. Thousand Oaks: Sage, 2005. xi-xiii.

Garber, Linda. *Identity Poetics: Race, Class, and the Lesbian-Feminist Roots of Queer Theory.* New York: Columbia UP, 2001.

Garnes, David. "*A Single Man,* Then and Now." *The Isherwood Century: Essays on the Life and Work of Christopher Isherwood.* Ed. James J. Berg and Chris Freeman. Madison: U of Wisconsin P, 2000. 196-202.

Garrity, Jane. "Mapping Queer Space." *English Language Notes* 45 (2007): 1-5.

---. *Step-Daughters of England: British women modernists and the national imaginary.* Manchester: Manchester UP, 2003.

Gifted and Challenged: The Making of 'Shortbus'. Dir. M. Shawn Kaminsky. Spectrum Media Productions, 2007.

Goffman, Erving. *The Presentation of Self in Everyday Life.* Garden City: Doubleday, 1959.

Gottlieb, Daphne. "pilot light." *Kissing Dead Girls.* Brooklyn: Soft Skull P, 2008. 6-7.

Gunn, Thom. "The Hug." *Collected Poems.* New York: Farrar, Straus & Giroux, 1994. 407.

---. "Touch." *Touch.* London: Faber & Faber, 1967. 26-27.

Gutierrez, Donald K. *Breaking Through to the Other Side: Essays on Realization in Modern Literature.* Troy: Whitston, 1994.

Haffey, Kate. "Exquisite Moments and the Temporality of the Kiss in *Mrs. Dalloway* and *The Hours.*" *Narrative* 18 (2010): 137-162.

Halberstam, Judith. *In a Queer Time and Place: Transgender Bodies, Subcultural Lives.* New York: New York UP, 2005.

---. *The Queer Art of Failure.* Durham: Duke UP, 2011.

Halbfass, Wilhelm. *India and Europe: An Essay in Understanding.* Albany: SUNY P, 1988.

Hall, Donald E. *Reading Sexualities: Hermeneutic theory and the future of queer studies.* New York: Routledge, 2009.

Hall, Radclyffe. *The Well of Loneliness.* London: Virago, 1982.

Halperin, David M. *How to Do the History of Homosexuality.* Chicago: U of Chicago P, 2002.

Hamill, Sam, and J. P. Seaton, eds. *The Poetry of Zen.* Boston: Shambhala, 2004.

Hart, Angie, Derek Blincow, with Helen Thomas. "Resilient Therapy: Strategic Therapeutic Engagement with Children in Crisis." *Child Care in Practice* 14 (2008): 131-145.

Heights. Screenplay by Amy Fox and Chris Terrio. Dir. Chris Terrio. Merchant Ivory, 2005.

Heuving, Jeanne. *The Transmutation of Love and Avant-Garde Poetics.* Tuscaloosa: U of Alabama P, 2016.

Hellekson, Karen, and Kristina Busse, eds. *The Fan Fiction Studies Reader.* Iowa City: U of Iowa P, 2014.

Hemmings, Clare. *Bisexual Spaces: A Geography of Sexuality and Gender.* London: Routledge, 2002.

---. "Extract from *Locating Bisexual Identities: Discourses of Bisexuality and Contemporary Feminist Thought.*" *Bisexuality: A Critical Reader.* Ed. Merl Storr. London: Routledge, 1999. 193-200.

Hitzlsperger, Thomas. Interview by Carolin Emcke and Moritz Müller-Wirth. "Thomas Hitzlsperger: 'Homosexualität wird im Fussball ignoriert'." *Die Zeit* 9. Jan. 2014.

---. Interview by Raphael Honigstein. "Thomas Hitzlsperger: 'I finally figured out that I preferred living with a man'." *The Guardian.* The Guardian, 8 Jan. 2014. Web. 20 Oct. 2017. <https://www.theguardian.com/football/2014/jan/08/thomas-hitzlsperger-gay-footballer-interview>.

Hotz-Davies, Ingrid. "Scham in den Romanen Jane Austens, oder: Wie die Gender Studies auf den Affekt gekommen sind." *Ins Wort gesetzt, ins Bild gesetzt: Gender in Wissenschaft, Kunst und Literatur.* Ed. Ingrid Hotz-Davies and Schamma Schahadat. Bielefeld: transcript, 2007. 181-206.

Hughes, Mary Joe. "Michael Cunningham's *The Hours* and Postmodern Artistic Re-Presentation." *Critique* 45 (2004): 349-361.

Human Rights Campaign. *Growing Up LGBT in America: HRC Youth Survey Report Key Findings.* New York: Human Rights Campaign, 2012.

Hunt, Lynn. "Introduction: Obscenity and the Origins of Modernity, 1500-1800." *The Invention of Pornography: Obscenity and the Origins of Modernity, 1500-1800.* Ed. Lynn Hunt. New York: Zone Books, 1993. 9-45.

Hutcheon, Linda. *The Politics of Postmodernism.* 2nd ed. London: Routledge, 2002.

Hüther, Gerald. *Die Macht der inneren Bilder: Wie Visionen das Gehirn, den Menschen und die Welt verändern.* 9th ed. Göttingen: Vandenhoeck & Ruprecht, 2015.

Iser, Wolfgang. *The Act of Reading: A Theory of Aesthetic Response.* Baltimore: Johns Hopkins UP, 1978.

Isherwood, Christopher. *A Single Man.* London: Vintage, 2010.

Isin, Engin F., and Greg M. Nielsen, eds. *Acts of Citizenship.* London: Zed Books, 2008.

Jackson, Roger R. "śūnyatā," *Encyclopedia of Buddhism. Vol. 2.* Ed. Robert E. Buswell. New York: Macmillan Reference, 2004. 809-810.

Jarnot, Lisa. *Robert Duncan: The Ambassador From Venus. A Biography.* Berkeley: U of California P, 2012.

Jenkins, Henry. *Textual Poachers: Television Fans & Participatory Culture.* New York: Routledge, 1992.

Johnson, Mark Andrew. *Robert Duncan.* Boston: Twayne, 1988.

Jordan, Judith V. "Relational Resilience in Girls." *Handbook of Resilience in Children.* Ed. Sam Goldstein and Robert B. Brooks. 2nd ed. New York: Springer, 2013. 73-86.

Juhasz, Suzanne. "The Queer Poetics of May Swenson." *Body My House: May Swenson's Work and Life.* Ed. Paul Crumbley and Patricia M. Gantt. Logan: Utah State UP, 2006. 181-194.

Jung, Susanne. "Prisms of Desire: The Art of Postpornography." *queere (t)ex(t) perimente.* Ed. Franziska Bergmann, Jennifer Moos and Claudia Münzing. Freiburg: fwpf, 2008. 67-88.

Kaplan, Carola M. "Working through Grief in the Drafts of *A Single Man.*" *The American Isherwood.* Ed. James J. Berg and Chris Freeman. Minneapolis: U of Minnesota P, 2015. 37-47.

Kast, Verena. *Imagination: Zugang zu inneren Ressourcen finden.* Ostfildern: Patmos, 2012.

Kent, Martha, and Mary C. Davis. "The Emergence of Capacity-Building Programs and Models of Resilience." *Handbook of Adult Resilience.* Ed. John W. Reich, Alex J. Zautra and John Stuart Hall. London: Guilford P, 2010. 427-449.

Kent, Martha, Mary C. Davis, and John W. Reich. "Introduction." *The Resilience Handbook: Approaches to Stress and Trauma.* Ed. Martha Kent, Mary C. Davis and John W. Reich. New York: Routledge, 2014. xii-xix.

Keown, Daniel. *Buddhism: A Very Short Introduction.* Oxford: Oxford UP, 1996.

---. *A Dictionary of Buddhism.* Oxford: Oxford UP, 2013.

---. "Ethics." *Encyclopedia of Buddhism*. Ed. Damien Keown and Charles S. Prebish. London: Routledge, 2007. 337-348.

Kilian, Eveline. *GeschlechtSverkehrt: Theoretische und literarische Perspektiven des gender-bending*. Königstein: Ulrike Helmer, 2004.

Kilian, Eveline, and Hope Wolf. "Introduction: The Spatial Dimensions of Life Writing." *Life Writing and Space*. Farnham: Ashgate, 2016. 1-21.

Kinnard, Jacob N. "Art and Zen." *Encyclopedia of Buddhism*. Ed. Damien Keown and Charles S. Prebish. London: Routledge, 2007. 58-60.

Kosslyn, Stephen M., Giorgio Ganis, and William L. Thompson. "Neural Foundations of Imagery." *Nature Reviews Neuroscience* 2 (2001): 635-642.

Kosslyn, Stephen M., William L. Thompson, Irene J. Kim, and Nathaniel M. Alpert. "Topographical representations of mental images in primary visual cortex." *Nature* 378 (1995): 496-498.

Krell, Claudia, and Kerstin Oldemeier. *Coming-out – und dann...?! Coming-out-Verläufe und Diskriminierungserfahrungen von lesbischen, schwulen, bisexuellen, trans* und queeren Jugendlichen und jungen Erwachsenen in Deutschland*. Opladen: Barbara Budrich, 2017.

Kristeva, Julia. *Powers of Horror: An Essay on Abjection*. Trans. Leon S. Roudiez. New York: Columbia UP, 1982.

Kushner, Tony. *Angels in America*. London: Nick Hern, 2007.

Lackner, Eden, Barbara Lynn Lucas, and Robin Anne Reid. "Cunning Linguists: The Bisexual Erotics of *Words/Silence/Flesh*." *Fan Fiction and Fan Communities in the Age of the Internet: New Essays*. Ed. Karen Hellekson and Kristina Busse. Jefferson: McFarland, 2006. 189-206.

Laplanche, Jean, and Jean-Bertrand Pontalis. *Das Vokabular der Psychoanalyse*. Trans. Emma Moersch. Frankfurt: Suhrkamp, 1972.

Leavenworth, Maria Lindgren. "'A Life as Potent and Dangerous as Literature Itself': Intermediated Moves from *Mrs. Dalloway* to *The Hours*." *The Journal of Popular Culture* 43 (2010): 503-523.

Le Guin, Ursula K. *The Wave in the Mind: Talks and Essays on the Writer, the Reader, and the Imagination*. Boston: Shambhala, 2004.

Levine, Peter. *In an Unspoken Voice: How the Body Releases Trauma and Restores Goodness*. Berkeley: North Atlantic Books, 2010.

Local Government Act. Section 28. 1988. *UK Legislation Homepage*. Web. 20 Jan. 2017. <http://www.legislation.gov.uk/ukpga/1988/9/section/28>.

Lopez, Donald S. *Buddhism*. London: Allen Lane, 2001.

---. *Elaborations on Emptiness: Uses of the Heart Sūtra*. Princeton: Princeton UP: 1996.

Lösel, Friedrich, and David P. Farrington. "Direct Protective and Buffering Protective Factors in the Development of Youth Violence." *American Journal of Preventive Medicine* 43 (2012): 8-23.

Love, Heather. *Feeling Backward: Loss and the Politics of Queer History*. Cambridge: Harvard UP, 2007.

Lucas, John. "From Realism to Radicalism: Sylvia Townsend Warner, Patrick Hamilton and Henry Green in the 1920s." *Outside Modernism: In Pursuit of the English Novel, 1900-30*. Ed. Lynne Hapgood and Nancy Paxton. London: Macmillan, 2000. 203-223.

Lucas, Rose. "Drifting in the Weeds of Heaven: Mary Oliver and the Poetics of the Immeasurable." *Rhizomes* 13 (2006).

Lutz, Ralf. *Der hoffende Mensch: Anthropologie und Ethik menschlicher Sinnsuche*. Tübingen: Francke, 2012.

Mailander, Jane. "The Advantages of Erotic Fan Fiction As an Art Form." *Jane Mailander Personal Homepage*. Web. 28. Nov. 2007. <http://members.aol.com/janemort/erotic. html>.

Malpas, Simon. *The Postmodern*. London: Routledge, 2005.

Mansfield, Katherine. "Leves Amores." *Katherine Mansfield: A Secret Life*. By Claire Tomalin. London: Penguin, 1987. 259-260.

Massey, Doreen. *Space, Place and Gender*. Minneapolis: U of Minnesota P, 1994.

Masten, Ann S., and Margaret O'Dougherty Wright. "Resilience over the Lifespan: Developmental Perspectives on Resistance, Recovery, and Transformation." *Handbook of Adult Resilience*. Ed. John W. Reich, Alex J. Zautra and John Stuart Hall. London: Guilford P, 2010. 213-237.

Maupin, Armistead. "Foreword." *The Isherwood Century: Essays on the Life and Work of Christopher Isherwood*. Ed. James J. Berg and Chris Freeman. Madison: U of Wisconsin P, 2000. xi-xv.

McEvilley, Thomas. *The Shape of Ancient Thought: Comparative Studies in Greek and Indian Philosophies*. New York: Allworth P, 2002.

McKellen, Ian. "How I Came Out, Live on National Radio." *Official Homepage*. Web. 20 Jan. 2017. <http://www.mckellen.com/activism/activism_coming_out.htm>.

---. *Inside the Actor's Studio*. Episode 9.5. Bravo. 8 Dec. 2002.

---. "Stonewall UK." *Official Homepage*. Web. 20 Jan. 2017. <http://www.mckellen.com/ activism/activism_stonewall.htm>.

---. "Visiting UK Schools with Stonewall." *Official Homepage*. Web. 20 Jan. 2017. <http://www.mckellen.com/activism/education_for_all.htm>.

McMahan, David L. "Meditation (Chan/Zen)." *Encyclopedia of Buddhism*. Ed. Damien Keown and Charles S. Prebish. London: Routledge, 2007. 500-502.

McNew, Janet. "Mary Oliver and the Tradition of Romantic Nature Poetry." *Contemporary Literature* 30.1 (1989): 59-77.

Medd, Jodie. "Encountering the past in recent lesbian and gay fiction." *The Cambridge Companion to Gay and Lesbian Writing*. Ed. Hugh Stevens. Cambridge: Cambridge UP, 2011. 167-184.

Milk, Harvey. "A City of Neighborhoods: First Major Address I and II." *An Archive of Hope: Harvey Milk's Speeches and Writings*. Ed. Jason Edward Black and Charles E. Morris. Berkeley: U of California P, 2013. 166-172.

---. "Gay Freedom Day Speech." *An Archive of Hope: Harvey Milk's Speeches and Writings*. Ed. Jason Edward Black and Charles E. Morris. Berkeley: U of California P, 2013. 215-220.

---. "Harvey Speaks Out." *An Archive of Hope: Harvey Milk's Speeches and Writings*. Ed. Jason Edward Black and Charles E. Morris. Berkeley: U of California P, 2013. 159-165.

---. "Political Will." *An Archive of Hope: Harvey Milk's Speeches and Writings*. Ed. Jason Edward Black and Charles E. Morris. Berkeley: U of California P, 2013. 245-249.

---. "You've Got to Give Them Hope." *An Archive of Hope: Harvey Milk's Speeches and Writings*. Ed. Jason Edward Black and Charles E. Morris. Berkeley: U of California P, 2013. 145-155.

Mitchell, John Cameron. "here! with Josh and Sara #58". *Heretv.com*. 2006. Web.

Morris, Charles E., and Jason Edward Black. "Introduction: Harvey Milk's Political Archive and Archival Politics." *An Archive of Hope: Harvey Milk's Speeches and Writings*. Ed. Jason Edward Black and Charles E. Morris. Berkeley: U of California P, 2013. 1-59.

Montefiore, Janet. *Men and Women Writers of the 1930s: The Dangerous Flood of History*. London: Routledge, 1996.

Moseley, Nick. *Acting and Reacting: Tools for the Modern Actor*. London: Nick Hern, 2005.

Muñoz, José Esteban. *Cruising Utopia: The Then and There of Queer Futurity*. New York: New York UP, 2009.

---. *Disidentifications: Queers of Color and the Performance of Politics*. Minneapolis: U of Minnesota P, 1999.

My Own Private Idaho. Dir. Gus Van Sant. New Line Cinema, 1991.

Nodin, Nuno, Elizabeth Peel, Allan Tyler, and Ian Rivers. *The RaRE Research Report: LGB&T Mental Health – Risk and Resilience Explored*. London: PACE, 2015.

Nussbaum, Martha C. *Love's Knowledge: Essays on Philosophy and Literature*. Oxford: Oxford UP, 1992.

O'Brien, Wendy. "Exercise of Hope." *The Resilience of Hope*. Ed. Andrea M. Stephenson and Janette McDonald. Leiden: Brill, 2010. 29-39.

O'Day, Deirdre. "Judith Radstone." *The Guardian*. The Guardian, 13 Feb 2001. Web. 20 Sept 2017.

Oliver, Mary. *New and Selected Poems: Volume One*. Boston: Beacon P, 2004.

Onega, Susana. *Jeanette Winterson*. Manchester: Manchester UP, 2006.

Oparei, DeObia. *Crazyblackmuthafuckin'self*. London: Royal Court, 2002.

---. *Personal Interview*.

Palmer, Paulina. *Contemporary Lesbian Writing: Dreams, Desire, Difference*. Buckingham: Open UP, 1993.

Parker, Pat. "My lover is a woman." *Movement in Black: The Collected Poetry of Pat Parker 1961-78*. Trumansburg: Crossing P, 1983. 98-100.

Paul, Annie Murphy. "Your Brain on Fiction: The Neuroscience of Your Brain on Fiction." *New York Times*. New York Times, 17 Mar. 2012. Web.

Payne, Peter, Peter A. Levine, and Mardi A. Crane-Godreau. "Somatic experiencing: using interoception and proprioception as core elements of trauma therapy." *Frontiers in Psychology* 6 (2015): 1-18.

Penley, Constance. *NASA/TREK: Popular Science and Sex in America*. New York: Verso, 1997.

Pennebaker, James W. *Opening Up: The Healing Power of Expressing Emotions*. New York: Guilford P, 1997.

Po, Li. "Zazen on Ching-t'ing Mountain." *The Poetry of Zen*. Ed. Sam Hamill and J. P. Seaton. Boston: Shambhala, 2004. 42.

Pramaggiore, Maria. "Extracts from *Epistemologies of the Fence*." *Bisexuality: A Critical Reader*. Ed. Merl Storr. London: Routledge, 1999. 144-149.

---. "Straddling the Screen: Bisexual Spectatorship and Contemporary Narrative Film." *RePresenting Bisexualities: Subjects and Cultures of Fluid Desire*. Ed. Donald E. Hall and Maria Pramaggiore. New York: New York UP, 1996. 272-297.

Pykett, Lyn. "A New Way With Words? Jeanette Winterson's Post-Modernism." *'I'm telling you stories': Jeanette Winterson and the Politics of Reading*. Ed. Helen Grice and Tim Woods. Amsterdam: Rodopi, 1998. 53-60.

Quinto, Zachary. "10.16.11. nyc..." *Official Homepage*. Web. 20 Jan. 2017. <http://www.zacharyquinto.com/news/2011/10/post.html#more>.

Rachman, Shalom. "Clarissa's Attic: Virginia Woolf's *Mrs. Dalloway* Reconsidered." *Twentieth Century Literature* 18 (1972): 3-18.

Rall, Veronika. "Die neue Leiblichkeit: Zum Fall der Hüllen im Autorenkino." *Entfesselung des Imaginären? Zur neuen Debatte um Pornografie*. Ed. Antonia Ingelfinger and Meike Penkwitt. Freiburg: Jos Fritz, 2004. 315-330.

Rapport, Nigel, and Joanna Overing. "Myth." *Social and Cultural Anthropology: The Key Concepts*. London: Routledge, 2000. 269-282.

---. "Narrative." *Social and Cultural Anthropology: The Key Concepts*. London: Routledge, 2000. 283-290.

Reddemann, Luise. *Eine Reise von 1000 Meilen beginnt mit dem ersten Schritt: Seelische Kräfte entwickeln und fördern*. Freiburg: Herder, 2004.

---. *Imagination als heilsame Kraft: Ressourcen und Mitgefühl in der Behandlung von Traumafolgen*. Stuttgart: Klett-Cotta, 2016.

---. *Psychodynamisch Imaginative Traumatherapie PITT: Das Manual*. Stuttgart: Klett-Cotta, 2004.

---. *Überlebenskunst*. Stuttgart: Klett-Cotta, 2006.

Reynolds, Margaret, ed. *The Penguin Book of Lesbian Short Stories*. London: Penguin, 1994.

Reynolds, Margaret, and Jonathan Noakes. *Jeanette Winterson: The Essential Guide*. London: Vintage, 2003.

Richardson, Michael. *Georges Bataille*. London: Routledge, 1994.

Ricoeur, Paul. "Life in Quest of Narrative." *On Paul Ricoeur: Narrative and Interpretation*. Ed. David Wood. London: Routledge, 1991. 20-33.

---. "Narrative Identity." *On Paul Ricoeur: Narrative and Interpretation*. Ed. David Wood. London: Routledge, 1991. 188-199.

Robinson, Frank M. "Foreword: 'Harvey'." *An Archive of Hope: Harvey Milk's Speeches and Writings*. Ed. Jason Edward Black and Charles E. Morris. Berkeley: U of California P, 2013. xvii-xxiii.

Rogers, Robbie. Interview by Donald McRae. "Robbie Rogers: why coming out as gay meant I had to leave football." *The Guardian*. The Guardian, 29 March 2013. Web. 20 Oct. 2017. <https://www.theguardian.com/football/2013/mar/29/robbie-rogers-coming-out-gay>.

Rönnau-Böse, Maike, and Klaus Fröhlich-Gildhoff. *Resilienz und Resilienzförderung über die Lebensspanne*. Stuttgart: Kohlhammer, 2015.

Rooney, David. "Career Zigzag, Changing Coasts And Galaxies." *New York Times*. New York Times, 21 Oct. 2010. Web. 20 Jan. 2017. <http://www.nytimes.com/2010/10/24/ theater/24quinto.html>.

Royle, Nicholas. *After Derrida*. Manchester: Manchester UP, 1995.

Rubin, Gayle. "Thinking Sex: Notes for a Radical Theory of the Politics of Sexuality." *Pleasure and Danger: Exploring Female Sexuality*. Ed. Carole S. Vance. London: Pandora, 1992. 267-293.

Rüsen, Jörn. *Historische Orientierung: Über die Arbeit des Geschichtsbewusstseins, sich in der Zeit zurechtzufinden*. Köln: Böhlau, 1994.

Rusk, Lauren. *The Life Writing of Otherness: Woolf, Baldwin, Kingston, and Winterson*. New York: Routledge, 2002.

Russell, Sue. "Mary Oliver: The Poet and the Persona." *Harvard Gay and Lesbian Review* 4.4 (1997): 21-22.

Sadowski, Michael. *In a Queer Voice: Journeys of Resilience from Adolescence to Adulthood*. Philadelphia: Temple UP, 2013.

---. *Safe Is Not Enough: Better Schools for LGBTQ Students*. Cambridge: Harvard Education P, 2016.

Sandten, Cecile, and Kathy-Ann Tan. "Home: Concepts, Constructions, Contexts – An Introduction." *Home: Concepts, Constructions, Contexts*. Ed. Cecile Sandten and Kathy-Ann Tan. Trier: Wissenschaftlicher Verlag Trier, 2016. 1-8.

Sarao, K.T.S. "anātman." *Encyclopedia of Buddhism. Vol. 1*. Ed. Robert E. Buswell. New York: Macmillan Reference, 2004. 18-20.

Schechner, Richard. *Performance Studies: An Introduction.* New York: Routledge, 2006.

Schleip, Robert, and Heike Jäger. "Interoception: A new correlate for intricate connections between fascial receptors, emotion, and self recognition." *Fascia: The Tensional Network of the Human Body.* Ed. Robert Schleip, Thomas W. Findley, Leon Chaitow and Peter A. Huijing. München: Elsevier, 2012. 89-94.

Schneider, Rebecca. *The Explicit Body in Performance.* London: Routledge, 1997.

Schwarzer, Alice, ed. *PorNo: Opfer und Täter, Gegenwehr und Backlash, Verantwortung und Gesetz.* Köln: Kiepenheuer & Witsch, 1994.

Sedgwick, Eve Kosofsky. *Between Men: English Literature and Male Homosocial Desire.* New York: Columbia UP, 1985.

---. *Epistemology of the Closet.* Berkeley: U of California P, 1990.

---. *Tendencies.* Durham: Duke UP, 1993.

---. *Touching Feeling: Affect, Pedagogy, Performativity.* Durham: Duke UP, 2003.

---. *The Weather in Proust.* Ed. Jonathan Goldberg. Durham: Duke UP, 2011.

shalott. "Limestone." *fanfic by astolat.* Web. 20 Jan. 2017. <http://intimations.org/fanfic/stargate/Limestone.html>.

shalott. "A Beautiful Lifetime Event." *fanfic by astolat.* Web. 20 Jan. 2017. <http://www.intimations.org/fanfic/stargate/lifetime_event.html>.

Shilts, Randy. *The Mayor of Castro Street: The Life and Times of Harvey Milk.* New York: St. Martin's P, 1982.

Shortbus. Dir. John Cameron Mitchell. Fortissimo Films, 2006.

Sierz, Aleks. "In-Yer-Face Theatre: Mark Ravenhill and 1990s Drama." *British Drama of the 1990s.* Ed. Bernhard Reitz and Mark Berninger. Heidelberg: C. Winter, 2002. 107-121.

Sinclair, Anthony. "Art of the ancients." *Nature* 426 (2003): 774-775.

Singh, Anneliese A. "Transgender Youth of Color and Resilience: Negotiating Oppression and Finding Support." *Sex Roles* 68 (2013): 690-702.

---, Sarah E. Meng, and Anthony W. Hansen. "'I Am My Own Gender: Resilience Strategies of Trans Youth." *Journal of Counseling & Development* 92 (2014): 208-218.

Sleigh, Tom. "Thom Gunn's New Jerusalem." *At the Barriers: On the Poetry of Thom Gunn.* Ed. Joshua Weiner. Chicago: U of Chicago P, 2009. 241-256.

Smith, Patricia Juliana. "Introduction: Icons and Iconoclasts. Figments of Sixties Queer Culture." *The Queer Sixties.* Ed. Patricia Juliana Smith. New York: Routledge, 1999. xi-xxvi.

Sontag, Susan. "Notes on 'Camp'." *Against Interpretation.* New York: Farrar, Straus & Giroux, 1964. 275-292.

Stargate Atlantis. Prod. Brad Wright and Robert C. Cooper. Metro Goldwyn Mayer, 2004-2009.

Stasi, Mafalda. "The Toy Soldiers from Leeds: The Slash Palimpsest." *Fan Fiction and Fan Communities in the Age of the Internet: New Essays.* Ed. Karen Hellekson and Kristina Busse. Jefferson: McFarland, 2006. 115-133.

Stein, Claudius. "'Imagine – it is easy if you try:' Imagination – eine jahrtausendealte Ressource." *Psychotherapeut* 62 (2017): 128-135.

Storr, Merl, ed. *Bisexuality: A Critical Reader.* London: Routledge, 1999.

---. "Introduction." *Bisexuality: A Critical Reader.* Ed. Merl Storr. London: Routledge, 1999. 1-12.

Stryker, Susan, and Jim Van Buskirk. *Gay by the Bay: A History of Queer Culture in the San Francisco Bay Area.* San Francisco: Chronicle Books, 1996.

Supernatural. Prod. Eric Kripke. The CW Television Network, 2005-2018.

Swenson, May. "Neither Wanting More." *The Love Poems of May Swenson.* Boston: Houghton Mifflin, 1991. 74.

---. "The Process." *Collected Poems.* Ed. Langdon Hammer. New York: Penguin, 2013. 113-114.

---. "Question." *Collected Poems.* Ed. Langdon Hammer. New York: Penguin, 2013. 43-44.

---. "Standing Torso." *Collected Poems.* Ed. Langdon Hammer. New York: Penguin, 2013. 562-563.

Swenson, Paul. "A Figure in the Tapestry: The Poet's Feeling Runs Ahead of Her Imagination (Greenwich Village, 1949-50)." *Body My House: May Swenson's Work and Life.* Ed. Paul Crumbley and Patricia M. Gantt. Logan: Utah State UP, 2006. 27-39.

Tan, Kathy-Ann. *Reconfiguring Citizenship and National Identity in the North American Literary Imagination.* Detroit: Wayne State UP, 2015.

Tarnation. Dir. Jonathan Caoutte. Wellspring Media, 2003.

Thomson, Jeffrey. "'Everything Blooming Bows Down in the Rain': Nature and the Work of Mourning in the Contemporary Elegy." *Ecopoetry: A Critical Introduction.* Ed. J. Scott Bryson. Salt Lake City: U of Utah P, 2002. 153-61.

Tomalin, Claire. *Katherine Mansfield: A Secret Life.* London: Penguin, 1987.

Tomkins, Silvan. *Shame and Its Sisters: A Silvan Tomkins Reader.* Ed. Eve Kosofsky Sedgwick and Adam Frank. Durham: Duke UP, 1995.

Traub, Valerie. *The Renaissance of Lesbianism in Early Modern England.* Cambridge: Cambridge UP, 2002.

Ullyatt, Gisela. "'The Only Chance to Love This World': Buddhist Mindfulness in Mary Oliver's Poetry." *Journal of Literary Studies* 27.2 (2011): 115-131.

Ungar, Michael. "Cultural Dimension of Resilience among Adults." *Handbook of Adult Resilience.* Ed. John W. Reich, Alex J. Zautra and John Stuart Hall. London: Guilford P, 2010. 404-423.

---. "Introduction: Resilience Across Cultures and Contexts." *Handbook for Working With Children and Youth: Pathways to Resilience Across Cultures and Contexts.* Ed. Michael Ungar. Thousand Oaks: Sage, 2005. xv-xxxix.

van der Kolk, Bessel. *The Body Keeps the Score: Mind, Brain and Body in the Transformation of Trauma.* London: Penguin, 2014.

---. "Posttraumatic stress disorder and the nature of trauma." *Dialogues in Clinical Neuroscience* 2 (2000): 7-22.

van Dijk, Lutz, and Barry van Driel, eds. *Sexuelle Vielfalt lernen: Schulen ohne Homophobie.* Berlin: Querverlag, 2008.

Wachman, Gay. *Lesbian Empire: Radical Crosswriting in the Twenties.* New Brunswick: Rugers UP, 2001.

Wallace, Benjamin. "What's Up, Spock?" *New York Magazine.* New York Magazine, 17 Oct. 2011. Web. 20 Jan. 2017. <http://nymag.com/movies/features/zachary-quinto-2011-10/>.

Walther-Ahrens, Tanja. *Seitenwechsel: Coming-Out im Fussball.* München: Gütersloher Verlagshaus, 2011.

Warner, Sylvia Townsend. *Lolly Willowes or The Loving Huntsman.* New York: New York Review Books, 1999.

---. *Summer Will Show.* New York: New York Review Books, 2009.

Weeks, Jeffrey. *Sex, Politics and Society: The Regulation of Sexuality since 1800.* 2nd ed. London: Longman, 1989.

Werner, Emmy E. "Risiko und Resilienz im Leben von Kindern aus multiethnischen Familien." *Handbuch Resilienzförderung.* Ed. Margherita Zander. Trans. Gerrit Pohl. Wiesbaden: Springer, 2011. 32-46.

White, Hayden. *Metahistory: The Historical Imagination in Nineteenth-Century Europe.* Baltimore: Johns Hopkins UP, 1973.

Williams, Linda. *Hard Core: Power, Pleasure, and the "Frenzy of the Visible".* Berkeley: U of California P, 1989.

---, ed. *Porn Studies.* Durham: Duke UP, 2004.

Winterson, Jeanette. *Art Objects: Essays on Ecstasy and Effrontery.* London: Vintage, 1996.

---. *Oranges Are Not the Only Fruit.* London: Vintage, 1985.

---. *Why Be Happy When You Could Be Normal?* London: Vintage, 2011.

Wolfreys, Julian. "Narrative." *Critical Keywords in Literary and Cultural Theory.* Basingstoke: Palgrave Macmillan, 2004. 162-169.

---. "Reader/Reading." *Critical Keywords in Literary and Cultural Theory.* Basingstoke: Macmillan, 2004. 212-220.

Woods, Gregory. *A History of Gay Literature: The Male Tradition.* New Haven: Yale UP, 1998.

---. *Homintern: How Gay Culture Liberated the Modern World.* New Haven: Yale UP, 2016.

Woolf, Virginia. *Mr Bennett and Mrs Brown*. London: Hogarth P, 1924.

---. *Mrs Dalloway*. London: Penguin, 1992.

Wright, Les. "San Francisco." *Queer Sites: Gay Urban Histories Since 1600*. Ed. David Higgs. London: Routledge, 1999. 164-189.

Wright, Margaret O'Dougherty, Ann S. Masten, and Angela J. Narayan. "Resilience Processes in Development: Four Waves of Research on Positive Adaptation in the Context of Adversity." *Handbook of Resilience in Children*. Ed. Sam Goldstein and Robert B. Brooks. 2nd ed. New York: Springer, 2013. 15-37.

Wunderlich, Mark. "The Trick". *The Anchorage: Poems*. Amherst: U of Massachusetts P, 1999. 7-8.

Zautra, Alex J. "Resilience Is Social, After All." *The Resilience Handbook: Approaches to Stress and Trauma*. Ed. Martha Kent, Mary C. Davis and John W. Reich. New York: Routledge, 2014. 185-196.

Zautra, Alex J., John Stuart Hall, and Kate E. Murray. "Resilience: A New Definition of Health for People and Communities." *Handbook of Adult Resilience*. Ed. John W. Reich, Alex J. Zautra and John Stuart Hall. London: Guilford P, 2010. 3-29.

Zeeman, Laetitia, Kay Aranda, Nigel Sherriff, and Chris Cocking. "Promoting resilience and emotional well-being of transgender young people: research at the intersections of gender and sexuality." *Journal of Youth Studies* 20 (2017): 382-397.

GPSR Authorized Representative: Easy Access System Europe, Mustamäe tee
50, 10621 Tallinn, Estonia, gpsr.requests@easproject.com

www.ingramcontent.com/pod-product-compliance
Lightning Source LLC
Chambersburg PA
CBHW061729120626
46550CB00005B/1748